Experiencing Emergence in Organizations

The perspective of complex responsive processes draws on analogies from the complexity sciences, bringing in the essential characteristics of human agents, understood to emerge in social processes of communicative interaction and power relating. The result is a way of thinking about life in organizations that focuses attention on how organizational members cope with the unknown as they perpetually create organizational futures together.

Providing a natural successor to the editors' earlier series *Complexity and Emergence in Organizations*, this series, *Complexity as the Experience of Organizing*, aims to develop this work further by taking very seriously the *experience* of organizational practitioners, and showing how adopting the perspective of complex responsive processes yields deeper insight into practice and so develops that practice.

In this book, all the contributors work as consultants or managers in organizations. They provide narrative accounts of their actual work, addressing questions such as:

- How do widespread or global patterns, such as government or corporate policies, emerge and evolve in the local interactions between people?
- What actually happens in global change programmes such as installing competencies, managing diversity and assuring quality?
- What does this imply about the relationship between the local and the global?

In considering such questions in terms of their daily experience, the contributors explore how the perspective of complex responsive processes assists them to make sense of their experience and so to develop their practice. *Experiencing Emergence in Organizations* offers a different method for making sense of experience in a rapidly changing world by using reflective accounts of ordinary everyday life in organizations rather than idealized accounts. The editor's commentary introduces and contextualizes these experiences as well as drawing out key themes for further research.

Experiencing Emergence in Organizations will be of value to readers from among those academics and business school students and practitioners who are looking for reflective accounts of real life experiences of *researching* in organizations, rather than further prescriptions of what life in organizations ought to be like.

Ralph Stacey is Director of the Complexity and Management Centre at the Business School of the University of Hertfordshire and Director of the Doctor of Management programme run by the Centre. He is one of the editors of the *Complexity and Emergence in Organizations* series, and the editor of five books in this series.

Experiencing Emergence in Organizations

Local interaction and the emergence
of global pattern

Edited by
Ralph Stacey

Routledge
Taylor & Francis Group

LONDON AND NEW YORK

First published 2005
by Routledge
2 Park Square, Milton Park, Abingdon, Oxon OX14 4RN

Simultaneously published in the USA and Canada
by Routledge
270 Madison Ave, New York, NY 10016

Routledge is an imprint of the Taylor & Francis Group

Typeset in Times by Keystroke, Jacaranda Lodge, Wolverhampton
Printed and bound in Great Britain by TJ International Ltd, Padstow, Cornwall

British Library Cataloguing in Publication Data
A catalogue record for this book is available from the British Library

Library of Congress Cataloging in Publication Data
Experiencing emergence in organizations : local interaction and the
    emergence of global pattern / Ralph Stacey [editor]. – 1st ed.
        p. cm.
    Includes bibliographical references and index.
    1. Organizational change. 2. Organizational behavior. 3. Corporate culture.
    4. Organizational learning. 5. Communication in organizations. 6. Social
    interaction. I. Stacey, Ralph D.
    HD58 . 8 .E98 2005
    302.3'5–dc22   2004026096

ISBN 0–415–35132–4 (hbk)
ISBN 0–415–35133–2 (pbk)

Contents

Contributors

Alison Donaldson is an independent writer and consultant, based in London. She completed her Doctor of Management in Organizational Change at the University of Hertfordshire in 2003.

Stig Johannessen is Associate Professor in Organization and Management at the University College (HINT) in Levanger, Norway. He holds a Ph.D. in corporate management from the Norwegian University of Science and Technology (NTNU) in Trondheim, where he also teaches. He is Chairman of the Board of the Complexity and Management Center, Norway.

Michael Nolan is a consultant with Sheppard Moscow Ireland. He consults in the area of organizational change, leadership development and facilitation of group processes. He was awarded the degree of Doctor of Management at the University of Hertfordshire in 2003.

David Scanlon is R&D Business Analyst at AstraZeneca. He was awarded an MA in Organizational Change at the University of Hertfordshire in 2002.

Ralph Stacey is Professor of Management at the Business School of the University of Hertfordshire and Director of its Complexity and Management Centre. He is also a member of the Institute of Group Analysis.

Richard Williams was CEO of Westminster Kingsway College, and in July 2004 he left the further education sector to take up a new role as CEO of a charity working with young people and adults across the UK. He has completed the Doctor of Management programme at the University of Hertfordshire.

Series preface
Complexity as the Experience of Organizing

Edited by Ralph Stacey, Douglas Griffin and Patricia Shaw

Complexity as the Experience of Organizing is a sequel to the highly successful series *Complexity and Emergence in Organizations* also edited by the editors of this series. The first series has attracted international attention for its development of the theory of complex responsive processes and its implications for those working in organizations. The perspective of complex responsive processes draws on analogies from the complexity sciences, bringing in the essential characteristics of human agents, namely consciousness and self-consciousness, understood to emerge in social processes of communicative interaction, power relating and evaluative choice. The result is a way of thinking about life in organizations that focuses attention on how organizational members cope with the unknown as they perpetually create organizational futures together. This second series aims to develop that work by taking seriously the experience of organizational practitioners, showing how adopting the perspective of complex responsive processes yields deeper insight into practice and so develops that practice.

Contributors to the volumes in the series work as leaders, consultants or managers in organizations. The contributors provide narrative accounts of their actual work, addressing such questions as: What does it mean, in ordinary everyday terms, to lead a large organization? How do leaders learn to lead? What does it mean, in ordinary everyday terms, to consult managers in an organization? How does the work of the consultant assist managers when the uncertainty is so great that they do not yet know what they are doing? What does executive coaching achieve? What happens in global change programs such as installing competencies, managing diversity and assuring quality? Why do organizations get stuck in repetitive patterns of behavior? What kinds of change can be facilitated? In considering such questions in terms of their daily experience, the

xii • Series preface

contributors explore how the perspective of complex responsive processes assists them in making sense of their experience and so develop their practices.

The books in the series are addressed to organizational practitioners and academics who are looking for a different way of making sense of their own experience in a rapidly changing world. The books will attract readers looking for reflective accounts of ordinary everyday life in organizations rather than idealized accounts or further prescriptions.

Other volumes in the series:
A Complexity Perspective on Researching Organizations
Taking experience seriously
Edited by Ralph Stacey and Douglas Griffin

Complexity and the Experience of Leading Organizations
Edited by Douglas Griffin and Ralph Stacey

Experiencing Risk, Spontaneity and Improvisation in Organizational Change
Working live
Edited by Patricia Shaw and Ralph Stacey

Complexity and the Experience of Managing in Public Sector Organizations
Edited by Ralph Stacey and Douglas Griffin

1 Introduction: emergence and organizations

Ralph Stacey

- ● **Rational and magico-mythical ways of thinking**
- ● **The perspective of complex responsive processes**
- ● **The properties of complex responsive processes of relating**
- ● **The consequences of taking a complex responsive processes perspective**
- ● **The implications for thinking about the global and the local**
- ● **The chapters in this book**

Over the period 2000 to 2002, a number of us at the Complexity and Management Centre at the Business School of the University of Hertfordshire published a series of books called *Complexity and Emergence in Organizations* (Stacey *et al.*, 2000; Stacey, 2001; Fonseca, 2001; Griffin, 2002; Streatfield, 2001; Shaw, 2002). These books developed a perspective according to which organizations are understood to be ongoing, iterated processes of cooperative and competitive relating between people. We argued that organizations are not systems but the ongoing patterning of interactions between people. Patterns of human interaction produce further patterns of interaction, not some *thing* outside of the interaction. We called this perspective *complex responsive processes of relating*.

Since 2000, some of the authors in the series, together with other Complexity and Management Centre colleagues in association with the Institute of Group Analysis, have been conducting a research program on organizational change leading to the degrees of Master of Arts by research or Doctor of Management. This is necessarily a part-time program because the core of the research method (see another volume in this series: Stacey and Griffin, 2005) involves students taking their own experience seriously. If patterns of human interaction produce nothing but further patterns of human interaction, in the creation of which we are all participating, then there is no detached way of understanding organizations from the position of the objective observer. Instead, organizations have to be understood in terms of one's own personal experience of participating with others in the co-creation of the patterns of interaction that are the organization. The students' research is, therefore, their narration of current events they are involved in together with their reflections on themes of particular importance emerging in the stories of their own experience of participation with others to create the patterns of interaction that are the organization. The research stance is, then, one of detached involvement.

The purpose of this volume is to bring together the work of a number of program participants who have been concerned with what, in hindsight, has emerged as a common theme. The theme has to do with how widespread or global patterns, such as government policies and corporate ways of doing things, are iterated, and so repeatedly emerge and potentially evolve, in the local interactions between people. Usually, government and corporate policies, as well as national and organizational cultures, are felt and understood as forces arising outside of local interaction and acting on that local interaction, often in a constraining, even oppressive manner. These outside forces are taken as powerful, stable givens, arising outside of our own direct experience and beyond our influence, with which we must comply. The chapters in this volume present a different way of thinking about these matters, moving away from the taken-for-granted notion of outside forces to an exploration of just how people are affected in their local interactions with each other by the global patterns they may feel to be outside forces. What these chapters describe, it seems to me, is the experience of emergence in organizations, rather than the experience of outside forces.

At the end of this introductory chapter, I give a brief indication of what each of these authors cover and what the central themes of the volume are. I will also be introducing each chapter with an editorial comment. Before doing that, however, there is a brief review of ways of thinking about organizations followed by a short, and so necessarily compact, summary of what I mean by the theory of complex responsive processes, what it implies about the relationship between the local and the global and how this differs from other traditions of thought about these matters. Further details of these arguments are also set out in Chapter 2, which focuses on complex responsive processes ways of thinking about what are usually regarded as outside forces.

Rational and magico-mythical ways of thinking

In his book on involvement and detachment, Elias (1987) distinguishes between two modes of thinking. As an example of the first mode, which he refers to as involved thinking, he refers to the way people in the West viewed nature in the pre-scientific age. People experienced nature as rather mysterious forces acting upon them, often with great violence, which they found very difficult to understand, let alone control. When people find themselves in such situations they become anxious, and this arouses high levels of emotion, creating a vicious circle in which it becomes harder and harder to formulate explanations of what is happening to them. They become deeply involved in the experience; that is, they think in highly emotive ways, finding it increasingly difficult to stand back and reflect in a 'reality congruent' fashion. The anxiety is dealt with, to some extent, by developing what Elias calls 'magico-mythic' explanations according to which nature is understood either in terms of impersonal forces acting upon people in a way they cannot control or as personalized gods and spirits also beyond human control. Such explanations call forth responses of acceptance, submission and conformity.

The second mode of thinking, which Elias calls detached thinking, is exemplified by the scientific method. By overcoming fears of the unknown, the scientific method enables people to stand back and reflect on nature in a way that is more 'reality congruent'. By taking the position of the objective observer, they feel less involved in their experiences with nature, less emotional and more rational. The result is a virtuous circle in which levels of anxiety diminish so enabling a more detached attitude, leading to greater control over nature and so even further decline in levels of anxiety.

Even in relation to nature, however, Elias argues that humans never display pure forms of either detached or involved thinking. He says that it is only very young children or extremely mentally disturbed adults who come anywhere near the complete involvement of being totally submerged in their own experience. The neuroscientist, Damasio (1994, 2000), argues that a person is only completely rational, or detached, when particular areas of the brain are damaged. Such people show no emotion but also have no moral capacity or ability to select sensible action options from an array of options which they can still rationally formulate. This is because the same areas of the brain deal with both emotion and rational selection of action options. For normal people, then, thinking is always paradoxically involved and detached at the same time; thinking rationally always also involves emotion at the same time. However, the paradox of involvement and detachment is transformed as ways of thinking that differ from one situation to another. In some situations, the aspect of involvement is more apparent while in others it is the aspect of detachment that is more apparent. This leads to how we might characterize thinking in the social sciences. Here, Elias argues that it is much harder to think in ways that are more detached because in the social sciences the phenomena we are concerned with are ourselves. Elias appeals to us to face up to the fact that we do not have 'reality congruent' ways of thinking about social phenomena such as organizations. He ascribes this to a basic fact to be found in all human experience, namely that we depend upon each other. None of us can survive on our own; indeed, there is hardly anything that any of us can do on our own. Even more fundamentally, even our very selves/identities are formed in interaction with each other. What each of us does affects others and what they do affects each of us. We inevitably both constrain and enable each other. Thus each of us is continually forming intentions and making choices of our next action but because we are interdependent none of us can control the consequences of what we do. The consequences emerge in the interplay of all our intentions and those consequences prompt further action on the part of all of us, the consequences of which will also emerge, and so on, in a process that has no beginning or end. Elias uses a vivid metaphor to depict this situation. It is as if we are chained to others who are chained to yet others. Each time one moves, the others are tugged in the same direction by these invisible chains, and as they move the first is pulled as are yet others. We are moved hither and thither in ways we find difficult to comprehend and over which we have no control.

This experience of the social nowadays is thus similar to the experience people had long ago in their encounter with nature, and the same kind of anxiety is therefore aroused. This makes it very difficult to adopt detached thinking in relation to the social and so the paradox of detached involvement tends to be transformed as 'magico-mythic' thinking. People come to talk about social forces acting on them and organizations as 'things', systems, even living systems, that exist outside of their interaction. As an example of this 'magico-mythic' thinking, Elias refers to the way in which social scientists talk about societies, institutions and organizations as 'wholes' or 'systems', which he says is the creation of a mystery in order to solve a mystery. What he calls for to generate an alternative, more detached mode of thought is a focus on the actual processes of our interdependence and this is what the perspective of complex responsive processes seeks to do.

It seems to me that mainstream organizational and management literature, the business schools and the management and leadership development programs of major organizations are all, for the most part, promoting what Elias has called magico-mythic thinking. For example, we talk about culture as a system that someone can design and move about. However, the magico-mythic nature of our explanations of organizational life is covered over by the rational sounding language in which they are presented. They promote the illusion of control, so providing social defenses against anxiety, but in the process distancing us from our actual experience and making rationally invisible what we actually do in organizations. Increasingly I have come to the view that most of the explanations of, and prescriptions for, acting in organizations amount to a massive construction of a fantasy world so that we can preserve the illusion that someone is in control. Let me give an example.

There have been many occasions when I have taken sessions with highly intelligent, highly competent senior managers on, say, leadership development programs, when the response to my suggestion that they focus attention on their own experience has been that this is not practical. They want to know how to 'apply' what I am saying. They call for prescriptions, 'tools' and techniques in the belief that this is what is practical. I may then ask them whether they derived anything practical from the session prior to mine and, if so, what that was. I am then told that the previous session did provide them with a practical tool that they could apply when they returned to the office on Monday morning. The 'tool' they refer to takes the form of a list of actions or behaviors, for example, the seven habits of effective people, or even more frequently the ubiquitous two-by-two matrix. So, for example, they may point to the 'tool' for changing their organization's culture. This diagram will have some variable measured on the vertical axis, say, solidarity. Another variable will be measured on the horizontal axis, say, open-mindedness. Four possible ways of combining these variables are depicted to yield four different categories of culture. Low solidarity and low open-mindedness leads to culture type A. Low solidarity and high open-mindedness leads to culture type B. High solidarity and low open-mindedness leads to culture type C. High solidarity and high open-mindedness leads to culture type D. The participants are then asked to locate their organization's culture on the matrix and they often discover it is the least attractive type, A. They then decide that what they need in order to succeed is culture type D, which most people think is the 'right' culture to have. The prescription is then for them to return to the office on Monday morning and promote solidarity and open-mindedness in the belief that this will enable them to shift their corporation's culture from type A to type D. What is truly astonishing is that anyone for a moment believes that this is remotely possible, let alone practical. I only have to ask them whether they actually believe they can do this for the whole fantasy to be punctured.

What is happening when people talk like this is a taken-for-granted process of reifying the organization. It feels natural to think that the organization actually exists as a thing which may be moved around. Not only do people tend to reify organizations, they quite easily slip into anthropomorphizing them. Not only is the organization a thing, it is also a kind of person with a purpose and a direction of its own, both of which may be chosen by its most powerful members. It is now not uncommon for people to talk about an organization as a living thing, a living system just like the systems in nature. It is then a short step to call for a return to ancient wisdom when thinking about organizations so as to find a simpler way that is more connected to nature. Calls are made for the re-sacralization of nature and of work. What we see here is a progressive move to highly involved, magico-mythical thinking about organizations, highly reminiscent of how people used to view nature. It is then quite natural to think of organizational life in terms of forces acting upon us to which we must submit.

What I believe the chapters in this book are doing is moving in the opposite direction to the one I have outlined above. They show how taking seriously one's experience of what one is actually doing in local interactions with others, taking seriously our interdependence, leads to very different views of what is practical. Taking this route, we come to see that there are no mysterious social forces acting upon us. Instead, we see how we are taking up global patterns in our local interactions, so reproducing and potentially transforming those global patterns. This call to focus on experience should not be mistaken for a utopian ideal for a 'return' to some primal harmony. By experience, I mean the actual experience of interaction in which we express hatred, aggression and greed, as well as love, compassion and care.

I want to turn now to a brief review of the perspective of complex responsive processes, a somewhat expanded account of which may be found in Chapter 2 of this volume. The first series of books referred to at the start of this chapter provides a detailed development of the perspective.

The perspective of complex responsive processes

From the perspective of complex responsive processes, organizations are viewed as patterns of interaction between people that are iterated as the present. Instead of abstracting from the experience of human bodily interaction, which is what we do when we posit that individuals create a system in their interaction, the perspective of complex responsive processes stays with the experience of interaction which produces nothing but further interaction. In other words, one moves from thinking in terms of a spatial metaphor, as one does when one thinks that individuals interact to produce a system outside them at a higher level, to a temporal processes way of thinking, where the temporal processes are those of human relating. Organizations are then understood as processes of human relating, because it is in the simultaneously cooperative–consensual and conflictual–competitive relating between people that everything organizational happens. It is through these ordinary, everyday processes of relating that people in organizations cope with the complexity and uncertainty of organizational life. As they do so, they perpetually construct their future together as the present.

Complex responsive processes of relating may be understood as acts of communication, relations of power, and the interplay between people's choices arising in acts of evaluation.

Acts of communication

It is because human agents are conscious and self-conscious that they are able to cooperate and reach consensus, while at the same time conflicting and competing with each other in the highly sophisticated ways in which they do. Drawing on the work of the American pragmatist George Herbert Mead (1934), one can understand consciousness (that is, mind) as arising in the communicative interaction between human bodies. Humans have evolved central nervous systems such that when one gestures to another, particularly in the form of vocal gesture or language, one evokes in one's own body responses to one's gesture that are similar to those evoked in other bodies. In other words, in their acting, humans take the attitude, the tendency to act, of the other, and it is because they have this capacity that humans can know what they are doing. It immediately follows that consciousness (knowing, mind) is a social process in which meaning emerges in the social act of gesture–response, where the gesture can never be separated from the response. Meaning does not lie in the gesture, the word, alone, but in the gesture taken together with the response to it as one social act.

Furthermore, in communicating with each other as the basis of everything they do, people do not simply take the attitude of the specific others with whom they are relating. Humans have the capacity for generalizing so that when they act they always take up the attitude of what Mead called 'the generalized other'. In other words, they always take the attitude of the group or society to their actions – they are concerned about what others might think of what they do or say. This is often unconscious and it is, of course, a powerful form of social control. According to Mead, self-consciousness is also a social process involving the capacity humans have to take themselves as an object of subjective reflection. This is a *social* process because the subject, 'I', can only ever contemplate itself as an object, 'me', which is one's perception of the attitude of society towards oneself. The 'I' is the often spontaneous and imaginative response of the socially formed individual to the 'me' as the gestures of society to oneself. Self is this emergent 'I–me' dialectic so that each self is socially formed while at the same time interacting selves are forming the social. The social may be understood as a social object. A social object is not an object in the normal sense of a thing that exists in nature but is a tendency on the part of large numbers of people to act in a similar manner in similar situations. The social object is a generalization that exists only when it is made particular in the ordinary local interaction between people. Communication, then, is not simply the sending of a signal to be received by another, but rather complex social, that is, responsive, processes of self-formation in which meaning and the society-wide pattern of the social object emerge.

Relations of power

Drawing on the work of Elias (1939), one understands how the processes of communicative interacting constitute relations of power. For Elias, power is not something which one possesses but is rather a characteristic of all human relating. In order to form, and stay in, a relationship with someone else, one cannot do whatever one wants. As soon as we enter into relationships we constrain and are constrained by others and, of course, we also enable and are enabled by others. Power is this enabling–constraining relationship where the power balance is tilted in favor of some and against others depending on the relative need they have for each other. Elias showed how such power relationships form figurations, or groupings, in which some are included and others are excluded, and where the power balance is tilted in favor of some groupings and against others. These groupings establish powerful feelings of belonging which constitute each individual's 'we' identity. These 'we' identities, derived from the groups to which we belong, are inseparable from each of our 'I' identities. As with Mead, then, we can see that processes of human relating form and are formed by individual and collective identities, which inevitably reflect complex patterns of power relating.

Choices arising in acts of evaluation

In their communicative interacting and power relating, humans are always making choices between one action and another (see Chapter 2 in this volume for a fuller development of this aspect). The choices may be made on the basis of conscious desires and intentions, or unconscious desires and choices, for example, those that are habitual, impulsive, obsessive, compulsive, compelling or inspiring. In other words, human action is always evaluative, sometimes consciously and at other times unconsciously. The criteria for evaluating these choices are values and norms, together constituting ideology. We are thus using the notion of ideology in the sense of Elias (1970), who argued that we always act according to some ideology and negating one ideology immediately gives rise to another one. Here ideology arises in the experience of bodies interacting with each other rather than as some 'whole' abstracted from experience with the potential for this to give rise to 'false' consciousness where people are alienated from their direct experience.

Norms (morals, the right, the 'ought') are evaluative criteria taking the form of obligatory restrictions which have emerged as generalizations and become habitual in a history of social interaction. We are all socialized to take up the norms of the particular groups and the society to which we belong, and this restricts what we can do as we particularize the generalized norms in our moment-by-moment specific action situations. Elias' work shows in detail how norms constitute major aspects of the personality structures, or identities, of interdependent people.

Values (ethics, the 'good') are individually felt voluntary compulsions to choose one desire, action or norm rather than another. Values arise in social processes of self-formation (Joas, 2000) – they are fundamental aspects of self, giving meaning to life, opening up opportunities for action. They arise in intense interactive experiences which are seized by the imagination and idealized as some whole to which people then feel strongly committed. Mead (1938) describes these as cult values which need to be functionalized in particular contingent situations, and this inevitably involves conflict.

Together, the voluntary compulsion of value and the obligatory restriction of norms constitute *ideology*. Ideology is the basis on which people choose desires and actions, and it unconsciously sustains power relations by making a particular figuration of power feel natural. We can see, then, that complex responsive processes of human relating form and are formed by values, norms and ideologies as integral aspects of self/identity formation in its simultaneously individual and collective form.

In describing the fundamental aspects of the complex responsive processes of human relating, we have referred on a number of occasions to *patterns* of communicative interaction, *figurations* of power relations, and *generalizations/idealizations* that are *particularized/ functionalized* in specific situations. These patterns, figurations, generalizations/idealizations and particularizations/functionalizations may all be understood as themes, taking both propositional and narrative forms, which emerge and re-emerge in the iteration in each succeeding present of the interactive processes of communication, power and evaluation. These themes organize the experience of being together, and they can be understood, in Mead's terms, as social objects and the imagined wholes of cult values which are taken up by people in their local interaction with each other in specific situations of ordinary, everyday life.

The properties of complex responsive processes of relating

By analogy with complex adaptive systems (Waldrop, 1992; Goodwin, 1994; Kauffman, 1995), the thematic patterning of interaction is understood to be:

- *Complex*. Complexity here refers to a particular dynamic or movement in time that is paradoxically stable and unstable, predictable and unpredictable, known and unknown, certain and uncertain, all at the same time. Complexity and uncertainty are both often used to refer to the situation or environment in which humans must act and this is distinguished from simple or certain environments. Prescriptions for effective action are then related to, held to be contingent upon, the type of environment. However, from the complex responsive processes perspective it is human relating itself which is complex and uncertain in the sense described above. Healthy, creative, ordinarily effective human interaction is then always complex, no matter what the situation. Patterns of human relating that lose this complexity become highly repetitive and rapidly inappropriate for dealing with the fluidity of ordinary, everyday life, taking the form of neurotic and psychotic disorders, bizarre group processes and fascist power structures.

• *Self-organizing and emergent.* Self-organizing means that agents interact with each other on the basis of their own local organizing principles, and it is in such local interaction that widespread coherence emerges without any program, plan or blueprint for that widespread pattern itself. In complex responsive processes terms, then, it is in the myriad local interactions between people that the widespread generalizations such as social objects and cult values emerge. These are particularized in the local interactions between people.

• *Evolving.* The generalizations of social object and cult value are particularized in specific situations, and this inevitably involves choices as to how to particularize them in that specific situation, which inevitably means some form of conflict. The generalizations will never be particularized in exactly the same way and the nonlinear nature of human interaction means that these small differences could be amplified into completely different generalizations. In this way, social objects and cult values evolve.

The consequences of taking a complex responsive processes perspective

I am suggesting, then, that we think about organizations in a way that is close to our ordinary, everyday life in them. We understand organizations to be the widespread patterns of interaction between people, the widespread narrative and propositional themes, which emerge in the myriad local interactions between people, both those between members of an organization and between them and other people. Thinking in this way has two important consequences.

First, no one can step outside of their interaction with others. In mainstream thinking, an organization is viewed as a system at a level above the individuals who form it. It is recognized that this organizational system is affected by patterns of power and economic relations in the wider society and these are normally thought of as forces, over and above the organization and its individual members, which shape local forms of experience. Individuals and the social are posited at different levels and causal powers are ascribed to that social level. In the kinds of process terms I am trying to use, there are no forces over and above individuals. All we have are vast numbers of continually iterated interactions between human bodies and these are local in the sense that each of us can only interact with a limited number of others. It is in the vast number of local (in this specific technical sense) interactions that widespread, global patterns of power and economic relations emerge. The widespread patterns emerge as repetition and potential transformation at the same time. We can then see highly repetitive patterns iterated over long time periods. The general comments we make about such patterns refer to what is emerging rather than to any force over and above those in whose interaction it is emerging. In their local interaction people will always be particularizing, taking up in their local interactions, these generalizations, and they may not be aware of doing so. No one can step outside of interaction to design that interaction, and from this perspective it does not make sense to think of leaders setting directions or designing widespread patterns of interaction which they can then realize. When leaders set directions or formulate organizational designs, they are in effect articulating what Mead means by social objects and cult values. What happens as a result of doing this depends upon how people take up such social objects and cult values in their local interactions with each other.

Second, then, there is no overall program, design, blueprint or plan for the organization as a 'whole'. Designs, programs, blueprints and plans exist only insofar as people are taking them up in their local interactions. Any statements that the most powerful make about organizational designs, visions and values are understood as gestures calling forth responses from many, many people in their local interactions. The most powerful can choose their own gestures but will be unable to choose the responses of others so that the outcome of their gestures will frequently produce surprising outcomes.

If one views organizations as widespread narrative patterns emerging in local interaction, how are we to think about what feel like global 'forces' operating on us?

The implications for thinking about the global and the local

From a complex responsive processes perspective, we come to question the whole idea of external 'forces' operating on us and see such an idea as a form of magico-mythical thinking applied in the social sphere. As Alison Donaldson argues in Chapter 7 of this volume, the development of the technologies of writing and printing has produced a detached way of thinking in terms of abstract categories. The technology makes it easy for us to slip into reifying the abstract categories of thought and we come to think that they actually exist. In this way we have covered over the magico-mythical nature of mainstream thinking about organizations with a rational sounding jargon of abstract categories, such as social forces. This is now so taken for granted that it is almost impossible to question it. However, the perspective of complex responsive processes does provide an alternative way of thinking by stressing human interdependence, and so focuses our attention on the detail of local interaction because it is only in the experience of local interaction that a global pattern is to be found. Global patterns are understood to be social objects and cult values, iterated over and over again in many, many local interactions, and as they are iterated they evolve because of the human capacity for spontaneity and the property of nonlinear interaction of amplifying small differences.

A very important conclusion follows from this way of thinking, namely that it is impossible to design global patterns of order simply because such patterns emerge in local interaction. Emergence means that pattern arises in the complete absence of any plan, blueprint or program for that global pattern. It follows that when people do articulate some global pattern and attempt to design it, they are doing nothing more than making a gesture, which could be a very powerful gesture. The pattern which emerges, however, is to be found only in the local responses to that global gesture. We think in a very different way about organizational change and corporate and national governance if we take this perspective. This view is explored in Chapter 2 of this volume, and Chapters 3, 4 and 5 give accounts from experience of what such a perspective means.

We also come to think about technology in a different way. Instead of focusing on technology simply as a physical object, we come to understand it as also, at the same time, a social object. This idea is developed further in Chapter 6 of this volume. Technologies have meaning for us and while we shape them, they shape us. The shaping effect of writings and printings, as social objects, is explored in Chapter 7.

The perspective of complex responsive processes is built on a social action model of communication in which meaning emerges in local interactions between people. Meaning is not located in any individual but emerges, and is continually iterated, in interaction between individuals. This is a very different model of communication to the sender–receiver model of mainstream thinking. Instead of regarding communication as an engineering problem, the perspective of complex responsive processes regards communication as human relating where power, ideology, ethics and morality are central.

The chapters in this book

In what follows I give a very brief indication of what each chapter in this volume is about. A fuller commentary on each may be found in the Editor's introduction to each chapter.

In Chapter 2, I point out how mainstream writing on organizations understands global change, government policies and technology in terms of impersonal forces or systems that become increasingly divorced from ordinary human interaction as we move from the local to higher and higher global levels. This distances us from our own experience. I then explore another way of thinking about the relationship between the local and the global from the perspective of complex responsive processes. This perspective leads to a very different view of the relationship between the local and the global in which global patterns emerge without design from local interactions.

Chapter 3 by David Scanlon, an internal consultant, is an account of a major initiative in a global corporation which seeks to design and roll out a global pattern to deal with increasing diversity in cultural terms and growing requirements for equal opportunities. This narrative reveals what happens when people try to design global patterns without realizing that such patterns cannot be designed because they emerge in myriad local interactions as described in Chapter 2. The global pattern of dealing with diversity is actually emerging in many, many local interactions. Not surprisingly, the initiative does not lead to much, at least in the two years covered by Scanlon's narrative. What people seem to be doing is preparing plans and designing indicators against which people can be measured for compliance, without discussing why they are doing it. It seems that the motivation for programs of this kind has to do with the fantasy of being able to control diversity by obliterating it and covering this over with rational jargon, while refusing to talk about what people are actually doing. For me, this is an example of the magico-mythical thinking that Elias talks about.

Chapter 4, by Michael Nolan, describes how people in a small consultancy company in Ireland, of which he is a member, have come to be stuck in their practice and explores ways in which that stuckness might shift. Nolan explores how the global pattern, which may be understood as a social object, of a particular professional practice is dynamically iterated from one present to the next in local interaction. The social object of a particular practice is taken up in local interaction in a way that sustains its stability. He explains just how this is happening and how it is only in local interaction that it could shift.

Chapter 5 moves from the situation of both large and small commercial corporations to that of a major organization in the public sector. Richard Williams, who was at the time of writing Head of the Westminster Kingsway Further Education College in the UK, describes in some detail just how the global education policies of the government, taking the form of social objects and cult values to do with performance and targets, are taken up in the local interaction between college CEOs and those charged with implementing government policies. In particular he identifies the anxieties aroused by the threats to identity to which the government's global education management policies give rise.

Chapter 6, by Stig Johannessen and myself, explores mainstream ways of thinking about technology and proposes a way of thinking about technology as social object.

In Chapter 7, Alison Donaldson, a consultant in the UK, reviews the literature on how the move from oral to literate cultures has affected the way in which we think. In doing this, she is clarifying how technology as social object is formative of our very identities. The rational, abstract thinking that literateness engenders is very evident in how people in organizations now communicate with each other.

References

Damasio, A. R. (1994) *Descartes' Error: Emotion, Reason and the Human Brain*, London: Picador.

Damasio, A. R. (2000) *The Feeling of What Happens: Body and Emotion in the Making of Consciousness*, London: Heinemann.

Elias, N. (1939) *The Civilizing Process*, Oxford: Blackwell.

Elias, N. (1970) *What is Sociology?*, Oxford: Blackwell.

Elias, N. (1987) *Involvement and Detachment*, Oxford: Blackwell.

Fonseca, J. (2002) *Complexity and Innovation in Organizations*, London: Routledge.

Goodwin, B. (1994) *How the Leopard Changed its Spots*, London: Weidenfeld & Nicolson.

Griffin, D. (2002) *The Emergence of Leadership: Linking self-organization and ethics*, London: Routledge.

Joas, H. (2000) *The Genesis of Values*, Cambridge: Polity Press.

Kauffman, S. A. (1995) *At Home in the Universe*, New York: Oxford University Press.

Mead, G. H. (1934) *Mind, Self and Society*, Chicago, IL: Chicago University Press.

Mead, G. H. (1938) *The Philosophy of the Act*, Chicago, IL: Chicago University Press.

Shaw, P. (2002) *Changing Conversations in Organizations: A complexity approach to change*, London: Routledge.

Stacey, R. (2001) *Complex Responsive Processes in Organizations: Learning and knowledge creation*, London: Routledge.

Stacey, R. (2003) *Strategic Management and Organizational Dynamics: The Challenge of Complexity* (4th edn), London: Pearson Education.

Stacey, R. and Griffin, D. (eds) (2005) *A Complexity Perspective on Researching Organizations: Taking experience seriously*, London: Routledge.

Stacey, R., Griffin, D. and Shaw, P. (2000) *Complexity and Management: Fad or radical challenge to systems thinking?*, London: Routledge.

Streatfield, P. (2001) *The Paradox of Control in Organizations*, London: Routledge.

Waldrop, M. M. (1992) *Complexity: The Emerging Science at the Edge of Chaos*, Englewood Cliffs, NJ: Simon & Schuster.

2 Local and global processes in organizational life

Ralph Stacey

● **The relevance of the complexity sciences for understanding human organizations**
● **Organizations understood as complex responsive processes of relating**
● **The relationship between local interaction and global patterns**
● **A different understanding of social forces/structures**

People in organizations accomplish whatever it is they accomplish through continually interacting with a relatively small number of others. We can describe this as local interaction. It does not matter where one is in the hierarchy of an organization, one is still interacting on an hourly, daily basis with a small group of others. Even the CEO of a huge corporation spends his or her day relating to only a small fraction of the organization's membership, just as any clerk much lower down the hierarchy does. The number of colleagues the CEO interacts with may well be larger than those the clerk interacts with, but both are limited and in that sense both are local. The power ratio is tilted substantially towards the CEO and away from the clerk so that the actions of the CEO may evoke responses from very large numbers of people while the actions of the clerk are attended to by only a few. However, although responses to the CEO's actions may be numerous, their very number means that they cannot be direct responses to him or her. Instead those responses will be expressed in many, many local situations. In all of these local situations people are interacting with each other according to patterns, themes, habits or routines, which they may spontaneously adapt at a particular time according to the contingencies of the particular situation in which they find themselves. All of this reflects their own personal histories and the histories of the local groupings in which they find themselves. The point is that no matter who we are, each of us is always interacting locally to get things done in organizations.

But at the same time, no matter who we are, we are constrained in what we do together locally by what may feel like major *external forces* beyond our control, widespread, overall *structures* we have to take as given, *institutionalized instruments of power* which we have no option but to submit to, pre-existing *technologies* that shape what we do, and *allocations of resources* about which we can do little. We can describe this as the global. For example, we are constrained by our organization's hierarchical structure, its authorizing and reporting procedures, particularly to do with the allocation of resources, and the accepted ways of talking and doing things that we call the organization's culture. Just as constraining are the 'forces' and 'structures' of the wider society of which our organization is a part (e.g. the law, government policies for regulating industries and controlling public sector organizations, market allocation of monetary resources, legislation and pressure to provide equal opportunities, collective campaigns to do with animal rights and ecological sustainability, trends such as globalization). To understand how we get things done in organizations, therefore, we need to understand the relationship between local interaction and the global, which may usually be felt as only constraining but which is, of course, at the same time enabling.

Nowadays, the most widespread way of understanding the relationship between the local and the global is in terms of systems. People interact locally in a team, project group or department and this is often thought of as a system produced by the interaction of individual members who are understood as parts of that system. So each team, group, department has its own purpose, objectives, missions, procedures and local ways of doing things, which together constitute a system, and members must conform to this system if it is all to work. In other words, in their interaction people form the system, and that system acts in turn as a causal force on their interactions. However, such a local system cannot operate in isolation but must interact with other teams, groups and departments, also understood as systems. In their interaction, these subsystems form the organizational system, and that organizational system is thought to act back on each subsystem as a causal force. Each subsystem must fit in with the purpose, objectives, missions, procedures and organization-wide ways of doing things. It is this higher level, global requirement that is felt as constraining, although it is also enabling.

Furthermore, no organizational system can operate in isolation but must interact with other organizational systems, together producing an even higher global level or suprasystem such as an industry, market, nation or society. Each organizational system must then fit in with the wider purposes, objectives, procedures and ways of doing things characteristic of the suprasystem. It is this requirement which is felt to be an external force that constrains members of every organization, although it enables cooperative action as well. The suprasystem, therefore, acts back on organizations as a causal force shaping organizational systems. Then there is an even higher level system of industries, nations and societies interacting with each other to produce global economies and international bodies, and these too act back as causal forces on the lower level systems.

In this way of thinking, then, we have the notion of a nested hierarchy of systems in which the higher levels act back as enabling constraints on the lower levels which in turn produce the higher levels. Down at the bottom of this hierarchy is the local interaction of people in their teams, groups and departments, and as one moves up this hierarchy one increasingly encounters the global. At the local level people are severely constrained in what they can do by the requirements of the various global levels. Furthermore, each level is understood to be subject to its own laws and these become the focus of different academic disciplines. Thus at the level of the individual we need to turn to psychology, and at the level of the team or group, ways of understanding group dynamics become relevant. Then at the level of the organization, explanations are provided by micro economics, and organizational and management theory. At the level of markets and industries, it is macro-economics that provides the required explanations. At the level of nations and societies, we turn to sociology and political theory.

What happens in this way of thinking is that we begin to understand what is happening in terms of impersonal forces or systems that become increasingly divorced from ordinary human interaction as we move from the local to higher and higher global levels. For example, neo-classical economics is built on a very simple assumption about humans, summarized in the phrase 'economic man' who is assumed to be a calculating, utility-maximizing agent. Thereafter, the modeling and theorizing of economic science broadly continues in terms of impersonal market forces or impersonal routines without much reference to people. The same may be said for the modeling and theorizing to be found in mainstream organizational theory and sociology. Throughout, people, ordinary human bodies, are conspicuous by their absence, and their ordinary everyday experiences as they go about their daily work in their local situations are disregarded as rather unimportant. They are thought to be so constrained by the operation of the higher level systems that the focus of attention is on the design of those impersonal higher level systems. It is thought that if we are to become more effective, if we are to change, then this requires designed change in some higher level system. It will not be enough if people try to change anything in their own local interactions. One result of this thinking, now so widely taken up, is that people at local levels feel powerless and alienated from their own experience. And it has important ethical implications in that when things go wrong, we think that the blame must be directed at the higher level systems and those senior people who are responsible for them. The recent Hutton Enquiry in the UK into allegations that the government distorted intelligence information to justify the Iraq War provides a very clear example. Hutton concluded that members of the government were not to blame and condemned the BBC for broadcasting the inaccurate allegations. In particular, it was concluded that the fault lay in the BBC's editorial system and that top executives of the BBC were to blame for this. The Chairman and the CEO were then forced to resign and assurances were given that the system would be improved.

What I have been describing thus far is a particular, widely prevalent way of understanding the relationship between local interaction and the global, which I find problematic because of the way it distances us from our own experience. The purpose of this chapter is to explore another way of thinking about the relationship between the local and the global. This other way is a perspective that colleagues and I have been calling complex responsive processes (Stacey et al., 2000; Stacey, 2001; Griffin, 2001). Some of the fundamental propositions upon which this perspective is based are drawn by analogy from the complexity sciences, particularly the notion of complex adaptive systems. The following section comments on complex adaptive systems and their relevance to human interaction, and the one after that gives a brief summary of the perspective of complex responsive processes. The subsequent sections go on to explore how this perspective leads to a very different view of the relationship between the local and the global compared to the one described briefly above.

The relevance of the complexity sciences for understanding human organizations

The complexity sciences are concerned with phenomena that are characterized by nonlinear dynamics and encompass a number of areas, for example, mathematical chaos theory (Gleick, 1988), dissipative structure theory (Prigogine and Stengers, 1984), and the theory of complex adaptive systems (Goodwin, 1994; Kauffman, 1995). The latter is of particular interest because the approach taken is that of agent-based modeling. A complex adaptive system consists of very large numbers of interacting entities known as agents. During their interaction they adapt to each other, forming a system that adapts to its environment. Examples of phenomena whose behavior is being modeled in this way are termites constructing large structures, ants signaling food locations, birds flocking, and billions of neurons interacting in a brain to produce coherent patterns of thought and action. This agent-based approach is of particular interest to social scientists because human groups, organizations and societies may also be thought of as agents interacting with each other. Phenomena such as these are explored through computer simulations in which each individual agent is represented by a set of computer instructions, or rules, which specify how the agent is to interact with a limited number of other agents. Each agent then *is* a set of computer instructions to do with interaction; that is, a big string of 0s and 1s arranged in a particular pattern. In other words, each agent is a pattern of digital symbols. There is no program or blueprint for any overall, global pattern, only the programs which are the individual agents. Large numbers of agents, or patterns of digital symbols, are then left to interact with each other and any overall or global patterns produced are observed and studied. The question is whether there can be any global coherence even though there is no global design, plan or program. What the simulation amounts to, then, is the continuing iteration over time of local interaction between agents, and what the scientists are looking for is global patterns in these iterations and for what may be deduced from them. The large numbers of simulations explored so far all reveal certain common properties.

First, the simulations demonstrate that local interaction between patterns of digital symbols produces emergent order or coherence of a widespread or global kind. This global order emerges in the complete absence of any blueprint, program or plan for that global order. Another way of putting this is to say that large numbers of agents interacting locally with each other can produce overall coherence without any overall plan. Local interaction means that each agent is following its own rules in interacting with a relatively few others and this local interaction is referred to as self-organization. It is through processes of self-organization, understood in this very specific sense, that global coherence emerges without any global plan.

In complex adaptive system theory, the emergent global coherence is understood to constitute a whole, a system, hence the name 'complex adaptive systems'. It is then an easy move to thinking that it is the system that is organizing itself and/or it is the agents who are organizing themselves to produce the whole. Furthermore, it may also be argued that the emergent whole, or system, displays properties that cannot be reduced to the level of the individual agents and, indeed, this is often put forward as a definition of emergence. The emergent whole may then be understood to have its own regularities, or laws, which depend upon but cannot be reduced to, or predicted from, the lower level (Gell-Mann, 1994). Thus chemical phenomena may be thought of as emerging from physics, with biology emerging from chemistry and human individuals emerging from biology. Each level may in turn be thought of as a complex adaptive system. One could then argue that groups, organizations and societies emerge from individuals, constituting higher levels as complex adaptive systems with their own regularities or laws.

The theory of complex adaptive systems, therefore, leads to much the same way of thinking about the relationship between the local and the global in human interaction as that based on earlier systems theories outlined at the beginning of this chapter. The major difference, however, is the insight that global order emerges from local interaction in the absence of a global plan. I will be arguing below that, while it may be useful to think in terms of nested systems in the natural sciences, it is not appropriate when it comes to thinking about human action. I will be arguing that what is emerging in the local – that is, self-organizing – interaction of human agents is not a system at all but further patterns of interaction both locally and globally at the same time. I will be arguing for a move from systems thinking, with its spatial metaphor of levels, to temporal process thinking (Stacey, 2003), and in doing so drawing analogously on the property that the simulations display of iterative interaction patterning itself over time. It is then not systems or agents organizing themselves but the patterns of interaction between the agents which may be said to be organizing themselves. I will suggest that this leads to a rather different way of thinking about the relationship between the local and the global when it comes to human action.

The second property displayed by simulations of complex adaptive systems has to do with diversity. It is important to draw a distinction between simulations in which the agents are homogeneous and those in which they are heterogeneous. Where the agents are all the same as each other, in the sense that they all follow exactly the same rules of interaction, then it is only possible for one global pattern to emerge from their interaction and there is no possibility of spontaneous movement to another pattern, let alone any possibility that new patterns could emerge (Allen, 1998a, 1998b). It is only when random events, or fluctuations, are introduced into the model that it displays the capacity to move to another global pattern, and it is only when the agents are different from each other that the possibility arises of the emergence of new patterns. In other words, it is only when the agents are different from each other that the global patterns emerging in their local interaction can evolve (Allen, 1998a, 1998b). The evolution occurs through the amplification of small differences in each iterative interaction and we see emerging global patterns displaying continuity and potential transformation at the same time.

The matter of diversity links to a third property displayed by simulations of complex adaptive systems, namely unpredictability. Some complexity scientists, it seems to me, identify unpredictability with the movement from one system level to another. For example, Gell-Mann (1994) describes how interaction between systems at one level, together with some chance or accidental events, produces emergent systems at a higher level, which cannot be predicted from the interaction at the lower level. However, he refers to the higher level system as a 'frozen accident' displaying regularities that enable prediction. Others (e.g. Kaufmann, 1995) regard unpredictability as an inherent ongoing characteristic of complex adaptive systems at all levels. It seems to me that if one is talking about a heterogeneous complex adaptive system, one that evolves, so producing novelty, then one has to be talking about unpredictability. A system which is continually evolving through amplifying small differences must be continually moving into an unknown future, but not any future, because the history of the system constrains its future possibilities. It is then probably more accurate to talk about a paradox of predictability and unpredictability at the same time.

To summarize, complex adaptive system simulations demonstrate that when agents (digital symbols) iteratively interact locally according to their own rules of interaction, then global patterns of order or coherence emerge, paradoxically predictable and unpredictable at the same time, in the absence of any global program or plan. Furthermore, when these agents are different to each other, both they and the global patterns emerging in their interaction evolve, so producing novelty. So, instead of thinking that local interaction is producing a global whole, or system, we could think of patterns of local interaction as producing further patterns of both local interaction and global patterns at the same time. There is then no need to think in terms of systems or wholes at all. However, even then, the simulations are highly abstract, showing the properties of certain kinds of abstract interaction between abstract agents in the domain of digital symbols. To be useful in any other domain, say, biology, it is necessary to bring to these abstract relationships the attributes of that particular domain. In other words, the simulations can only ever be a source domain for analogies that might be useful in some other domain when interpreted in terms of the attributes of that other domain. It is not admissible, I argue, to simply apply complex adaptive systems theory to some other domain, and this applies with particular force to the human domain.

In thinking about the implications of complex adaptive systems simulations for human action it is essential to take account of the nature of human agents. First, it is highly simplistic to think of human beings as rule-following beings. In our acting, we may take account of rules but can hardly be said to follow them blindly as do the digital agents in computer simulations. The essential and distinctive characteristic of human agents is that they are living bodies who are conscious and self-conscious beings capable of spontaneity, imagination, fantasy and creative action. Human agents are essentially reflexive and reflective. Furthermore, they are essentially social beings in a distinctive way in that they do not interact blindly according to mechanistic rules but engage in meaningful communicative interaction with each other in which they establish power relations between themselves. In addition, in interacting with each other humans exercise at least some degree of choice in how they will respond to the actions of others and this involves the use of some form of evaluative criteria. Human agents also use simple and increasingly complicated tools and technologies to accomplish what they choose to do. It is these embodied attributes of consciousness, self-consciousness, reflection and reflexivity, creativity, imagination and fantasy, communication, meaning, power, choice, evaluation, tool use and sociality that should be explicitly brought to any interpretation, as regards human beings, of the insights derived from complex adaptive system simulations.

As soon as one does explicitly take account of the above essential attributes of human agents, it becomes problematic to talk about human systems. Some 250 years ago, Kant introduced the notion of system as a useful way of understanding organisms in nature but cautioned against applying this notion to human action. A system is a whole produced by its parts and separated by a boundary from other wholes. A part is only a part insofar as it is doing what is required to produce the whole. If one thought of a human individual as a part then by definition that individual could not exercise choices. If individuals did make their own choices, they could not be said to be parts of a system because they would be acting in their own interests instead of in the interests of the system. In addition to making choices, humans form figurations of power relations in which they act in the interests of their own group, often in conflict with other groups. They are then not acting in the interests of a wider, more global system, but in their own interests. Human agents cannot, therefore, be thought of as parts of a system because individually and collectively they exercise choice and engage in power plays. If one is to think of humans designing a system, one encounters the problem that the designer has to be viewed as taking an observer position outside of the system in order to design it. But the designer, being human, is also part of the system. Second order systems thinking (Jackson, 2000; Midgley, 2000) tries to address this problem by widening the boundary of the system to include the observer. But this simply sets up the need for an outside observer of the wider system, so leading to an argument characterized by infinite regress.

Furthermore, with one exception, systems models cannot explain how anything novel could arise because a system is always unfolding the pattern already enfolded in it by its rules of operation. The one exception is complex adaptive systems consisting of agents characterized by diversity. Here, the model takes on a life of its own, as it were, evolving unpredictably in ways that no one has programmed. This is the same as saying that of its very essence no one can design its evolution as small differences are amplified into significant, unforeseeable changes. The agents in such a system are forming the system while being formed by it at the same time, but in a mechanistic way in which they display no consciousness, self-consciousness, imagination, reflexivity, choice, creativity or spontaneity. Furthermore, there are practical problems with such a system model. If the model takes on a life of its own, while the phenomenon being modeled also takes on a life of its own, it is highly unlikely that both will follow the same trajectory. The explanatory power of the model is then questionable. It also becomes unclear what might be meant by a 'boundary' or a 'whole' in relation to such a system model. If it is evolving in unpredictable ways, the 'whole' will always be incomplete and the boundary unclear. It seems to me that in pointing to the nature of their dynamics, heterogeneous complex adaptive system models begin to unravel the usefulness of thinking in systems terms at all. If we avoid thinking in terms of systems when it comes to human interaction then the explanation of the relationship between the local and the global in terms of a nested hierarchy of systems falls away.

What then is an alternative way of thinking about the relationship between local interaction and global pattern, one that takes explicit account of the central features of human agency listed above? The alternative is to take as analogies the properties of iterative interaction, or temporal process, from the domain of heterogeneous complex adaptive systems and to interpret them in terms of key human attributes. Colleagues and I have been attempting to do this in what we have called the perspective of complex responsive processes. The following section provides a brief summary of this perspective before turning, in the section after that, to what it implies for the relationship between local interaction and the global.

Organizations understood as complex responsive processes of relating

The book series 'Complexity and Emergence in Organizations' (Stacey *et al.*, 2000; Fonseca, 2001; Griffin, 2001; Stacey, 2001; Streatfield, 2001; Shaw, 2002) provides a detailed development of the theory of complex responsive processes. In this section, I will point to some of its key features that are relevant to the argument of this chapter. A key property of complex adaptive systems, referred to above, is that of processes of interaction in digital symbols patterning themselves as both local and global order at the same time. How might we take this abstract relationship from the domain of complex adaptive systems to the domain of human interaction? Well, human interaction is basically responsive communication between human bodies where each is conscious and self-conscious, and so capable of reflection, reflexivity, imagination and fantasy, thereby having some choice and displaying some spontaneity. The first key aspect of the complex responsive process of relating between human bodies is, therefore, communicative interaction, and

George Herbert Mead's (1934) theories of conversation provide a
powerful way of understanding this. It leads us to think of organizations
as ongoing temporal processes of human communicative interaction.

Communicative interaction

Drawing on the work of the American pragmatist George Herbert
Mead (1934), one can understand consciousness as arising in the
communicative interaction between human bodies. Humans have evolved
central nervous systems such that when one gestures to another,
particularly in the form of vocal gesture or language, one evokes in
one's own body responses to one's gesture that are similar to those evoked
in other bodies. Mead refers to this as communication in the medium
of significant symbols. In other words, in their acting, humans take the
attitude, the tendency to act, of the other and it is because they have this
capacity to communicate in significant symbols that humans can know
what they are doing. It immediately follows that consciousness (knowing,
mind) is a social process in which meaning emerges in the social act of
gesture–response, where the gesture can never be separated from the
response. Meaning does not lie in the gesture, the word, alone, but only
in the gesture taken together with the response to it.

Furthermore, in communicating with each other, as the basis of
everything they do, people do not simply take the attitude of the specific
others with whom they are relating at any one time. Humans have the
capacity for generalizing so that when they act they always take up the
attitude of what Mead called the generalized other. In other words, they
always take the attitude of the group or society to their actions – they are
concerned about what others may think of what they do or say. This is
often unconscious and it is, of course, a powerful form of social control.

Human society is a society of selves, and selves exist only in relation
to other selves. A self is an individual who organizes his or her own
response by the tendencies on the part of others to respond to his or
her act. Self exists in taking the role of others. According to Mead,
self-consciousness is thus a social process involving the capacity humans
have as subjects to take themselves as an object. This is a social process
because the subject, 'I', can only ever be an object to itself as 'me', and
the 'me' is one's perception of the attitude of society towards oneself.
The 'I' is the often spontaneous and imaginative response of the socially
formed individual to the 'me' as the gesture of society to oneself. Self is

this 'I–me' dialectic, where 'I' and 'me' are inseparable phases of the same action, so that each self is socially formed while at the same time interacting selves are forming the social. Communication, then, is not simply the sending of a signal to be received by another, but rather complex social, that is, responsive, processes of self-formation in which meaning and society-wide patterns emerge. One cannot, therefore, be a self independently of social interaction. Selves are social selves and society is a society of selves.

For Mead, mind is a private role play/silent conversation of a body with itself, and the social is the public, vocal interaction or conversation between bodies. Furthermore, such gestures indicate to the other how the social act is likely to unfold further. Mead explains what he means by an individual calling forth a similar response in herself as in the other. He means that she is taking the attitude of the other and he defines attitude as the tendency to act in a particular way. Mind then is the activity of experiencing a similar attitude, a similar tendency to act in a particular way, in response to gestures directed to others. Mind here is clearly a social phenomenon.

Simulations of complex adaptive systems demonstrate that it is possible for global order to emerge in local interaction in the medium of digital symbols. In an abstract sense interaction patterns itself as local and global order at the same time. In Mead's work we see a theory of consciousness and self-consciousness emerging in the social interaction between human bodies in the medium of significant symbols, and at the same time widespread social patterns also emerge. Human interaction forms and is formed by the social at the same time. To put this another way, local interaction forms and is formed by global pattern at the same time. Human interaction patterns itself, as does digital interaction, but the argument is conducted without any reference to rules, systems or 'wholes', focusing instead on key aspects of human agency as iterative temporal processes.

Particularly important in this way of understanding human interaction is the human capacity for generalizing, for taking the attitude of the generalized other as consciousness and the 'me' phase of the 'I–me' dialectic where the 'me' is the generalized attitude of the society to the 'I'. I will be exploring this notion of generalization in Mead's work in greater detail below because it is key to understanding the relationship between the local and the global. But before that consider the second key aspect of complex responsive processes of relating which has to do with power. Here the work of Norbert Elias is particularly instructive.

Relations of power

Drawing on the work of Elias (1939), one understands how the processes of communicative interacting constitute relations of power. For Elias, power is not something anyone possesses but, rather, is a characteristic of all human relating. In order to form, and stay in, a relationship with someone else, one cannot do whatever one wants. As soon as we enter into relationships, therefore, we constrain and are constrained by others and, of course, we also enable and are enabled by others. Power is this enabling–constraining relationship where the power balance is tilted in favor of some and against others depending on the relative need they have for each other. Elias showed how such power relationships form figurations, or groupings, in which some are included and others are excluded, and where the power balance is tilted in favor of some groupings and against others. These groupings establish powerful feelings of belonging which constitute each individual's 'we' identity. These 'we' identities, derived from the groups we belong to, are inseparable from each of our 'I' identities. As with Mead, then, we can see that processes of human relating form and are formed by individual and collective identities, which inevitably reflect complex patterns of power relating. Furthermore, Elias shows how these power figurations are sustained, unconsciously, by ideologies, which are in turn sustained by gossip and processes of shame.

Choices arising in acts of evaluation

In their communicative interacting and power relating, humans are always making choices between one action and another. This may be on the basis of conscious desires and intentions, or unconscious desires and choices (e.g. those that are habitual, impulsive, obsessive or compulsive). In other words, human action is always evaluative, sometimes consciously and at other times unconsciously. The criteria for evaluating these choices are values and norms, together constituting ideology. This aspect is explored more fully in Chapter 2 of another volume in this series of books (Griffin and Stacey, 2005).

Norms (morals, the right, the 'ought') are evaluative criteria taking the form of obligatory restrictions which have emerged as generalizations and become habitual in a history of social interaction (Joas, 2000). We are all socialized to take up the norms of the particular groups and the society to which we belong, and this restricts what we can do as we particularize the generalized norms in our moment-by-moment specific action situations. Elias' work shows in detail how norms constitute major aspects of the personality structures, or identities, of interdependent people.

Values (ethics, the 'good') are individually felt voluntary compulsions to choose one desire, action or norm rather than another. Values arise in social processes of self-formation and self-transcendence (Joas, 2000; Dewey, 1934) – they are fundamental aspects of self, giving meaning to life, opening up opportunities for action. They arise in intense interactive experiences which are seized by the imagination and idealized as some 'whole' to which people then feel strongly committed. Mead (1938) described these as cult values which need to be functionalized in particular contingent situations, and this inevitably involves conflict.

Together the voluntary compulsion of values and the obligatory restriction of norms constitute *ideology*. Ideology is the basis on which people choose desires and actions and it unconsciously sustains power relations by making a particular figuration of power feel natural (Dalal, 1998). We can see, then, that complex responsive processes of human relating form and are formed by values, norms and ideologies as integral aspects of self/identity formation in its simultaneously individual and collective form.

The thematic patterning of human experience

In the above description of the fundamental aspects of the complex responsive processes of human relating, I have referred to *patterns* of communicative interaction and *figurations* of power relations. These patterns and figurations may be understood as themes, taking both propositional and narrative forms, which emerge and re-emerge in the iteration, in each succeeding present, of the interactive processes of communication, power and evaluation. Particular themes are values, norms and ideologies. These themes organize the experience of being together.

Complex responsive processes of relating are, therefore, simultaneously processes of communicative interaction, power relating and ideological evaluation in which local individual selves/identities and the global patterns of the social emerge at the same time, each forming and being formed by the other at the same time. They are continually iterated as continuity and transformation which is possible because of the spontaneity of the 'I' and the possibility of small differences being escalated into transformed patterns. And pattern means the largely narrative themes that are individual selves and social phenomena at the same time.

The use of tools

Communicative interaction between people in organizations frequently involves the use of highly sophisticated tools. Obvious examples are telephones, the Internet, email, documents of all types and the wider media of television and newspapers. Less obvious, perhaps, are management systems of information and control, including budgets, plans of all types, monitoring, evaluation and appraisal systems, databases and so on. National and international financial systems may also be thought of as tools in communicative interaction, so entering into the patterning of the themes of communicative interaction in organizations and other groups. When people interact with each other in their local situations they talk to each other in ways that have reference to these systems and procedural tools. In fact, these tools shape the themes of communicative interaction, both enabling and exercising powerful constraints on that communication. However, meaning does not lie in the tools but in the gestures–responses made with the tools.

In order to explore in more detail the broad statements made in the previous paragraphs about the relationship between the local and the global, I want to return to the points Mead makes about human capacities for generalization.

Generalizing/idealizing and functionalizing: social objects and cult values

Mead's main concern was not simply with a dyadic form of communication but with much wider, more complex patterns of interaction between many people. He was concerned with complex social acts in which many people engage in conversations through which they accomplish the tasks of fitting in and conflicting with each other to realize their objectives and purposes. People do not come to an interaction with each other afresh each time because they are born into an already existing, socially evolved pattern and they continue to play their part in its further evolution. This leads Mead to his concept of the generalized other. In order to accomplish complex social acts, it is not enough for those involved to be able to take the attitude of the small numbers of people they may be directly engaged with at a particular time. They need to be able to take the attitude of all of those directly or indirectly engaged in the complex social act. It would be impossible to do this in relation to each individual so engaged, but humans have developed the capacity to generalize the attitudes of many. In acting in the present, each individual is then taking up the attitude of a few specific others and at the same time the attitude of this generalized other, the attitude of the group, the organization or the society. These wider, generalized attitudes are evolving historically and are always implicated in very human action. In play, the child takes the role of another. But in the game the child must take on not only the role of the other but of the game; that is, of all participants in the game and its rules and procedures. The generalized other is the taking of the attitude of all other participants.

In the evolution of society many generalizations emerge which are taken up, or particularized in people's interactions with each other. This is a point of major importance. Mead draws attention to paradoxical processes of generalization and particularization at the same time. Mental and social activities are processes of generalizing and particularizing at the same time. Individuals act in relation to that which is common to all of them (generalizing) but responded to somewhat differently by each of them in each present time period (particularizing).

Mead provided a number of formulations of these generalizing–particularizing processes. One such formulation is his explanation of self-consciousness referred to above. In understanding self-consciousness Mead talked about a person taking the attitude of the group to himself, where that attitude is the 'me'. It is important to bear in mind that Mead was saying something more than that the self arises in the attitude, the tendency to act, of specific others towards oneself. Mead was talking about a social, generalizing process where the 'me' is a generalization across a whole community or society. For example, what it means to be an individual, a person, a man or a woman, a professional and so on does not arise in relation to a few specific people but to a particular society in a particular era. We in the West think of ourselves now as individuals in a completely different way to how people in the West did 400 years ago and in a different way to people in other cultures. In the 'I–me' dialectical, then, we have a process in which the generalization of the 'me' is made particular in the response of the 'I' for a particular person at a particular time in a particular place. For example, I may take up what it means to be a man in my society in a particular way that differs in some respects from how others see themselves as men in my own society, in other societies and at other times.

Mead's discussion of what he called the social object is yet another formulation of this generalizing and particularizing process. Mead distinguishes between a physical object and a social object. A physical object exists in nature and is the proper object of study in the natural sciences, while the social object is the proper object of study in the social sciences. While the physical object may be understood in terms of itself, the social object has to be understood in terms of social acts. Mead referred to market exchange as an example of a social act. When one person offers to buy food this act obviously involves a complex range of responses from other people to provide the food. However, it involves more than this because the one making the offer can only know how to make the offer if he or she is able to take the attitude of the other parties to the bargain. All essential phases of the complex social act of exchange must appear in the actions of those involved and appear as essential features of each individual's actions. Buying and selling are involved in each other.

Mead, therefore, defined the social act as one involving the cooperation of many people in which the different parts of the act undertaken by different individuals appear in the act of each individual. The tendencies to act as others act are present in the conduct of each individual involved, and it is this presence that is responsible for the appearance of the social object in the experience of each individual. The social act defines the object of the act and this is a social object which is to be found only in the conduct of the different individuals engaged in the complex social act. The social object appears in the experience of each individual as a stimulus to a response not only by that individual but also by the others involved – this is how each can know how the others are likely to act and it is the basis of coordination. A social object is thus a kind of gesture together with tendencies to respond in particular ways. Social objects are common plans or patterns of action related to the existent future of the act. The social object is a generalization which is taken up, or particularized, by all in a group/society in their actions. Social objects have evolved in the history of the society of selves and each individual is born into such a world of social objects. The conduct of individuals marks out and defines the social objects which make up their environment in which the nature of the social objects and the sensitivities of individuals answer to each other. In other words, individuals are forming social objects while being formed by them in an evolutionary process.

Mead linked social objects to social control. Social control is the bringing of the act of the individual into relation with the social object, and the contours of the object determine the organization of the act. The social act is distributed among many, but the whole social object appears in the experience of all of them. Social control depends upon the degree to which the individual takes the attitude of the others; that is, takes the attitude which is the social object. All institutions are social objects and serve to control individuals who find them in their experience.

Mead also linked social objects to values and, in another formulation of the interaction between the general and the particular, he draws a distinction between cult values and their functionalization. Cult values are idealizations that emerge in the evolution of a society. Mead said that they were the most precious part of our heritage and examples of cult values are democracy, treating others with respect, regarding life as sacred, belief in being American or British and so on. Other examples are mission and vision statements in organizations. Such cult values present people with the image of an idealized future shorn of all constraints. If such values are applied directly to action, without allowing for variations contingent on a specific situation, then those undertaking such action form a cult in which they exclude all who do not comply. In the usual course of events, however, this does not happen as people act on present interpretations of cult values. For example, a cult value to do with the sacredness of life is not directly applied in some places leading to conflict regarding, for example, abortion. Functionalization of cult values inevitably leads to conflict and the negotiation of compromises around such conflict. Functionalizing of values is the enactment of values in the ordinary, local interactions between people in the living present. In his notion of cult values, Mead points not only to the generalizing tendencies of interacting people but also to the idealizing tendencies characteristic of their interaction. Such idealizations may be good or bad depending upon who is doing the judging.

Mead's notions of social objects and cult values have something in common with the notions of social structure, habit and routine. What was distinctive about Mead's approach to these matters, however, is how he avoided positing social structure as a phenomenon that exists outside individuals. Social objects and cult values are generalizations and idealizations that only have any existence in their particularization in the ordinary, everyday interactions between people in the living present.

It is important to note how Mead used the term 'object' in a social sense as a 'tendency to act' rather than as a concept or a thing, which are meanings appropriate to physical objects. In a social setting, then, Mead used the term 'object' in tension with the usual understanding of object as a thing in nature. The pattern or tendency Mead calls an object is in a sense an object in that it is what we perceive in taking it up in our acting, but this is perception of our own acting not a thing. We seem to have a strong tendency to reify patterns of acting and this makes it important to emphasize that Mead's social object is not a thing.

To summarize, social objects are *generalized tendencies*, common to large numbers of people, *to act in similar ways in similar situations*. These generalized tendencies to act are iterated in each living present as rather repetitive, *habitual patterns of action*. However, in their continual iteration, these general tendencies to act are normally *particularized* in the specific situation and the specific present in which the actors find themselves. Such particularization is inevitably a *conflictual process* of interpretation as the meaning of the generalization is established in a specific situation. The possibility of *transformation*, that is, further evolution, of the social object arises in this particularizing because of the potential for *spontaneity* to generate variety in human action and the capacity of nonlinear interaction to *amplify* consequent small differences in their particularization. While physical objects are to be found in nature, social objects can only be experienced in their particularization in complex social acts in the living present. Social objects do not have any existence outside of such particularizing social acts.

As well as being generalizations, social objects may also take the form of *idealizations* or cult values. Such cult values present to people a future free of conflicts and constraints, evoking a sense of enlarged personality in which they can accomplish anything. Such values have the effect of *including* those who adhere to them and *excluding* those who do not, so establishing collective or *"we" identities* for all the individuals in both groupings. Social objects/cult values are thus closely linked to *power*. Social objects as generalized tendencies to act in similar ways both enable and constrain the actors at the same time. Social objects are thus forms of *social control* reflected in figurations of power relations between people.

The relationship between local interaction and global patterns

In all his formulations of human communicative interaction, Mead presented the same paradox. Gesture and response are inseparable phases of one social act in which meaningful patterns of interaction arise. I suggest that these meaningful patterns take the form of narrative and propositional themes that organize the experience of being together. Such themes are iterated in each present taking the paradoxical form of habit, or continuity, and potential transformation at the same time. The essentially reflexive nature of human consciousness and self-consciousness means that we have the capacity to reflect imaginatively on these patterns, articulating both the habitual and the just emerging transformations and in doing so either sustain the habitual or reinforce the transformation of habit.

In our reflection we generalize the tendencies we observe across many current situations, creating imaginative 'wholes' that have never existed and never will (Dewey, 1934). What we are doing in creating these imaginative 'wholes' is constructing in our interaction perceptions of unity in the patterning of our interactions. That imaginatively perceived unity is then a generalized tendency to act in similar situations in similar ways. What is emerging is the imaginative generalization that is one phase of what Mead calls social object. The other phase, which is inseparable from the generalization, is the particularizing of the general in the specific contingent situations we find ourselves in. The general may only be found in its particularization in our local interaction and that particularizing inevitably involves conflict. A particularly important form of social object is the norms, the obligatory constraints, that serve as the moral basis for choosing one action rather than another. In reflecting upon our patterns of interaction, in generalizing those patterns and in imaginatively constructing some kind of unity of experience, we employ the tools of writing to codify habits or routines (for example, as law), and even design changes in them. However, any intentionally designed change can only ever be a generalization and what that means can only be found in the particularization; that is, in the interplay between the intentions of the designers of the generalization and the intentions of those who are particularizing it.

We not only generalize habitual patterns of interaction to construct some kind of unity of experience, we also inevitably idealize our imaginatively constructed unities or 'wholes'. It is in this process that we experience value, the voluntary compulsions that serve as criteria for selecting what we feel to be good actions (Dewey, 1934). Here again, Mead presented a paradoxical formulation in his distinction between cult and functional values. The idealization must be functionalized in specific contingent situations – the meaning of the idealization is only to be found in the experience of its functionalization. The functionalizing process inevitably involves conflict. Once again, we may employ the tool of writing to articulate and codify the idealizations in the form of ethical propositions, myths and inspiring narratives. They may be presented as intended, crafted vision statements for a corporation, for example. However, although someone can design and intentionally present statements about values, they can only ever be cult values which have no meaning on their own. In other words, the cult value is the first phase of a social act which can never be separated from the other phase, namely functionalizing.

Ideology may also be thought of in paradoxical terms as the simultaneous voluntary compulsion of value and the obligatory restriction of norm. Ideology provides criteria for choosing one action rather than another and it serves as the unconscious basis of power relations, making it feel natural to include some and exclude others from particular groups, thereby sustaining the power difference between those groups.

Given the points made above, we can now understand what we mean by the local and the global and how they are related to each other. The global is the imaginatively created unity we perceive in our patterns of interaction – it is the generalization and the idealization as one phase of social object. The local is the particularizing of the general and the functionalizing of the idealization. However, these are phases of one social act and can never be separated. The general is only to be found in the experience of the particular – it has no existence outside of it. The idealization is only to be found in the experience of the particular – it too has no existence outside of it. The process of particularizing is essentially reflective, reflexive, and quite possibly imaginative and spontaneous. It is possible for individuals and groups of individuals, particularly powerful ones, to intentionally articulate and even design the general and the ideal but the particularizing and the functionalizing involves an interplay of many intentions and values, and this interplay cannot be intended or designed, except temporarily in fascist power structures and cults. Furthermore, the generalizations and idealizations will further evolve in their particularization and functionalization. In short, the global and the local are paradoxical processes of generalizing and particularizing at the same time.

This point about the particularization of generalizations is of great importance and reinforces, for me, the inappropriateness of simply applying the notion of complex adaptive systems, or any notion of systems for that matter, to human interaction. In complex adaptive systems, the agents follow rules; in effect, they directly enact generalizations and idealizations. If humans simply applied generalizations and idealizations in their interactions with each other then there would be no possibility of individual imagination and spontaneity, and hence no possibility of creativity. We would simply be determined by the generalizations and idealizations. It is in the essentially conflictual particularizing of the generalizations and idealizations, which have emerged over long periods of human interaction, that socially constructed, interdependent individuals display spontaneity, reflection, reflexivity, imagination and creativity as well as conflict. Spontaneity, it seems to me, should be distinguished from impulse. In humans, impulse is an unreflective compulsion to do something, on the spur of the moment as it were. Impulsive actions, however, are still socially formed and reflexive. Humans are reflexive in that their actions are formed by their own histories. Whatever we do, whether impulsive or not, depends upon who we are, upon identity/self, which is socially formed. Humans are also socially reflexive in that what they think and what they do is formed by the group, community, society they are part of and has a history. This social reflexivity is also shaping whatever we do, impulsive or not. Spontaneity is often spoken of as if it were the same as impulse and the opposite of reflection in that spontaneous action also has that spur-of-the-moment quality. However, this is to chop out one event from an ongoing flow of interaction. I would argue that if we pay attention to the interactions preceding the selected moment of spontaneous interaction, we find people exploring the situation they face in ways that are reflective and it is because of this 'preparation' as it were that someone takes spontaneous action, having the appearance of 'on the spur of the moment'. What distinguishes this kind of spontaneous interaction from mere impulse is that it is a skillful performance, not just a reaction. Spontaneity is what makes it possible for people to deal with the unique contingencies of the situations they always face. Spontaneity generates variety in responses, often as small differences that have the potential for being escalated. In other words, human spontaneity is closely associated with the possibility of transformation and novelty in human interaction. Spontaneity in humans, I would argue, is reflexive, just as impulse is, but unlike impulse, the spontaneous act emerges in a history of skillful, reflective performance. Furthermore, spontaneity is never simply located in the individual, or the 'I', because the 'I' can never be separated from 'me', the social.

An example

Consider government policy relating to the National Health Service in the UK as an example of what I have been describing above. The NHS may be thought of as a collective identity, a 'we' identity that is inseparable from the 'I' identities of all who work for it and all who are concerned with its governance. Such an identity is a social object; that is, generalized tendencies to act in similar ways by large numbers of people in similar situations. On closer inspection, however, there is not one monolithic identity, one social object, but many linked ones. Each hospital, for example, has a distinctive identity, as do the groups of different types of medical practitioners and managers. There are, therefore, many social objects, many generalized tendencies by large numbers of people to act in similar ways in similar situations. Furthermore, the medical profession, the NHS and the many different institutions and groupings it comprises are all idealized. Cult values, such as 'proving free health care', 'doing no harm', 'providing all with the highest standard of care' and 'providing the same standard of care in all geographical locations to all classes of person', are essential features of what the NHS means. 'Performance' and 'quality' are recent additions to these cult values. The generalizations and idealizations can all be recorded in written artifacts, sound recordings and films as propositions and/or narratives. These artifacts may take the form of policy documents, legal contracts, procedures, instructions from the Department of Health and so on. Such artifacts are then used as tools in the communicative interaction and power relating between members within the NHS and between them and those concerned with its governance. However, the artifacts recording the generalizations and idealizations are just artifacts, not the generalizations and idealizations themselves. Whether recorded or not, the generalizations and idealizations only have any meaning in the local interactions of all involved in each specific situation – they are only to be found in the experience of local interaction.

So, for example, when groups of policy-makers in the Department of Health and each of the main political parties get together to decide what to do about the NHS, they are clearly interacting locally. What they will be reflecting upon and discussing are the generalizations and idealizations of the NHS or parts of it. They may issue a consultation document, a green paper, to large numbers of people for comment. This is then taken up for discussion in the professional bodies representing different groups in the NHS. Again the discussion is local interaction, as is the subsequent negotiation of changes in any of the policies. What they are discussing and negotiating in this local interaction is changes to the global, to the generalizations and idealizations. Eventually a white paper, or policy statement, is produced and instructions sent to, say, all the hospitals in the country setting out what new targets they must meet in order to demonstrate quality and performance and in what way they will be punished if they do not. What I have been describing is processes of local interaction, local negotiation, in which emerges articulations of the general and the ideal as far as the NHS is concerned. The process is one in which people have been trying to design the general and the ideal and, in the way they currently do this in the UK, they reflect a particular way of thinking about the NHS. In setting targets and establishing monitoring processes they display a way of thinking derived for cybernetics systems thinking. They are trying to design and install a self-regulating system.

However, the NHS is not a self-regulating system, but many local patterns of interaction in which the general is continually emerging as continuity and change as it is iterated from one present to the next. What then becomes important is how people are taking up, in their local interactions, the generalizations and idealizations articulated in the artifacts of written instructions and procedures. The meaning cannot be located simply in the gesture which these artifacts represent but at the same time in the myriad responses this gesture calls forth. In a specific situation on a specific day, there may simply not be the physical capacity to achieve the targets set. In each specific situation there will always be conflicts on what the targets mean and how they are to be adhered to. The target may then become something that has to be avoided, manipulated, even falsified. For example, a specific decision might be to meet, say, a target of reducing waiting lists, by sending people home too early after an operation, leading to a rise in readmissions. The cult value of 'equal treatment' has to be functionalized in a specific situation at a specific time, and may mean giving expensive medication to one person and not to another. The global generalization/cult value that the policy-makers designed is thus being transformed in the local interaction so that it comes to mean something different – instead of uniform high performance it may come to mean 'cover up' and 'deceit'.

As the unexpected emerges in many, many local interactions, the global pattern is transformed and, of course, in their local interactions, the policy-makers are reflecting upon this. They may then conclude that the now burgeoning number of targets is proving too much of an embarrassment and should be scrapped. However, still thinking in system terms, they feel that they must design some other form of generalization to stay in control and secure adequate performance. The proposal now in the NHS is that 700 targets should be abandoned but only to be replaced with twenty-two qualitative standards. Once again, however, the meaning does not lie in the generalization alone but in its particularization in many local situations. It will be interesting to see what emerges from this new move.

The argument I am presenting here has an immediate implication for processes of policy-making. This is that the almost exclusive focus on the design of a generalization in policy-making will lead to continual cycles of surprise. Greater attention needs to be paid to the process of particularizing if policy-makers are to avoid some of the endless policy reversals that characterize policy-making, at least in the NHS.

Norbert Elias is another writer who presents a very similar argument about the relationship between the local and the global.

Elias on long-term social trends

In his explanation of the civilizing process in Europe over the past few hundred years, Elias described in some detail the relationship between local interaction and the slowly evolving global patterns of society. He did not use macro-models and was dismissive of employing concepts such as systems or 'wholes'. He said that using the term 'whole' simply created a mystery in order to solve a mystery. He argued that social evolution could not be understood in terms of social forces, cultural systems, supra-individuals, suprasystems, spirit, *élan vital*, or any other kind of whole outside of experience. Instead, he argued for a way of understanding the global that stayed with the direct experience of interaction between people, the local. Thus, instead of using macro-models, Elias explored the ordinary patterns of relating between people in their local situations, showing how global patterns emerge in these local interactions and how, at the same time, those global patterns are structuring the very personalities of locally interacting people.

> Though it is unplanned and not immediately controllable, the overall process of development of a society is not in the least incomprehensible. There are no 'mysterious' social forces behind it. It is a question of the consequences flowing from the intermeshing of

the actions of numerous people. . . . As the moves of interdependent players intertwine, no single player nor any group of players acting alone can determine the course of the game no matter how powerful they may be. . . . It involves a partly self-regulating change in a partly self-organizing and self-reproducing figuration of interdependent people, whole processes tending in a certain direction.

(Elias, 1970, pp. 146–147)

In *The Civilizing Process*, published in 1939, Elias argued that as Western society evolved, social functions became more and more differentiated under the pressure of competition. He was pointing here to global patterns. However, this differentiation meant that the number of social functions increased so that any individual had to depend upon more and more others to do anything. As this interdependence rose, more and more people had to attune their actions to each other, making it necessary for them to regulate their conduct in increasingly differentiated, more even and more stable ways. He was pointing here to patterns of local interaction and how they could not be separated from the global patterns. The requirement for more complex control had to be instilled into each individual from infancy if society was to function. The more complex forms of control became increasingly automatic, taking the form of unconscious self-compulsion that individuals could not resist even if they consciously desired to do so. Self-restraint became habitual, or unconscious, through the evolution of societies. Without this local pattern, people could not operate in increasingly differentiated societies, the global, and without such societies such self-restraint would not be required.

Elias also linked the growth of self-control in local interaction to the global patterns of the growth of centralized organs of society and the monopolization of force by those organs. In societies in which force is not monopolized, individuals are caught more directly and more frequently between pleasure and pain. The local relationships between individuals are more volatile as people engage more frequently in physical violence against each other. Life is uncertain and risks cannot be calculated so that people live more impulsively in the present. As society develops in the direction of the monopolization of physical force, global patterns, the individual no longer engages in local feuds but rather in the more peaceful local functions of economic exchange and the pursuit of prestige. The monopolization of force created pacified social spaces that were normally free from acts of violence so that the free use of physical violence by the physically strong was no longer possible. Non-physical forms of violence became more frequent, for example, from economic monopolies and from the loss of self-control by individuals when driving cars. Both danger and control, therefore, came less frequently from physical force and more frequently from the very nature of self-control.

Elias argued that global social evolution results in local fears to do with socially correct behavior. These fears are banished to an individual's own personality and to interactions with others that are shielded from public visibility 'behind the scenes', for example, in the bedroom. Self-control encompasses an individual's whole conduct, and many impulses and affects no longer reach the level of consciousness. The consequence of growing interdependence in larger groups and the exclusion of physical violence was that social constraints were transformed into unconscious self-constraints as 'habitus'. Perpetual hindsight and foresight is instilled from childhood, becoming conscious self-control and unconscious automatic habit.

Elias attached particular importance to shame, embarrassment and repugnance in the formation of 'habitus'; that is, individual-social habits. Elias put rising levels of shame and embarrassment at the center of the evolution of a society of individuals. He argued that there had been a gradual removal of sexuality behind the scenes of social life, reflecting the advancing threshold of shame and embarrassment and the shift in the balance of external and internal controls, accompanied by the increasing psychological difference between childhood and adulthood. The same process applied to aggressiveness and cruelty.

Elias also described the civilizing process in terms of the global dynamics between the established and the outsiders. As one grouping emerges as established and privileged, others press for emancipation from their outsider status. Initially, the larger group of outsiders, who are poorer 'lower classes' oppressed by the established 'upper classes', tend to follow their drives and affects more spontaneously. Their local conduct is characterized by less self-control than the established upper classes. In the evolution of Western society this contrast between the behavior of the upper and lower classes decreased considerably due to the growing necessity of all people to earn their living in regulated work. As the upper classes came to have to work in similar ways to the lower classes and as the manners of the upper classes spread to the lower, the differences in conduct between them diminished. It is important to note how Elias understood the simultaneous evolution of society and individuals in terms

of power relations, and in terms of competition and cooperation.
He talked about the characters and attitudes of people who form
power figurations being formed by these figurations. Elias described
how particular kinds of interdependence between people had set in
motion global processes of feudalization and how the competition
between feudal lords had led to the emergence of absolutist states.
He showed how these reorganizations of human relationships went
hand in hand with changes in manners and personality structures,
the local. He talked about personality structures forming the social
while being formed by it at the same time.

A different understanding of social forces/structures

The notions of social forces and social structures are easily reified so
that we slip into the habit of regarding them as things with an independent
existence outside of our interaction with each other, even following their
own laws. We may even anthropomorphize them and come to think
of them as organisms with their own lives quite apart from our own.
However, on careful consideration it becomes clear that what we are
referring to when we use these terms is nothing more than widespread
enduring and repetitive patterns of interaction with each other that we
call routines or habits. When we reify or anthropomorphize these routines
and habits, we tend to think of them as external powers causing our
interactions. The perspective of complex responsive processes avoids
such anthropomorphizing and reifying, and does not view routines and
habits as causal powers with regard to our interactions. Instead, we come
to see that global routines and habits emerge in our local interactions
and continue to be sustained as they are iterated from present to present
in those local interactions. Social forces, social structures, routines and
habits can all be understood as generalizations that are particularized
over and over again in each specific situation we find ourselves.
In other words, they are social objects, generalized tendencies to act.
Furthermore, these generalizations are often idealized and come to
form the cult values we repeatedly have to functionalize in our
interaction.

This way of understanding routines and habits focuses attention on the
inevitably conflictual nature of particularizing the general and the
idealized. If people simply apply some generalization or idealization in an
absolutely rigid way there need be no conflict, but particularizing them in

specific, unique situations means making choices. Since different individuals and different groupings of those individuals will be making different interpretations of the situation, they will be pressing for different choices to be made. Which of those conflicting choices is actually made will be the result of negotiation and this immediately raises the matter of power. The particular choices made will reflect the figurations of power – the choices of individuals and groups will prevail when the power ratio is titled in their favor. Power figurations emerge in the interaction between people and, like all other organizing themes, there is a strong tendency for them to become habitual, generalized and even idealized. From a complex responsive processes perspective one understands institutionalized instruments, or technologies, of power to be just such generalized/idealized/habitual figurations of power relations. They too are iterated and particularized in each present and it is in such particularization that they evolve. They are not to be found as things or forces outside of our experience of interaction but only in that experience.

Power ratios are tilted towards those who have something that others need or want. The connection between power figurations and resources then becomes obvious. Since money is the key to controlling resources, power ratios are tilted towards those who can exert more control over money and away from those with little access to it. At this point it becomes important not to slip into reifying money and regarding it as the external cause of our interactions. Money too is a social object, a generalized tendency to act on the part of a large number of people in similar ways in similar situations. This generalization also exists only in its particularization in many, many local interactions. In those local interactions, the power ratio will continue to be titled towards those individuals and groups whose activities enable them to control more money.

This way of thinking about social structures, institutionalized instruments of power and resources focuses our attention on local interaction as the way of understanding the global. It is an invitation to take our experience seriously.

References

Allen, P. M. (1998a) 'Evolving complexity in social science', in G. Altman and W. A. Koch (eds), *Systems: New Paradigms for the Human Sciences*, New York: Walter de Gruyter.

Allen, P. M. (1998b) 'Modeling complex economic evolution', in F. Schweitzer and G. Silverberg (eds) *Selbstorganization*, Berlin: Dunker and Humbolt.

Dalal, F. (1998) *Taking the Group Seriously*, London: Jessica Kingsley.

Dewey, J. (1934) *A Common Faith*, New Haven, CT: Yale University Press.

Elias, N. (1939/2000) *The Civilizing Process*, Oxford: Blackwell.

Elias, N. (1970/1978) *What is Sociology?*, Oxford: Blackwell.

Fonseca, J. (2002) *Complexity and Innovation in Organizations*, London: Routledge.

Gell-Mann, M. (1994) *The Quark and the Jaguar*, New York: Freeman.

Gleick, J. (1988) *Chaos: The Making of a New Science*, London: Heinemann.

Goodwin, B. (1994) *How the Leopard Changed its Spots*, London: Weidenfeld & Nicolson.

Griffin, D. (2002) *The Emergence of Leadership: Linking self-organization and ethics*, London: Routledge.

Griffin, D. and Stacey, R. (2005) 'Experience and method: a complex responsive processes perspective on research in organizations', in R. Stacey and D. Griffin (eds), *A Complexity Perspective on Researching Organizations: Taking experience seriously*, London: Routledge.

Jackson, M. C. (2000) *Systems Approaches to Management*, New York: Kluwer.

Joas, H. (2000) *The Genesis of Values*, Cambridge: Polity Press.

Kauffman, S. A. (1995) *At Home in the Universe*, New York: Oxford University Press.

Mead, G. H. (1932) *The Philosophy of the Present*, Chicago, IL: University of Chicago Press.

Mead, G. H. (1934) *Mind, Self and Society*, Chicago, IL: University of Chicago Press.

Mead, G. H. (1936) *Movements of Thought in the Nineteenth Century*, ed. M. H. Moore, Chicago, IL: University of Chicago Press.

Mead, G. H. (1938) *The Philosophy of the Act*, Chicago, IL: University of Chicago Press.

Mead, G. H. (1977) *George Herbert Mead on Social Psychology*, ed. A. Strauss, Chicago, IL: University of Chicago Press.

Midgley, G. (2000) *Systemic Intervention: Philosophy, Methodology, and Practice*, New York: Kluwer.

Prigogine, I. and Stengers, I. (1984) *Order out of Chaos: Man's New Dialogue with Nature*, New York: Bantam Books.

Shaw, P. (2002) *Changing Conversations in Organizations: A complexity approach to change*, London: Routledge.

Stacey, R. (2001) *Complex Responsive Processes in Organizations: Learning and knowledge creation*, London: Routledge.

Stacey, R. (2002) *Strategic Management and Organizational Dynamics: The Challenge of Complexity* (4th edn), London: Pearson Education.

Stacey, R. (2003) *Complexity and Group Processes: A radically social understanding of individuals*, London: Brunner-Routledge.

Stacey, R., Griffin, D. and Shaw, P. (2000) *Complexity and Management: Fad or radical challenge to systems thinking?*, London: Routledge.

Streatfield, P. (2001) *The Paradox of Control in Organizations*, London: Routledge.

Editor's introduction to Chapter 3

The globalization of commerce and industry has had the effect of greatly increasing cultural diversity, creating issues that leaders and managers cannot ignore. Furthermore, in North America and Europe there has been an enormous growth in legislation promoting equal opportunities and prohibiting discrimination on grounds of race, nationality, gender, sexual orientation and age. This too creates issues, not the least being legal issues, that leaders and managers cannot ignore. In the terms used in Chapter 2 of this volume, what we are experiencing is the emergence of social objects and cult values; that is, widespread generalized and idealized tendencies to act in similar ways on the part of enormous numbers of people. Leaders and managers in many organizations, particularly in North America and Europe, are trying to respond to these emerging phenomena, and in this chapter, David Scanlon, who works in the UK for a globalized corporation, explores a particular instance of how they are doing this.

Typically, organizations take large-scale initiatives involving the establishment of working parties whose remit is to formulate strategies and design overall, global action plans to bring about respect for difference and diversity, as well as achieve equality and avoid discrimination. The approach to this work is to set global goals, prepare overall action plans covering communication and training, measure and monitor relevant indicators of performance in achieving the goals, and articulate the values which leaders should propagate to realize the required outcomes. Supposed best practice is identified in other organizations and used to provide benchmark prescriptions for dealing with diversity in every organization. Here, people are thinking in macro terms about a global design which is to be rolled out across the organization and applied uniformly in all local situations.

What is distinctive about the chapter by Scanlon is his narrative, which sets out, with a directness and honesty rarely found in the organizational literature, just what happens when groups of highly competent managers try to design the kind of global diversity initiative outlined above. He describes just how political the diversity program is, pointing to how people, including him, use such programs to further their own ambitions. He points to the conflict and power struggles generated by the initiative and provides a clear picture of people trapped in their own procedures, and the confusion they experience as to what they are actually doing.

He also describes how the initiative amounts to an attempt to directly apply cult values (see Chapter 2). In their discussions, those involved in the program subscribe, willingly or otherwise, to a taken-for-granted cult value of harmony and tolerance of difference. The effect of this, however, is to block the exploration of actual differences in the present between those engaged in the work. It becomes politically incorrect to name and explore the actual differences being expressed at the micro-level of the detail of the interactions between people. This attempt to insist on inclusion actually has the effect of excluding those who disagree with the blanket requirement to include. The insistence on inclusion then itself excludes. Instead of being explored as an important aspect of the main activity of the initiative, difference is then expressed in frustrated gossiping. The 'process' which the consultants to the project use also amounts to a cult value, and Scanlon describes how in applying it rigidly they end up using it as an instrument of control which creates an oppressive climate. What Scanlon is describing is just how the particularization/functionalization of such cult values actually takes place in the local situation of trying to develop a global initiative.

When Scanlon tries to draw attention to the patterns described above and to encourage ordinary conversations about what is going on and about what people are actually trying to do, he is misunderstood. His seniors simply keep repeating the call to 'roll out a dialogue' and 'prepare plans and measures that people can walk away with'.

For me, this narrative reveals what happens when people try to design global patterns without realizing that such patterns cannot be designed because they emerge in myriad local interactions as described in Chapter 2. The global pattern of actually dealing with diversity is actually emerging in many, many local interactions. Not surprisingly, the initiative does not lead to much, at least in the two years covered by Scanlon's narrative. In my experience, what Scanlon describes around one diversity initiative is typical of global initiatives in general (for example, those to do with quality, competences and values).

In reading this narrative, I am struck by the lack of real motivation to engage with their own actual experience of diversity. What people seem to me to be doing is preparing plans and designing indicators against which others can be measured for compliance, without discussing why they are doing it. One reason for the program, not mentioned in the chapter, no doubt has to do with the need to be able to demonstrate that procedures are in place to outlaw discrimination which may then be used by the corporation as a defense if litigation is brought by anyone claiming to be discriminated against. Apart from this, however, it seems to me that the motivation for programs of this kind has to do with the fantasy of being able to control diversity by obliterating it and covering this over with rational jargon, while refusing to talk about what people are actually doing. For me, this is an example of the magico-mythical thinking that Elias talks about (see Chapter 1).

3 The local experience of a global diversity initiative in a multinational pharmaceutical company

David Scanlon

Introduction

Diversity programs became popular in the USA some time ago. Popularity in the USA may be seen in that 'According to a study by the society for Human Resource Management in Alexandria, Virginia, 3 out of 4 Fortune 500 companies have formal diversity programs in place, over half of which (58 per cent) have staff members dedicated to these issues' (Caudron 1998: 91). More recently diversity programs have been taken up in Europe. Often cited reasons for the present need are: increased globalization in organizations through mergers and acquisitions and the required cultural integration; equal opportunities legislation which looks to prevent discrimination; increasing emphasis on corporate social responsibility brought on by triple bottom-line accounting, whether environmental, financial and social (PriceWaterhouseCoopers 2001). There have been legal implications with regard to equal treatment for many years; politicians have made strides in making society more inclusive. In Europe, the major driving force is The Treaty of Rome 1957, further supported in European Law by the Convention for the Protection of Human Rights and Fundamental Freedoms 1998, article 14, Prohibition of Discrimination. While these laws have been in place for some time, discrimination and issues around equal opportunity and pay continue to attract attention today. This link between HR and legal, the protection from potential expensive litigation, provides me with a picture of HR as protecting the organization, policing practices to ensure that organizations are compliant. The focus is both on protecting the 'organization' and on the rights of individuals in the organization; a situation that is fraught with inconsistencies when policies seem to be more focused upon 'organizational' needs.

Diversity is a popular concept in the world of HR. Diversity management is quoted as being a new paradigm for human resource management (Thomas and Ely 1996). Thomas and Ely differentiate between different strategic perspectives, the discrimination and fairness paradigm, the access and legitimacy paradigm, and the learning and effectiveness paradigm. The latter is stated as the paradigm which gives rise to successful diversity initiatives, as defined by actual improvements in business performance. They talk of eight pre-conditions for making the shift: leadership must truly value variety of opinion and insight embodied from different perspectives of a diverse workforce; leadership must recognize the difficulties that different perspectives present; the culture must create an expectation of high standards and performance from everyone; the culture must stipulate personal development through the design of jobs and the provision of training; the culture must encourage openness to sustain debate and constructive conflict; the culture must make people feel valued; a well-articulated vision is essential to ensure work discussions stay focused on the accomplishment of goals; and it must be a egalitarian and non-bureaucratic organization.

In terms of likely benefits, a recent article, based on interviews with human resource managers of fortune 100 companies, cited the five top reasons for engaging in diversity management as: better utilization of talent; increased marketplace understanding; enhanced breadth of understanding in leadership positions; enhanced creativity; and increased quality of team problem-solving (Gilbert and Ivancevich 2000). In another study, the initiatives most frequently carried out are: formal induction programs for new recruits; criteria for selection and advancement that are open to all; and having a policy on equal opportunities. Most cited benefits include: retention of employees; enhanced organizational flexibility; improved public image; and better morale. Driving forces behind initiatives were: good personnel practice; legislation; business sense; and organizational commitment to equal opportunities (Kandola and Fullerton 1994). A comprehensive guide for all HR is available, which gives all the information needed to be successful (Kandola and Kandola 1998).

Diversity in the sense described above is calling for greater creativity and productivity by closing the gap between the idealized state and the present state, 'detecting and correcting errors' which can be planned towards and achieved.

This dominant discourse, which I was involved in, emphasizes OD at the macro-level, an abstraction, which when combined with my need to find the 'truth' meant that I located OD not in experience but in theory and books; books that I could read, acquire the knowledge and apply. This focus meant that writing about my real experience of work was challenging in the early phase of study on the Master of Arts. The feelings associated with the statement 'Things "ought" to be different' meant that I sought knowledge in books and did not pay attention to my actual experience, which did not fit the idealized versions of life. It seemed as if my real experience was not a legitimate thing I could talk about for fear of ridicule or accusations of incompetence. In this chapter, however, I want to explore my own actual experience of a diversity initiative.

For two years I was involved in the 'diversity initiative' in my organization, a major international corporation which had grown rapidly through mergers and acquisitions. The cultural diversity of the company was therefore considerable. During the same period I was involved in a Master of Arts/Doctor of Management program in organizational change at the University of Hertfordshire. The MA program was an intense experience which challenged my understanding of the nature of change. Fellow participants came from many countries and so constituted a very diverse group. There was, therefore, a parallel between my work in my organization and the research work on the program. In both, I was trying to understand the nature of organizational change, in particular the impact of diversity and how to deal with it. The narrative in this chapter aims to describe some experiences of the diversity initiative and the research program.

My early involvement in the diversity initiative

In the course of interviewing the senior management team of R&D in late 1999, as part of my official role in the organization as in internal consultant supporting the implementation of a balanced score-card, 'diversity' came to my attention. I had been aware of activities in the area of diversity within my company and was pleased that it became a central plank of the R&D strategy. One of five key drivers in the R&D strategy was 'Build, develop and diversify our talent'. I was surprised, therefore, when we interviewed the senior management team in R&D and found that hardly anyone seemed to know what the 'diversify' piece meant. So what should be done? We proposed to the team that a definition and action plan might be a good first step.

Helen in HR, returning part-time from maternity leave, took up the challenge presented by the senior management team's objectives and started work on the diversity initiative in March 2000. Because of my close involvement with people in HR, the score-card work, other connections with Helen, and mutual issues arising from having a young family, we developed a close working relationship. I had access to senior managers and strategic business information; Helen held the key to my involvement in the diversity work. In August 2000, Helen's work led to a workshop in R&D to discuss diversity, define what it meant, and work up an action plan. I used my connections and relationship with Anders, Head of R&D Facilities and my head of department, to secure an invitation to the event.

A process consultant, Clare, who had supported Helen in the preparation and delivery of the workshop, ran the whole process. Her style was soft, gentle and non-confrontational. Clare brought external information about other companies' experience. This all seemed to fit with the comments in the session about how the organization might feel, a focus on harmony. Throughout the sessions music caressed the room. During one of the sessions we were asked to describe how it would feel to work in a diverse organization. Our comments were written on post-it notes. I was struck by how the other participants used words such as excitement, happiness, smiles, understanding, creativity and warmth. As I heard all of this, I reflected on how it had felt for me over the past few months while studying in a diverse group on the MA program. The experience of movement to a different way of thinking had promoted anxiety, feelings of being rejected, angry responses coming from habitual patterns in my past, and a lack of spontaneity. So I said, 'I think that an organization which was like this would give rise to a great deal of anxiety, and conflict would be commonplace.' I caught people's attention and was asked to explain why this was the case. It felt at that moment as though I was not playing the game. I felt anxious, I explained my rationale: 'In a diverse group there would be times where I would be confronted by issues that challenge my own values which would lead to anxiety. I would need to be able to manage myself in the face of the anxiety to go on working with the group.' This seemed to change the nature of the conversation.

Towards the end of the meeting, volunteers were sought to lead the various streams of work. I sensed that people were happy to commit to a few days to talk about the issues but were less willing to devote more time. In many ways this was the start of a pattern that has continued. I volunteered to lead diversity training. At the moment of nomination, I wondered what the response would be. I was anxious. As I offered my services, I looked up to see a number of faces nodding in agreement. The anxiety passed, I seemed to be accepted. The outcome of this meeting, and other conversations, was that I also attended the corporate diversity meeting along with Helen, and Ivan, head of legal, and senior management team sponsor. Clearly, something I was saying or doing was helping to achieve my desire to be involved. It became clear to me that the aim of programs such as 'Diversity' was about defining idealized situations in which there was no conflict or anxiety and about generating plans to get there. I was interested in joining the conversation with a different view.

A global workshop of thirty people gathered in October 2000 to define the 'corporate diversity strategy'. When I thought about the event and read the attendance list it was like reading a 'Who's Who' of my organization. I felt very humble and privileged to attend but also a little nervous. I had never worked before in such exalted company – from Board member to me. Before I set off for the event, I read through the list and recognized some of the names, recalled the situations and conversations with the few people I recognized and wondered about how the event would go. This pattern of planning for future events is familiar to me and one that can give rise to anxiety as I wonder about how I will be accepted.

A well-known consultancy firm who specialize in the area of diversity facilitated the event, and the task was to develop in 'real time' a strategy we could walk away with. I reflected how many times recently I had been involved in these situations, how often they broaden their purpose to include many other organizational issues, and how often I have felt either railroaded or that the answer was already there. I knew in some ways what was to come.

As I walked through the door, I saw the familiar face of Helen. We smiled warmly at each other and I made my way to an empty chair at the end of the room. I came in part way through the presentation of the lead consultant who called herself a futurologist. I thought, 'I know what is coming!' She was in the process of describing the process. It was very familiar to me: unfreeze, mobilize, realize, reinforce and sustain, and then focus on diversity leadership, communication and involvement, change skills and competencies, and measurement. These were the words of mainstream change management. We were going to hear best practice in each area and build the strategy over the next day and a half. The consultant spoke at a very fast pace and appeared to me to have a very large ego; everything was centered on what 'I' have done. I was wondering if the Swedes in the room were picking up everything and how they were responding to this brash American. I knew from previous experience that they often switch off in these situations and do not respond well to an overt focus on individual success. For my part, I tried to stay focused and attentive, but I soon slipped into checking out the room and working with my own internal reflections. The group broke up for an exercise in understanding our own diversity and I was able to join in fully. The message being sent by the consultants was 'we need to learn from the vast experience around us and focus on the future'. The message I received, however, was 'aren't we important, don't we know our stuff, and we've done this many times before'. There was a certain lack of originality, more in line with template consulting.

Next we were offered a model in which there were four concentric circles, meant to represent different levels of diversity: organizational (functional, work content, division, seniority, work location, union affiliation, management status); secondary (geographic, income, personal habits, recreational habits, religion, education, work experience, appearance, parental status, marital status); primary (age, gender, sexual orientation, physical ability, ethnicity, race); and core personality. We were all asked to write what we saw in ourselves for each circle. A woman who was warm and felt authentic led the session. She talked in a very calming voice and I saw her as a therapist. She used a number of Gestalt terms and talked of systems extensively. I was amazed at how compliant everyone was. People got involved. We were also introduced to John, who was very matter of fact and constantly reiterated, 'So what I am hearing you say is. . . .' I found myself feeling irritated at this refrain.

As the day went on a number of things started to happen which created conflict. A number of people from the USA started to dominate the discussion. They were clearly very passionate about the issue of race and repeated themselves over and over again. One of them was a constant voice all day and often cut people off as they were speaking. I started to wonder why she was doing this. What was she out to prove? I started to notice that whenever she spoke, people looked away in complete disinterest, in much the same way I was doing myself. The room was starting to feel tense.

Even in a syndicate room where we were looking at strategic objectives, the same person attempted to dominate. Many of her words were thrown out as though no one else knew what they were talking about. I had made my own attempt to start the ball rolling in the room: 'We talked a great deal about this last week and I could share with you the R&D work as a way to start.' This was not taken up. I did not push. The conversation went on in a very disjointed way, partly because the work was being done in parallel with other groups and we could not define objectives without the other work. As we left the room, someone turned to me with an aside: 'I thought what you said was spot on the mark.' He had said nothing during the meeting. In his silence he had participated; I felt validated and listened to.

Prior to breaking up into syndicates, best practice was shared from other companies. The next syndicate looked at methodologies for data collection. We were informed that there were only four methods of collecting the data: questionnaires; focus groups; interviews; and personal narratives. The message in the syndicate was that we had a great deal of data and would be making use of this. The 'push-back' from the consultants seemed to ignore this and advocated focus groups. The meaning I was making was that this was a push for business in supporting these focus groups. I agreed to present this back in plenary. It seemed a simple message: 'We have lots of data, might want to collect more, but we should promote dialogue on the issues both within the business and external to the business.' As I finished my presentation, John, the facilitator, stated that I had missed something and went on to say, 'We agreed that focus groups should be supported by external consultants.' Once again he gave me the same impression; I did not challenge him. The control I was experiencing was heightening. The other groups presented a force field analysis. Everyone was still very compliant.

The following day after a strange incident in the car-park involving bathrobes and fire alarms, we moved back into the same routine: best practice, discussion. Having all this information, it seemed that the right answer was on the overheads. The opportunity to discuss was limited. The energy dropped completely and the emphasis moved over to affirmative action. A number of attempts at taking the conversation somewhere else were made but all were rejected in favor of the process. The final straw came when Ivan, head of legal, stated, 'I'm sorry, this isn't right. I know that in Europe we have a lot to learn from the US, but this is not the US. In Sweden we have different issues. We need a vision that captures everyone.' His language was direct and forceful; his face was flushed and emotive. The debate at that point was fixed on corporate branding to become 'Employer of choice'. I knew from previous conversations that this was not how the Swedes saw the issue. It was not about PR; it was about relationships. I offered an observation that seemed well received: 'The group seems to be split between those who are focusing on relationships and those focused on affirmative action.' As I made my comments I noticed Tony, the event organizer, and other people listening attentively to my comments. From their comments and engagement I felt validated. Once again I felt listened to but completely inadequate, since I was unable to break the pattern.

Conversations at coffee breaks started to become more animated. The Swedes started to speak together in their native tongue. The energy level outside the meeting room was very high. The learned behavior of compliance, mixed with feelings of wanting to say the right thing, combined with poor process with little flexibility, contributed to everything boiling over. The things people could not say in the room were said outside – 'This is not good.' 'Some of the meeting behavior is appalling.' Whereas inside the meeting the discussion was focused on future plans and issues of organizational change, outside the meeting the conversations I was involved in were focused on the very thing we were here to discuss: diversity; meaning; the pain and discomfort that different views generate; how particular characters were not being 'aware' of their impact; and cultural stereotyping. These conversations felt more like gossip aimed at pointing at and alienating people. This I had experienced in the main meeting, through body language, but it was not talked about. How can this be explained in the context of the meeting discussion about planning a better organization? This was the enlightened group, who knew the issues well and yet were still demonstrating intolerance of difference. Perhaps we could have been seen as an embodiment of the organization? Certainly we were in a mess. But the consultants were in control – or so they thought.

After lunch, Tony, the chair of the meeting who was to present the output to the Board, and later to become Executive Director for HR, stood up.

Tony is soft-speaking but carries intensity; he has real presence. He gave what sounded to me like a fair and accurate summary of the events before lunch and looked to people to decide what was needed now. People engaged with this and seemingly agreed a way forward. This was to define exactly what we meant by diversity and to generate a compelling story for the senior executive team. The tension seemed to have gone and it was handed back to the consultants. 'We have a process to do this' were the first words I heard. It was as though, as we went back to the process, the discussion had not occurred. We discussed the next topic at the table and I began to notice three out of the five of us looking at one another in amazement. The loud woman and another person, a facilitator by training, continued. More best practice and another syndicate. I had had enough: 'I'm losing the plot. This isn't what we agreed.' Other people seemed to agree, but the facilitator said, 'I know it is tiring, but let's stay with it.' More best practice and another syndicate. Another attempt: 'Is it just me or does anyone else feel that this practice isn't right? Many of the companies cited are struggling and yet we are saying this work adds to the bottom line.' The discussion changed, and those who had switched off came in strongly and added their own points.

The outputs of the two workshops were presented to the senior executive team of the company and the management teams of R&D. In R&D we had a definition, an action plan, an organizational structure, an organizational scope, were guided by a senior sponsor, and had a list of the perceived long-term benefits of the work. The benefits included: increased efficiency; effectiveness; creativity; innovation and problem-solving; valuing and enhancing the contribution of all employees to promote the release of latent talent; stimulating receptiveness to change and willingness to share best practice; increased ability to attract, retain and develop people from all groups; improved team effectiveness; and enhanced external image to maintain the organization's reputation as a good employer. We defined priority areas for action: diversity at all levels, with the objective of identifying and removing barriers to performance; development and progression enabling all employees to contribute to their full potential; ensuring that legal and practical requirements were being met in each country; diversity training to increase understanding of the issues and benefits of diversity in daily work; and a communication and marketing plan to inform all R&D employees and relevant external parties of R&D's commitment to diversity and the actions being taken. We expressed a desire to set up a steering group with representatives from all the major functions and had in place a sponsor Ivan, a leader Helen, and the Core Action Team made up of all the volunteers from the R&D workshop, including myself. At the end of 2000, R&D had achieved their goal. They had a definition and an agreed action plan. But what had actually changed?

Why are companies like mine interested in diversity initiatives similar to the one I have described above? At one level the benefits can be described, as above, and seem like legitimate targets for organizational work. In the ever-closer union between organizational units from different parts of the world, in the trend towards globalization, it may be seen that the need to work more effectively, by understanding the different cultures involved, is important. The consequence of not improving in this area might be inefficiency, duplication of effort and miscommunication. In taking the perspective of the whole organization as the unit of change, duplication and miscommunication would be seen by managers as something to be avoided in the constant search to add value and sustain continued growth. With the focus on measurement, tracking the numbers of particular groups and assessing whether they are representative of society, as a whole, would seem attractive.

How might I think about the events described thus far?

How else might we think of the events described above, the perceptions I held, and the tension of the corporate event? Looking at the preceding description, which covers the initial engagement in discussions around the diversity initiative, a number of issues can be highlighted.

I might think of the various people involved as coming from different discourses who have joined a unifying project called diversity. From this perspective we would tend to highlight the similar views held, as a unifying principle in line with the inclusive nature of the project, and dismiss from the discussion areas, where we might diverge, sources of tension. Yet given the different discourses, experiences and knowledge everyone brings to the workshop, attempts to suppress the differences and focus on sameness will inevitably alienate some, marginalizing and excluding them from the conversation. What might some of the discourses influencing the discussion be? Clearly, from the debate in the HR world, diversity has a particular meaning and is associated with particular actions; a view embodied both in the representatives from the HR community and the consultants supporting the work. This was a view I shared but it was beginning to shift as I paid more attention to what was actually happening in the living present of the meetings. Some people represented various groups which diversity often targets: women, ethnic minorities, and for a European company, senior US representation in decision-making. Some of these groups may have been part of networks of like-minded people and hold another set of views outside of the HR world. Others represented might include managers and interested parties, some of whom may have experienced support in their search for success, the chosen ones, and others who may have felt excluded or passed over. Each group would generate particular views of the company as an inclusive organization. Each of these groups had previously been involved in some form of discourse that had shaped their views. The overall group could in no way be seen to have the same views but were being asked to shape one view in two days – an impossible task. Overlaid on these views, for these experienced managers, is the dominant discourse of management, with its emphasis on planning and control, views learned through OD interventions, personal reading and further education.

All this seems to have come together with various perceptions of what ought to be done, the way people should behave and feelings of being chosen with the associated status. Just scratching the surface of the complex array of influences in this way highlights a melting-pot of potential tension. However, the overall passivity and conformity to the process may be what Mead has called 'cult values': 'collective idealizations that divert attention from the detail of interaction in the living present . . . overriding universal norms, conformity to which constitutes the requirement of continuing membership of the institution' (Griffin 2002: 94–95). The more people become lured into these processes the more efficient they become, and the less room for spontaneity exists.

Given the difference of likely views and potential conflicts, the group somehow managed to resist talking about these differences as they focused on planning and future events. Attempts to raise these issues were quashed under the guise of process, which I experienced as control, but came from both the group and the consultants. This subsuming of particular themes seemed to stir up the conversation as I, and many others, continued these themes as internal dialogues and bodily responses to what was going on. In not recognizing that these internal conversations were themes shaped in the room, but excluded, anxiety was raised, the release of which was gossip. Both the internal and external dialogues were contributing to the ongoing conversations as individuals were forming and being formed by the group at the same time in relationship: 'in the private role-play of silent conversation the attitude of one's group towards one's actions finds a voice. This is a social form of control, arising simultaneously in the group and the individual' (Stacey 2003: 8). The legitimate themes in the formal settings of the room were shaped by the expected norms, the power imposed by the consultants, and the anxiety of individuals as they struggled with airing different views, away from the dictated process. The excluded themes included any talk about the lack of tolerance for difference, which most people felt would not be accepted.

Power relations reflected the role of the consultants. Fear of insulting or alienating the consultants blocked many people. However, they found their voice in the shadow, in the informal discussions in the break periods. Discussions, based upon connections made between people who empathized with each other – shared experiences and similarities – talked of differences. Emerging subgroups seemed to function as a release for anxiety as they became self-supporting and polarized the differences. This event seems, on reflection, to identify how different cultures start to emerge in the living present. This observation starts to question the whole idea of a planned organizational change aimed at increasing inclusiveness without recognizing the excluding nature of many conversations. Inclusion and exclusion are simultaneously present in the generation of identity through the natural turn-taking of conversation, established through conflicting constraints in the power relations. All these themes of power, inclusion-exclusion and anxiety played a part in shaping the emerging event as each person dealt with his or her own anxiety in habitual ways. What then is the diversity initiative doing in taking the macro-picture and ignoring the micro-interactions in which diversity really happens?

This coming together of themes, which shape both individuals and group in a single process, is one of the central notions in the theory of complex responsive process of relating. In the unreflective act of speaking into a situation, which is informed by the dominant individual-based view of the world, it is easy to miss this shaping and being shaped aspect of group interaction, as events are perceived to be within the individual's control. Seeing this from the perspective of Stacey, in which the reflective individual is viewed as taking responsibility for his or her part in the ongoing activities that emerge from the interaction itself, the events described above would not be seen as poor process or ineffective individuals, but rather a group experience in which individuals were seeking to define their identity in a reflexive way. Organizational change from this perspective is unpredictable and happens because of the apparent tension and differences.

At the time of this meeting, I was still seeing my role as bringing about change and was looking for interventions that gave rise to desired outcomes, based upon my perceptions that this was possible. In this environment, as I was looking to involve myself in activities with HR, much of what I was doing might be seen as pushing myself forward and gaining an identity, based upon my own insecurities. In many ways I relate to what Laing articulated as a 'divided self'.

> For the individual whose own being is secure in this primary experiential sense, relatedness is potentially gratifying; whereas the ontologically insecure person is preoccupied with preserving rather than gratifying himself: the ordinary circumstances of living threaten his low threshold of security . . . ordinary circumstances of everyday life constitute a continual and deadly threat. . . . If the individual cannot take the realness, aliveness, autonomy, and identity of himself and others for granted, then he has to become absorbed in contriving ways of trying to be real, of keeping himself or others alive, of preserving his identity, in efforts, as he will often put it, to prevent himself from losing himself.
>
> (Laing [1959] 1965: 42–43)

In thinking about how divided selves are sustained in organizations one might draw reference to the fantasized state of harmony described in diversity plans which, when placed against the reality of existence described in this narrative, makes the expression of difference difficult. Working in organizations with this focus it is easy to see how this dissociation and alienation, the divided self, is sustained.

As the workshop ended, I concluded that it was all about control and had nothing to do with open conversation or exploring difference which is what diversity is. It closed down all creativity and everyone seemed to be dying but unable to respond.

A strange interaction

Immediately after the workshop a colleague with whom I was studying on the MA program sent a brilliant view on diversity. I was so impressed with his sentiments that I forwarded his views to the attendees of the workshop. My intention was to engage them in another view away from the more traditional equal opportunity views. In doing this I found myself asking if there was another motive. Am I trying to influence people with my expertise, demonstrate an identity, once again, for myself in the eyes of others? My e-mail read:

> I would like to share with you a very philosophical document from a friend, a CEO in a US teaching hospital, who are having similar discussions to ourselves. The views expressed are similar to my own and given that we are studying together this does not surprise me. My intention in sending this is to raise awareness of other views around 'Diversity', particularly diversity of views, opinions and cultures.
>
> 'Our differences are real but can't be understood as being just mine or yours, they are ours. I say this from a perspective that differences must be both held by the individual and held by the groups of others with whom the individual is a part. One does not exist without the other; they are a part of the same process of our interactions together. We create our differences together and they exist only from and in the presence of others. Our differences provide us with identity and each of us seeks to have our unique self understood. At the same time, we seek to be included with others and that need to be included often causes us to minimize our differences. I think each of us struggles with this paradox every day as we deal with ourselves and others: how to be a unique individual and how to be part of a group of individuals with whom we wish to relate. This is not an either/or question; it is a both/and challenge. Recognizing this tension between difference and sameness in our everyday conversations with each other (and with ourselves) is a start to being comfortable with the reality with which we live. The great potential of difference to lead to emergent change while the power of sameness works simultaneously to maintain the everyday patterns of our lives is that reality. Both are happening at the same time. I don't think it is so much about making it happen, as it is about understanding that it will and being comfortable in and attentive to talking with others about both difference and sameness.'

In writing this, I wondered what response might come given the discussion at the workshop, which was much more focused on what the organization 'ought' to be and how we might measure the change. A number of people responded, but Clare's response prompted me to pick up the phone.

Thanks for sending the e-mail – I agree wholeheartedly with this view
of difference – the challenge is to find ways to be able to live with the
paradoxes of difference (and sameness)
I hope you are well
Regards
Clare

In picking up the phone I anticipated the opportunity of a conversation
about these views. 'Hi Clare, it is David Scanlon, we met at the diversity
meeting.' After pleasantries, I mentioned the e-mail exchange and invited
a conversation. The response was not very forthcoming. I had the
experience of being pushed away, not wanting to talk. This made no sense
of our interactions at the workshop. It felt strange in light of the response.
I felt excluded. I knew that my expectations were not met but something
happened which was more than that. It felt to me as though I was not
worthy of the conversation. It was as though my predicted pleasure in
conversation was squashed. Rather than working with what was there
I was working with my fantasized outcome and disappointed in the result.
I seemed unable to talk in words that connected. My reason for drawing
attention to this short everyday conversation will be brought up again
later. Drawing attention in this way is an acceptance that change is located
in the everyday conversations of the organization rather than in planned
organization-wide initiatives, though these are powerful gestures, usually
from powerful people. Only when I reflected later, after subsequent
events, did I see the significance of this conversation, a process of making
sense that reconstructed an event in the past and provided a different
meaning in a reflexive way.

At this time I was starting to recognize how my overriding needs to be
accepted, and an unusual ability to empathize with others, had given
rise to isolation: I did not express my identity but rather merged into the
social with which I was working. This was my particular way of avoiding
anxiety as I focused on me, alienating myself, paradoxically, through my
ability to merge. In starting to recognize this, the rest of this narrative
covers an experience of myself trying to come to terms, and understand,
my part in the emerging social. Through the concept of complex
responsive process of relating, my reading about anxiety, a reflective
involvement in my work and the MA learning community I started to
emerge and take my own voice.

I started work in my role as leader of the diversity training initiative and
a member of a core action team. I did not want to begin work without a

meeting of the other members of the team. Rather, I wanted us to work collectively. I saw my role as facilitating the process. Over the next few months I attempted unsuccessfully on many occasions to engage the team. I sent out e-mails to engage the discussion. I forwarded relevant material I came across. I attempted to organize meetings but was unable to get everyone together. I left messages on voice-mail which were not responded to and when I could I talked on the phone. Given that this was not my full time role it seemed as if I spent too much time working without any success. I knew that the people involved were very busy and their schedules were difficult to coordinate. The level of interest seemed low and yet I had agreed to deliver something.

Five actions were agreed at the workshop, and were refined at a number of meetings with Helen and the other 'action area' leaders. In my desperation, and growing sense of inadequacy, I relinquished my desire to facilitate and started to work.

One of the activities we had agreed was to map ongoing training activities in the organization that might support the diversity initiative. I consulted widely. A number of issues occurred to me: there was no structure for global delivery of programs in R&D; there were many programs which supported 'awareness' raising and cultural understanding run at local level but no system for sharing the information across sites; different parts of the organization were approaching training from different perspectives and diversity was covered well by the leadership programs. I started to wonder what it was that I needed to do. The most obvious was to link all the activities across the various sites using the Intranet but this I saw as an HR system issue that was outside the scope of our project. I did wonder what effect my conversations were having. Here was someone from outside HR starting to work in areas formerly their own. I started to realize that we might need consultant help in this area and formed a relationship with a consultant from a leading HR consultancy who I had met in the course of my day work. Helen continued to push me to talk with Clare, but I resisted in the belief that Clare would not have the capability and credibility to make an impact in a global effort.

I pulled together the varied input from the many conversations and presented them to the team at the group's first meeting, which one member of a team of four was unable to attend, giving late notice. We made good progress at the meeting and hammered out what we needed to do and agreed who was doing what. I thought that we had begun.

Throughout this time, between October and December, Helen was pushing me to spend the money she had in the budget; yet I had no clear idea what was wanted or how to deliver it. In addition, it was not until December that Helen presented the material from the workshop to the Senior Management Team in R&D, though she had presented to all the other functional management groups. The diversity steering group was yet to be formed. In many ways the authority to act was not clear to anyone.

I was beginning to grow anxious about my performance. It was only when the core action team met in December that I realized I was not alone. All the other members of the team, who were responsible for other aspects of diversity, were equally unsuccessful at getting anything moving. It was particularly difficult to attract any interest from HR where this initiative was not in their objectives and so they were reluctant to contribute. Throughout the consultation phase I had experienced the most resistance from HR. I was starting to feel the politics of the situation. Ivan, the sponsor, had never hidden his views that this was not a HR project and that projects which come from HR always fail. I was beginning to wonder if I was being seen as a threat.

In the New Year, Johan was appointed the new VP for HR in R&D. He had formally held a role in implementing the 'balanced score-card' in Corporate HR and was responsible for the development and implementation of the global employee survey. Johan and I had met a number of times, as I represented R&D at corporate events around the balanced score-card. My first impressions of him, one year previously, had been of someone who did not have a dynamic presence. Yet in conversation now, I found him engaging, open and non-judgmental – a patient listener. At the same time, I had a new boss. In our initial discussions about roles and responsibilities, I talked about my involvement with diversity and HR activities, and it was agreed that I should work with Johan in support of the 'balanced score-card' work. These two changes meant that a different relationship emerged for me. Johan and I met and talked on the phone regularly.

Conversations with people from HR, an OD consultant and a director within the Discovery organization generated more feelings of anxiety. What I felt was needed was a discussion about what diversity meant for the teams in the way they interacted together, drawing attention to what was really going on using the language of complex responsive processes of relating, not something which was planning an 'ought to be' situation, with a focus on numbers. I still held the belief that this particular design might have a better chance of raising awareness of differences and bringing about change. Asking the question, 'What are we actually doing when we talk about diversity?' seemed to me to be a legitimate one. Taking this view into two separate conversations with people from HR, an OD consultant and a director, I was told what I needed to do: 'The teams need to walk away with a plan and measures about how they will bring about change.' I said, 'I think what you are trying to do is too abstract for people.' The reply was, 'Come to our meeting and talk us through your plans so that we can roll out the dialogues.' In both of the conversations I seemed unable to make contact; it was as though we were speaking a different language. We must both have experienced this in similar ways. I felt a strong feeling of being controlled and the conversations had an air of stuckness. I felt powerless. All attempts to talk in another way were either rejected or met with agreement couched in words that emphasized something different. Other conversations with people outside of HR did not have this characteristic and seemed to generate more spontaneous and interesting conversations. I started to see how a rule-based approach, dominant in HR and characterized by a 'box-ticking' approach to organizational change, gave rise to particular 'cult values' which made any different kind of conversation difficult. I also thought about my own flexibility and started to notice how I was able to manage some of my responses and stay in relationship, even though the frustration and anger generated in the conversations seemed to push me away. I was managing the anxiety generated in me by effort to control my action. Attempts at voicing this feeling also failed.

In February the steering group was in place and had their first meeting. It was a meeting that Helen prepared with the purpose of reviewing the work to date. The plans were once again scrutinized, analyzed and reviewed, and roles and responsibilities for the different groups were agreed. In March 2001 the pressures of work and family became too much for Helen and she decided to leave the company. Her parting was an emotional experience as she mentioned that this team was the best one she had ever worked with and she would miss it. It had taken a year to get this far and now there was no leader. We had however agreed that I would be the acting leader until a replacement could be found. Ivan asked if I might consider putting myself forward for the position. This I did, and was interviewed for the position by Johan, VP for HR, and Ivan, sponsor of the project, in May.

I was left with the same feeling I had at the R&D workshop – there was no real drive to make this happen, but a lot of fine words. People were happy to talk about diversity planning, however! I also sensed real protectionism from HR, defensiveness about its role expressed through the various conversations in the organization. Once again I experienced anxiety as I managed myself in the various situations in which I felt controlled. Over this period, I had a major insight around my negative and destructive responses to control. I was still struggling with this as I attempted to manage my responses in the situations described above. I was starting to pay increasing attention to the language and events emerging in interaction itself and how my own reveries, inner dialogue, were shaped in the social. I was starting to experience a detached connectedness. It was becoming clearer to me that I knew less about the emerging interactions but could recognize particular triggers in myself that I was beginning to manage. What I mean by manage is to live with the anxiety of not responding in a habitual way to inner voices and feelings called forth by others and to remain in the moment of interaction through the pain – anxious calm. While the bodily feeling was the same and I could hear my internal voice looking for evidence to blame the other person, both supporting my identity and dissociating myself from the experience, I also sensed a growing curiosity. 'What is going on?' 'What have I said which threatens this person?' 'How are we shaping this?' 'Am I giving some signals of incompetence?' Rather than dismissing the anxiety with habitual ways of responding, I found myself reflecting in interaction on my own responses, inner dialogue and sitting with the anxiety. My views around diversity and the types of conversations needed were shifting as I saw the difficulty of individual change. What was still evident as I reflect on this period was how I still held the view that I could use this experience to raise others' awareness – to direct and control others.

A meeting with the steering group

The meeting with the steering group felt like a seminal moment for my involvement in the diversity initiative. It was June and this was the first time I was able to talk to the steering group about our activities over the past few months. During the time I had been acting leader, I had ensured that the core action team talked regularly by teleconference which had enabled us all to understand the issues. The issues which members of the team wanted to raise were clear to me and the needs from the group were clear. The agenda had been sent out and the majority of people were attending. I had also invited Johan, the VP of HR, to the meeting to give a HR perspective on diversity. Unlike other meetings I did not feel too nervous. I knew my material and was well prepared for the questions, if anything, too prepared.

I started by saying, 'Rather than go through the actions from the last meeting I have tried to build the agenda around these inputs. Here is the agenda.' I placed the agenda on the overhead projector and talked through it briefly. I then asked Johan to give an update of the HR strategy. Johan talked without overheads for ten to fifteen minutes. Throughout the conversation, the major issues we wanted to raise came up; people seemed to be getting to grips with the issues. I was able to contribute many of the messages on the slides in informal conversation. There was a real sense of engagement in the group. It came to a noticeable head in reference to the corporate view of diversity.

External to R&D, people often have the feeling that R&D do what they like and do not listen or cooperate with other parts of the business. It is often referred to as 'Fortress R&D'. What emerged in this moment seemed to be a classic example of this. The movement happened when Johan was asked by Ivan to talk about the diversity appointment to replace Helen. He talked about how conversations had been held around the organization to share the resource across the business in support of the global initiative; all requests had been met with a mild disinterest. The conversation intensified around the idea of 'R&D showing the way'. Ivan expressed this from his perspective: 'All the management teams know that they are not very diverse, and really want to do something about it.' There was talk of subversion, rebellion, 'Doing it anyway'. This built up into fervor, everyone in the room engaged in the need to stand up for what they believed. A silence followed.

'It seems this might be a good point to move on,' I offered. 'Though it seems like the conversation is covering most of the key issues, we could continue like this.' 'No, we would like to hear about the progress', responded Ivan. We now moved into a more input-based session in which many questions were asked. Throughout the meeting I was sensing clear expressions of individuality, each person talking from a particular standpoint. For example, Mohammed, the Project Manager, focused on actions and plans.

Throughout the meeting I was paying close attention to the signals I was picking up, in terms of body language, eye contact and location of comments. It seemed for all the camaraderie that there was a great deal of frustration in the room. I noticed Ivan's reddening cheeks, his apparently disinterested stares out of the window in response to some comments. All of this was supported by occasional frustrated words, the most frequent being in response to a discussion about communicating diversity. Someone asked towards the end of the session if Gunvor, the leader of the communication team, was happy with what she now needed to do. Her response was that she did not have a clear view of the actions needed, a view supported by Mohammed. As this happened I was mulling over how I could not understand this view. What I thought had been agreed seemed clear. I noticed Ivan's frustration. I wanted to say something but decided not to. The conversation went on a little further, until Ivan seemed unable to contain himself any more and burst in: 'I have listened to this. Gunvor, it seems what we have agreed is . . .' and listed the activities which I had understood to have been discussed, a demonstration of power and control.

At one point I experienced a strong sense of anxiety as I wondered whether or not to say something. In talking of diversity training I took a risk and spoke: 'It seems that many people in HR view these types of conversations as something that will be the same and rolled out. I do not see this as being appropriate. Each management team is at a different place. We need to have different conversations focused on their own experiences of being a group.' It seemed like there was a pause. Johan spoke first with a supporting comment, and the conversation quickly picked up around this theme, with everyone contributing. At that moment I sensed a release as I saw that the views of the many HR people I had spoken with were not held by the group.

Feeling unable to move

Sitting in the office preparing a briefing paper on our present portfolio position, for release to the analysts, my phone rang. 'My name is Clare, do you remember me?' I responded positively, remembering earlier experiences we had shared, the R&D diversity workshop many months earlier, an e-mail exchange, and the rather strained telephone conversation in which I had felt pushed away. 'When Helen left she mentioned that I should call you, but I have left this some time: how is the diversity work going?' I recounted some of the difficulties. The conversation continued, and I was very open with information regarding the program. I felt Clare might be able to help us and informed her of the conversations. What I got in return felt like a strong pitch. We were missing each other in conversation. It was almost as though I was being pushed. I heard how Clare was mentoring the lead diversity person in Ford, how her group was sponsoring a diversity group, how she had personally helped Helen a great deal, how she was in demand from many people in my organization, how her business had grown, how she knew what was needed for leadership development, how she was an authorized user of Emotional Intelligence and was publishing a book. All of this was delivered in a soft, almost therapeutic tone. I was beginning to feel very irritated. I was in the midst of a very heavy sell for the use of 'Emotional Intelligence as a measure of leadership development'. Rather than take up the cudgels I listened, occasionally using humor to deflect this onslaught. I stated strongly on a number of occasions that we do not use emotional intelligence per se at all and that the right person to talk to is Mary, the head of management development. I kept trying to bring this back to the diversity work. I often held the phone away from my ear in frustration. 'Is this woman using her Emotional Intelligence in the conversation; if so she is not very good', my inner voice stated mockingly. 'What are we going to do as a consequence of this conversation?' Clare asked. The conversation shifted from sell to agreed actions. Like a Judo player I wanted to use the energy, holding off my own prejudices, and organized a meeting with Lucy, the HR representative on the steering committee.

After the conversation I phoned Mary, the corporate head of management development. I left a message describing the conversation, mentioning that she might get a call. The next day, from London, I checked my messages and found a voice-mail from Mary. It started very aggressively: 'Thank you David for the message. Clare has been trying to get into the organization for the last two years and anyway I do not respond to cold calls. I spoke with Clare before your message and told her that EQ is incorporated into our leadership work.' Mary went on to say that Clare mentioned she was meeting with Lucy and me.

A few days later, after leaving one message, I spoke with Mary. At first the conversation was a repeat of the earlier comment. Turning our conversation into a recommendation, Clare tried to use our relationship and others to get around Mary, something that angered both Mary and myself. I let rip about my own experience and thanked Mary for her views that were similar to my own. I resolved to stop the meeting I had arranged. My gut instincts, made many months ago, felt right and validated in this experience. The conversation with Mary however took another turn as I asked if she could recommend any consultants from he leadership program to work with us in R&D on the diversity dialogue. 'Have you seen the work I did two years ago?' 'What is it you are trying to achieve?' The detailed questioning went on. As I answered the questions with what felt like some confidence and assurance, in a controlled way, I started to feel very threatened, since these questions were a repeat of an earlier conversation I had had with Mary and were starting to represent views that others, including the sponsor and HR representative on the steering committee, disagreed with. It was again a pattern of stuckness, a repetition of the same conversation emerging in the current conversation. It was as though I was being told to stop and leave this to her, and yet I had a legitimate reason for asking in light of the request from the steering committee meeting. Remaining composed I talked of the discussions in the steering group, their request for dialogue. I spoke openly about Ivan's resistance to HR and whether this was an influence, and my own feelings of being stuck in the middle. I wondered why she was blatantly trying to bully me. 'Mary, I have a great deal of sympathy for your point, I do think the leadership program is addressing issues around diversity. However, this work is focused towards intact groups. Others in R&D have different views to yours.' The conversation ended with us both saying we had to leave for other appointments. I was very angry.

My initial reaction was to speak with Johan, or Ivan, and to seek support from them. However, this did not happen. At a meeting some days later, and calmed down, I met with Lucy, the HR representative on the steering committee. This was an update meeting as Lucy had missed the steering group meeting. Since Lucy had been mentioned in the conversation with Mary (Lucy is going through the leadership program), I asked her views about the leadership consultants for the diversity dialogue. She pulled a face and shook her head. I went on to ask why 'was diversity not covered in the program?' Rather than support Mary's views she felt that diversity was something different and required a slightly different approach. I suggested she might want to talk to Mary about this.

So what was happening? Certainly I felt like piggy in the middle unable to grasp the ball. I was starting to realize how these types of conversations were impossible to change; they were what they were – stuck. All I could try to do was to remain aware of what was going on.

The announcement of the appointment of the diversity director was to take place within a week after the steering group meeting. How I actually heard about the appointment was curious. Coming back on the train from

London, a week after the June meeting, I telephoned my boss, Ann-Katrin, who had been working with the R&D senior management team and was waiting for her plane. After talking through a number of work items I updated Ann-Katrin on the discussion at the diversity meeting, my first opportunity to do so. Simultaneously the hostess of the airplane which Ann-Katrin was boarding was hassling her to turn off the phone. In finishing off the conversation Ann-Katrin said, 'I know about this. I was talking with Ivan yesterday.' I mentioned that I hadn't heard from Ivan yet. 'Ivan mentioned it was a woman so I know you haven't got it.' The conversation came to an end after further pressure from the cabin steward. I was not overcome with anguish, rather with numbness and a racing mind, as I searched for the clues I might have missed. I reviewed the interview, and tried to analyze who might have got the position. Could I work with this person? Do I want to go on with this? Will I ever be allowed into this type of work? How do other people in the organization see me? I was amazed at how quickly my thinking readjusted, as though it was used to disappointment. I wondered what words of comfort would come from Ivan and Johan. I called Ivan the following week. 'Hasn't Johan talked to you yet?' I agreed to follow this up with Johan. As a part of regular meetings I have with Johan we arranged to meet in the London HQ offices. We talked for two hours about the business we needed to discuss and the issue of the diversity position was not pushed by either of us. As we broke for lunch, the conversation started. It was an informal discussion in which Johan talked very positively about my abilities and how it was a close call. He mentioned who had been appointed and the concerns he held. I was happy with the appointment and felt privileged to have been even close to the appointment.

References

Caudron, S. (1998) *Diversity Watch* 29, 2: 91–94.

Gilbert, J. A. and Ivancevich, J. M. (2000) 'Valuing diversity: a tale of two organizations', *Academy of Management Executive* 14, 2: 93–105.

Griffin, D. (2002) *The Emergence of Leadership: Linking self-organization and ethics*, London: Routledge.

Kandola, P. and Kandola, R. (1998) *Tools for Managing Diversity*, London: Institute for Personnel and Development.

Kandola, R. and Fullerton, J. (1994) *Managing the Mosaic: Diversity in Action*, London: Institute for Personnel and Development.

Laing, R. D. ([1959] 1965) *The Divided Self*, London: Penguin.

PriceWaterhouseCoopers (Winter 2001) Human Resource business briefing.

Stacey, R. (2003) *Complexity and Group Processes: A radically social understanding of individuals*, London: Brunner-Routledge.

Thomas, D. A. and Ely, R. J. (1996) 'Making differences matter: a new paradigm for managing diversity', *Harvard Business Review* (September to October): 81–87.

Editor's introduction to Chapter 4

While Chapter 3 described a large-scale change initiative in a major corporation, in this chapter Michael Nolan explores how practitioners in a small consultancy sustain highly stable patterns of practice which trap them in ways they do not notice, making it extremely difficult to further develop their own practice. He takes a particular practice in his organization known as 'contracting'. This involves what amounts to a ritual according to which people make explicit their expectations before they engage with each other in any way. In the terms used in Chapter 2 of this volume, Nolan is talking about a social object called contracting; that is, a generalized tendency on the part of himself and his colleagues to act in a similar way in similar situations. The accounts he gives of various meetings with colleagues and clients explore how this social object is taken up in many local situations where the effect of doing so is to sustain a stable practice. Nolan shows how this stability is dynamic rather than static in that it is continually co-created in an ongoing way.

Nolan links this dynamic stability with the question of identity, where identity may be understood as a social object. Members of a community of practice derive an important aspect of their individual identities from belonging to the community, and maintaining that membership in a stable form is thus of great psychological importance. In the terms used in Chapter 2 of this volume, Nolan brings out in his narrative how identity is sustained by the way in which people functionalize particular cult values. For example, one cult value has to do with 'good' relationships, focusing on achievements and strengths, and this is functionalized in such a way as to avoid exploring differences and the conflict this leads to with its potential for damaging 'good' relationships. It is part of the cult value to avoid being 'negative'. Another cult value which operates to block questioning is that of overvaluing outcomes and 'getting it right'. Nolan is emphasizing how a practice can get in the way of examining that practice.

He links the social formation of identity to the dynamics of inclusion and exclusion in that we derive our 'we' identities directly from the groupings we are included in as well as those from which we are excluded. The need to sustain identity, to remain included, functions as a powerful motive, often unconscious, for conforming and not questioning the taken-for-granted aspects of practice. The dynamics of inclusion-exclusion, of course, reflect patterns of power relations between people. Power relations and the interlocking of identities constrain people from inquiring into the nature of their practice in a way that might lead to its transformation. Such transformation would, naturally, shift patterns of power relations and so affect the experience of identity.

Practice becomes stuck through increasingly less reflection in the moment on what people are doing together. People become less spontaneous and more bound by ritual, procedures and rules. Nolan looks in great detail at how he and his colleagues are constraining each other. Their 'processes' stop them being spontaneous. He gives a good sense of how the social object of practice has evolved in the history of his company, how the fear of reigniting the conflicts of a particular period in that history operates to prevent people from questioning what they are doing, how a dominant way of accounting for practice is actively policed. He notices that when he does try to question, others interpret this as his not understanding the practice, or as a leadership challenge or a personality block on his part.

Nolan does not ascribe stuckness in a practice to 'resistance' to change. Stuckness is an actively constructed, an actively iterated and an actively policed form of social activity rather than an individual inability to be reflective. However, he also discusses how stuck practice evolves in processes of joint inquiry in which, basically, people are taking up the social object of their practice in ways that differ from what they usually do in an unthinking way. We change in reflecting in the moment, in action, when we are struck by what we are doing. Nolan describes joint inquiry as emergent, conversational, narrative inquiry which creates a disturbance to practice and so opens up the potential for transformation. He contrasts this with more mainstream ideas of designing changes in practice which are then implemented. Joint inquiry is itself change, not something which then has to be implemented.

4 The emergence of global stability in local interaction in a consulting practice

Michael Nolan

Indeed a crucial use of words is to 'move' or 'strike' others by
the saying or the writing of certain words at certain moments, to use
such words to draw their attention and ours to aspects of their own
sayings and doings, to unique details of their lives, that might
otherwise have passed us both by unnoticed, and particularly to
yet to be created relations between such details.

(Shotter, 1993, p. 28)

This sense of being constrained in a prison one is helping to sustain
can affect us all.

(Shaw, 2002, p. 96)

This chapter seeks to explore the process of organizational change in the company of organizational development consultants to which I belong. It examines in particular the idea of bringing about change in practice, from within, by an established practitioner. I ask the question: How does an established, perhaps stuck, practice transform itself?

While complexity thinking is more frequently associated with change/chaos, I ask here what complexity has to say about our frequent experience of being 'stuck'. I concentrate on the notion of actively created, or emergent, stuckness. This is then contrasted with the experience of being 'struck' by novelty or difference in conversation and the role of being struck in the development of practice.

I work as an organization development (OD) consultant in a company of forty OD practitioners, White Spirit Consulting. I wonder: How we are to think about the process of organizing in a company such as ours? Management literature, it seems to me, is full of prescriptions about how to apply business ideas to a consultancy: for example, marketing, performance management and branding. These fail to make sense of the world I live in. There is an alternative strand of thinking which examines practice as opposed to the *organization* which delivers the practice. Donald Schön (1983), and many since, advocate the need for a *reflective practitioner* as a way of transforming the very nature of what we do as well as the explanations we offer for its appropriateness. Recently Wenger (1998) focused on the fact that practitioners do not work alone but in *communities of practitioners* and explored the nature of these communities. I use the concept of practice in this chapter to understand and negotiate change in White Sprit Consulting.

Those of us with experience of a small 'professional' organization know how difficult change can be and how immutable the core offering or proposition of the company seems to be. It is particularly complex to lead change from within; that is, when one is part of the practice, caught up in all its taken-for-granted ways of thinking and doing. One puts oneself at risk by questioning the operation, yet as an insider that very questioning can disturb the current relationships in a way that an outsider cannot.

In this chapter, I examine what it means for one as a practitioner to question our collective practice from within and I narrate the sometimes unexpected responses to this inquiry. In doing so, I find that our practice is 'stuck', in my view repeating an approach given some time ago by the founders. However, we simultaneously struggle to account for the validity of the practice to ourselves and to outsiders.

There are three core themes in this chapter:

1 *Practice*. This chapter uses the concept of *practice* to make sense
   of my organization but in a way that I think has significance for other
   organizations. The concept of practice draws attention to what we do
   as well as the explanations we offer for the appropriateness of what
   we are doing. However, existing thinking in this area (e.g. Schön 1983;
   Argyris and Schön 1974, 1978 and 1986), representing a tradition
   that splits thinking from acting, emphasizes reified representations of
   practice, models and hidden assumptions. I argue, however, drawing
   on Elias (1939, 1998), Shotter (1993), Mead (1934), Wenger (1998)
   and Stacey *et al.* (2000), that practice is an emergent property of
   interaction among practitioners, drawing attention to the continuous
   further specification of practice among practitioners rather than the
   implementation of a practice as designed. Both Argyris and Schön
   base their thinking on the individual practitioner. I argue, however,
   that practitioners are always in community and that the practice
   emerges between practitioners.

2 *Stuckness*. Practice also, at the same time, forms the practitioners.
   This chapter uses the notion of *stuckness* to examine how stability
   as well as change needs to be understood. I put forward the view that
   organizational stability, as well as change, is actively created through
   the process of local interaction. I argue that from within this same
   process, identity and power relations are formed, and form, the
   process. Hence the experience of 'stuckness', in this case atrophied
   practice, arises actively. It is continually co-created as a pattern that
   can emerge from the particular set of constraints and identities that
   are involved. Thus the pattern of 'stuckness' is as likely to have
   emerged from intentions to change, as it is to have resulted from
   efforts to stay the same. Patterns arising from local interaction may
   not be the result of the predesigned interventions of any one person,
   so the stability or perhaps 'stuckness' that results is an actively created
   but not intended structure. I argue that traditional ways of
   understanding stuckness are taken from the physical sciences and
   imported into management thinking. The current state is seen as
   a dynamic balance of opposing forces that return to equilibrium
   thereby resisting change (Lewin 1951). Alternatively, stuckness is
   located in the mental models or hidden assumptions driving individual
   practitioners' behavior (Argyris and Schön 1996). I argue, using
   John Shotter (1993) in particular, that it is the taken-for-granted,
   the rationally invisible, between practitioners that renders the practice

difficult to articulate. I argue that stuckness is an active, unintended, emergent pattern whereby power relations between practitioners and the interlocking of their identities constrain the inquiry into practice which might lead to its transformation.

3 *Joint inquiry.* I propose ways of working within a community of practitioners which are different to mainstream organization analysis or individual practice development. Individual development of practitioners does not necessarily amount to engagement in the stuckness of current practice. What I call *joint inquiry* does not involve the traditional mapping out of the practice or representing it in models to be redesigned and then implemented. Rather joint inquiry is an emergent, conversational, narrative inquiry into the taken-for-granted collective practice through which emerges further forms as practice and practitioner are transformed together. While constrained by power relations and the threat to identity of practitioners, joint inquiry is a disturbance to, and thus changes in, the stuck practice.

How I explore stuckness

I experience myself as 'stuck' within the web of constraints, generated between my clients, colleagues, and myself through which our particular practice of organizational development emerges. I glimpse the possibility of doing things differently, but wonder as I act how it has come to be that I struggle to realize these possibilities. What is the nature of being 'stuck'? This chapter is an account of how, in my view, White Spirit Consulting has become 'stuck', how I have come to make sense of this experience, how I am informed by this sense-making in my day-to-day practice and how I am continually 'struck' as I practice in new ways.

I begin by describing how I experience constraint both in my work with clients and my practice with White Spirit colleagues. This is a strange mixture of knowing the way I wish to act but not being fully in control of how I respond within this pattern. The view of stability as a dynamic pattern has led me to wonder if perhaps the very actions I, and others, intend to result in change actually intensify patterns of stability. How do I know if my actions are stabilizing or changing? How do we actively stay stuck in our practice? What themes from the history of the company are enabling stability? The narratives in this chapter seek to explore these questions and illustrate how I am dealing with the issue of stability.

Practice, it seems to me, becomes stuck through increasingly less reflection in the moment of action, less spontaneity, more ritualistic or more rule-governed behavior. I believe that something of the original dynamic within White Spirit Consulting has been lost and the threat to identity involved in questioning or opening up to this possibility prevents genuinely responsive action. How is it that the spontaneity disappeared from our practice? What do we gain in the process? I have traced, through recent crucial events, how our history may hold clues to current patterns and I explore ways I am using with colleagues to develop a more reflective collective practice. In particular I examine how taken-for-granted OD techniques become embedded in the accepted practice. I highlight one technique in particular, *contracting*, as a metaphor for stuck practice. In each narrative, contracting is explored in different ways as I examine the theoretical roots of the concept while also exploring alternatives.

Rather than seeing meetings within the company as being boringly repetitive, it may be argued that high levels of policing and contention about the maintenance of practice are at work in these meetings. I illustrate how our identities are being expressed through two particular meetings: the 'Pharma review meeting' and the 'Practice Development meeting'. Here I describe how I am beginning to form ways of inquiring 'from within'. I encourage colleagues to examine the taken-for-granted aspect of our practice in the belief that exploring this realm of our experience through conversation opens us up to fresh understanding and spontaneity of action. However, I also draw attention to the challenge to power relations and identities that emerge as I do this, which in turn is shaping and confirming my ideas about the active co-creation of stuckness.

Stuck with Karl

Let us begin with one of those 'arresting moments' that heightens an already developing theme, in this instance the multiple strands of constraint I experience as I work. I was taking part in a workshop, acting in a routine/standard way, while at the same time noticing that this was no longer the way I desired to work. The narrative illustrates how I am constrained, in a hotel in Germany 500 miles away from the nearest fellow consultant, by my participation in the community of practice that is White Spirit Consulting.

I sat in Berlin with a group from Dollense, the German pharmaceuticals company, as they responded to my co-facilitator Karl's question, 'What are your expectations of this workshop?' Karl, their OD specialist, works very effectively in English. A torrent of interesting and complex issues emerged as the participants engaged with the question. Karl wrote these on colored cards. I wanted desperately to respond to the questions and see how the conversation would develop, but I felt that I needed to hold back and stay with the design Karl and I had agreed in Dublin months earlier. I mentioned to the group how we would come back to these ideas later, in the slot on the agenda called 'Live issues', when someone from the group would facilitate the discussion. I noticed how deadening it was to put away the excitement, to proceed as designed and contracted with Karl. I knew that this was probably true for the group as well. Many times I have noticed how it is difficult to return to a hot topic, how our 'processes' stop us being spontaneous.

This experience shows me that as a new assignment begins, rather than working without design, I still follow traditional White Spirit practice which leads me into designs that constrain subsequent work. In this case the standard two-day facilitation skills design, which I offered the client, enables willing participants to learn new skills but hinders open-ended discussion about organizational issues. The conservatism of my approach arises from the constraints of revenue generation within the business. I assume that a standard design is more likely to be accepted by the client. I also experience the client's request for assistance as being crafted from within an understanding of what White Spirit has done in the past. A certain reputation, or brand identity, built around in-depth personal development, which was, in this case, generated by work done for Dollense by a colleague six years before. At the moment I describe above, I am sitting alongside Karl as he engages in the practice of *contracting* with the group about their wants and concerns for the workshop. This is a standard White Spirit process consulting technique used at the beginning of events. Karl is familiar with the technique, so in preparing for the event I suggested he take this section, among others, as I would need to do the elements he did not know. If I had responded to questions, I imagine it would have unraveled our agreed process, possibly causing friction between Karl and myself. So I felt acutely aware, through my experience of Karl's use of contracting, how rigid that piece of practice has become.

I have realized that I rarely take radical steps towards new practice. I could, as I have traditionally done, see this as a theme of self-doubt but this would be individualistic thinking. I now see myself being stuck in a prison of my/our own making, held in a web of power relations that include White Spirit Consulting and its clients.

Stuck with Block

This very shift of my attention, from psychologizing about personal attributes to noticing the patterning of practice interaction, is a key change in thinking I am seeking to illuminate here. I am inquiring how both Karl and I account for what we are doing in the situation I describe above. The OD technique we draw on to explain ourselves is called *contracting*. Why am I highlighting this simple technique?

- I am drawn to reflect on the moments when we reach agreement about the nature of the work we are going to do together, or put another way, moments when the nature of the consulting role is situationally agreed. These moments are important because constraint (hence power) seems to be most evident at these times.
- During my recent practice development discussions with colleagues I have been drawing attention to contracting as an unexamined and routine piece of technique.

The concept of contracting refers to those times when we engage with clients and begin to clarify what is expected from the interaction, what the client or clients want and what they think the consultant brings to the situation. Peter Block, in *Flawless Consulting* (1981), began to bring to consulting, from therapeutic practice, the notion that surfacing and dealing with 'resistance' at the entry stage is crucial to the long-term success of consulting projects. 'A contract is simply an explicit agreement of what the consultant and client expect from each other and how they are going to work together' (Block 1981, p.x).

One of the difficulties here, I think, is that Block is codifying his successful practice into a set of rules to be followed by others, rules which become adopted in an unthinking way and can lead to engagement that, on the face of it, is relational but is fundamentally rule-driven, lacking in novelty, surprise or radical shifts in direction. In my view, the practitioner becomes immune to the questioning that led to the suggestion of the rule in the first place.

Block's ideas have informed White Spirit practice. We call rigorously for a clear expression of needs from both sides in the consulting relationship.

We particularly follow his suggestion that the essence of contracting is attending to the mutual surfacing of true wants, needs and concerns at the outset. In the spirit of 'practicing what we preach', contracting is part of our internal process as well and is so embedded that it is almost unthinkable, as we shall see below, that an internal meeting would happen without a certain amount of initial contracting taking place.

The ritual of contracting has become my metaphor for what I see as our atrophied practice. By lightly drawing attention to how we automatically, ritualistically engage in contracting, or indeed, by my running sessions without any contracting and drawing attention to the difference, I have engaged my colleagues in 'practice development'.

For example, in April, when we were 'doing practice development' in Scotland, I noticed how we automatically started the session by contracting for outcomes, so I asked Malcolm, who was running the meeting, how he accounted for what he had just done, his practice of contracting. As the conversation continued he began to see contracting as a part of his automatic White Spirit practice, and said, 'I just thought contracting was what we *do* . . . I never think about it as an *option*. . . . It's kind of scary . . . it was just drummed into me when I joined.' Both of us, I think, were struck by this moment and made significant connections that would alter, in different ways for both of us, the way we would go on together.

In this narrative so far, I am drawing attention to the core themes I outlined above. By drawing attention to elements of our practice, in this case contracting, I am engaging in a fundamentally different way of making sense within our company. I was struck by how little we had ever discussed the detail of our practice between us. The conversation has tended to be more focused on designing events, organizational issues such as shareholdings and targets, as well as dealing with other colleagues' difficulties at a psychological level. I am also illustrating how, as I look at practice, I discover stuckness, the idea that we hold each other in some pattern which seems difficult to discuss. Indeed, the absence of practice discussion led me to believe that we actively constrain each other from doing so because it would be threatening in some way. These were early discussions I initiated about our practice, drawing attention to the stuckness but also noticing that through the experience of the conversation the practice becomes further specified between us.

Stuck in White Spirit

How come I feel constrained, prevented by some invisible leash from changing my practice by an organization that regards itself as being at the leading edge of contemporary OD practice? How come Malcolm, a skilled process consultant, can act in such a repetitive way?

At an event which I will describe below, I realized that in order to change my practice further, I would have to tackle the issue head-on instead of avoiding it, and try to change the community of practice, thereby allowing some shifts in my own practice. I had noticed how we in White Spirit have become unable to account for our practice to one another, or to clients, without using such terms as 'White Spirit magic' or 'trust the process'. Thus Schön's exploration of this phenomenon as a generic issue facing professional practitioners captivated me. His idea that our practice is *knowledge-in-action* and that change in practice comes through *reflection-in-action* gave me a framework that I could use readily with colleagues. I could also see that Schön's ideas needed rethinking from the complex responsive processes (Stacey *et al.* 2000) perspective I am developing. For example, by concentrating on the individual practitioner Schön ignores the issue of group practice. At this stage I thought that, following Schön, our inability to articulate *knowledge-in-action* was the issue in White Spirit. However, I began to see how power relations emerging from our history resulted in a mutual constraining of our ability to reflect together that was more severe than Schön was describing.

To explain and illustrate this I would like to recount the story of our Future Search conference, which took place in January 2002, aimed at building our organization's future capability.

Finding the past in Future Search

I remember catching a glimpse of a sallow-faced, bearded man crossing the hall of the Imperial Hotel in Russell Square at lunchtime on the day we started this thing called Future Search. I reckoned he was part of our unusual gathering, perhaps a client, or some supplier I did not know about. Someone said he was David White. Had I not met him before? I certainly had not, although I was immediately intrigued to find out from him how he had created the company twenty years ago.

These were what we call our 'Development Days', a three-day gathering of the entire company, which happens twice every year and, I think, builds the community to continue enthusiastically with the business of consulting. However, on this occasion we were holding a Future Search conference facilitated by Sandra Janov, one of the originators of this form of large group intervention (Weisbord and Janov 2000). The idea was to both experience and learn from the process but also, more importantly, to address the theme of becoming a leading edge consultancy in the years ahead. We had, as proposed by the methodology, invited clients, consultant's life partners, suppliers and internal support staff. I had invited Patricia Shaw, my doctoral supervisor, as a 'supplier of ideas'.

How the Future Search itself works is not my main concern here. It was an event which marked a turning point for me in the widening circle of engagement in my changing practice. I had kept my growing critique from my colleagues on the basis that they would not understand the ideas or that I had not sufficient grounding to debate convincingly with people outside the research community of my doctorate. Yet I knew that Patricia's presence would require that I take a stand. I experienced this as quite anxiety-provoking, a sense of not being comfortable in either camp, both welcoming and resenting the clash of identities evoked.

The initial chunk of work was to map three histories: World, White Spirit Consulting and Personal milestones. When I looked at the completed White Spirit Consulting map, a twenty-five-foot time-line on flipchart paper, with individual recollections at their appropriate points, I was struck by the story emerging. It made me aware of my own identity within the organization and heightened my sense of anger that something of our intellectual roots had been lost in our practice over the years. At the 1970s end of the scroll, David wrote about how he had studied new ideas current in the USA and had seen a business need for UK managers to know how to manage change in the increasingly complex organizations of the time. Having completed his Ph.D. thesis on decision-making/commitment-building, he partnered with Richard to apply this thinking in industry. I was struck by their immersion in the ideas of that era and the explicit establishment of White Spirit Consulting practice on a theoretical and intellectual basis.

At the other end of the White Spirit Consulting history map was a profusion of comments of a different nature: 'the day I joined', 'the day John left', 'the time I became established', 'unhappy times', 'morale on an upswing', 'Mary's leadership'. Very personal or business-focused comments predominated, it seemed to me. I felt odd writing, 'Start of my MA/Doctorate program'.

But my 'arresting moment' came when staring at the blank spaces in the middle; at least one-third of the history was blank, white flipchart space. The few comments written came from outsiders, stating how they had heard about disquiet within the company. There were just a few consultants' comments about friction and unhappiness. This middle period ended with statements about several people leaving, upheaval and a splitting apart of the businesses. I was saddened. It must be that those of us who were around in the middle years did not wish to disclose publicly how difficult it had been. I realized how few of the people who had been involved then were now present at this gathering. But I was also connecting the early intellectual flourishing with the blank space in the middle and our current sense of inability to progress.

While talking with David at dinner that evening, I explained how the organization had grown after he sold it, how it had tried to develop a flat structure based around values of 'equality' and 'authenticity', but how very little new thinking had emerged or informed our practice. Increasingly, any attempt to question ideas was seen as either a personal failing in understanding, or a leadership challenge. Questioning was often turned back on the challenger as evidence of a deep psychological block that was getting in the way of their development as a consultant. The topics of discussion were largely the institutional aspects, such as shareholdings, structures and growth, although the ferocity of these discussions would indicate that major inclusion-exclusion issues were at stake.

Meeting David inspired me. I was encouraged by his continued interest in the company he had created. Over the following days of the Future Search conference I found a voice, which did not seek to educate others in complexity theory, but rather to argue that we had, as a community, lost our link with intellectual ideas because of those middle years, that we had been given a powerful practice by David and Colin but lost our ability to account for it, and increasingly relied on the notion of White Spirit magic to explain ourselves. In essence we were still working off Richard and David's ideas, not having developed our practice in new ways since.

I began to realize that by becoming repetitive, the taken-for-granted nature of what we do leaves us stuck in our practice, isolated from its roots, unable to transform, destined to repeat. I began to realize how our particular stifling history and the realities of power relations within the company had resulted in the atrophied practice I experience. By the end of the meeting I was clear that it is the *process of developing practice* that would make us leading edge, rather than any particular set of ideas we might adopt. I began to argue that unless each consultant was on a journey of inquiry, together with colleagues, new ideas would flounder.

But as I develop my argument here, I revise my view of that history and acknowledge that a pattern emerged within our organization, the network of constraining relationships, which was characterized by the active creation of a stifling environment jointly sustained by all of us. The difficult bit is to acknowledge my attraction to and maintenance of the culture that I subsequently found damaging. One of my concerns (perhaps also an unconscious influence on my position) since the departure of many of the people mentioned here is that we will unintentionally revisit this pattern.

The Pharma review meeting: struck by stuckness

Since that January meeting I have engaged colleagues, at every opportunity, in conversations about practice. As I reflect on this process I am struck by how, in small but significant ways, our practice is changing through my involvement in this process. By this I mean that I notice that as I ask different questions, or have an intense interest in conversation, people have themselves been struck by the different nature of their reflection *while engaging in these conversations*.

I have suggested some processes whereby all of us could engage in reflective inquiry. As I do this I am very aware of the political nature of my actions. I am trying to maintain the interest of colleagues because we are in my view anti-intellectual, and at the same time establish processes that will generate a more fundamental, long-term questioning of our practice. I begin to wonder what conditions would be necessary for a significant joint inquiry. Is it enough to get some groups together and start a questioning process or do we need collectively to be challenged from another theoretical perspective? In attempting to establish conditions for a reflective practice, how can I account for myself in ways that are consistent with the ideas of organization and practice I now hold?

The following narrative will illustrate some of these dilemmas from within the inquiry and also, through my reflections, expand on these questions.

Let us go back in time to January, about three weeks after our development days, to a meeting of the Pharma team, held to discuss a major intervention in the Pharma organization. The intervention is a three-module, leadership development program for senior people from across the Pharma world. The White Spirit Consulting team is Helen (leading), Jane, Alison and myself as the four original designers who have been joined by Barbara, Gwen and recently Ian. Peter is the Pharma client who co-facilitates the events and has developed a very close relationship with all of us. The event is different for White Spirit because, for much of the time, we are separately facilitating groups of six people in ways that are not standard White Spirit practice. Therefore, in contrast say, to, an 'Influence Skills' event, we have no established ways of reviewing how we are doing at the end of each day. Yet, for a number of reasons – Helen's style, Peter's needs and the complexity of the program – we are actually spending uncharacteristically long periods of reflection at the end of these days, but with mixed results. I have been stirring up lots of thinking about our practice at these daily reviews. The meeting I am about to describe came as a suggestion that we should hold a separate meeting in London and not involve Peter so that we could perhaps delve deeper into our own thinking and thoughts about one another.

As I arrive in our London office, I notice how excited I am about this meeting because of some conversations we had about our practice in Lisbon the previous week, and I feel I am making headway in opening up other ways of inquiring into White Spirit practice.

We sit around the table, joined by Ian who has not yet worked on Pharma but will be shortly. He is a new consultant in White Spirit, brought in from one of the 'Big Six' to increase our understanding of 'systemic change'. However, his joining has been difficult. I immediately notice how his involvement shifted my willingness to contribute. Four old mates challenging how we do things in Lisbon is very different to opening up that conversation with a newcomer. I do not want to engage in an intellectual debate, which might suit Ian but lose the others, and I feel a sense of needing to help Helen and Jane with Ian's joining by taking a more party line 'this is the way we do it in White Spirit' approach. I think this is how it always feels: some institutional constraint, or in other words a felt constraint to sustain the institution, holds us back from questioning what we do.

Helen speaks: 'Well, shall we get started? In the memo I wrote, and got *some* replies to, I outlined what we might talk about.' Helen, who is both a leader in the English business and the Pharma project, is experimenting with a more directive style of leading. Gwen catches my eye and we laugh. I push my glasses down my nose chairman-style. We are aware of how different Helen's behavior is, how on the one hand it would be normal at business meetings in other companies but different for us, so we rebel slightly. Alison then says, in her oblique style, 'We had some great conversations in Lisbon and I made some notes. Would it be helpful if I read them to start us off?'

I, and I expect others, think, 'no it wouldn't'. Although I was engaged at the time, I think our ideas might not travel well, like a poor Portuguese wine! I am becoming acutely aware of our practice around contracting and think, 'Here we go again trying to chunk up an agenda and feeling all anxious or competitive about whether the proposed items will address the issue.' But I decide not to draw attention to this. I feel it is in the air, that sense of coming here to do something different but immediately stuck in some conflict over the agenda. I have a sense of 'here we go again, we will never change' being present. However, I also add to the list generation and say, 'I thought it would be important to talk about our proposition on leadership.' Gwen replies, 'I am all for that as long as,' looking at Ian rather than me, 'we don't unravel everything.' A message for Ian, I guess.

A tense moment: I feel the compelling urge to say that you cannot prevent unraveling but I fear I would be seen as Mr Theory if I mention this. At that moment I experience the bind of our practice. We think we are engaged in best business practice, that is, contracting, and there is a strong urge to 'get on with it' around the table, yet the more we individually say what we want from the meeting the more constraint there seems to be, which in turn generates some frustration. More of an emergent pattern as we speak than a holding back of thoughts, I think. Yet it feels highly disruptive at that stage to question what we are doing or to suggest we 'let our interests emerge during the course of the meeting'. I would like to point out that I am very aware of the interplay between the 'models and procedures' we use with clients and the effect these have on organizing within our own practice. I am struck by how difficult it is to get going, how tense and competitive it is. There is a real inability to know how to hold the conversation we think we need, or perhaps each of us thinks we need a different conversation. The outcome of this discussion will be some pattern unintended but familiar to all of us.

Helen, clearly unhappy with the way things are heading, suggests a ten-minute quiet time for individual reflection to write down what we have learned about leadership, Pharma and ourselves. This is accepted.

Dispersal, cigarettes, coffee, and we return to write down our thoughts. Barbara says, 'Isn't this *so* difficult', to which I reply, 'If we were in the lobby of the Ritz after a hard day we would be full of insights, this is what I mean by when I speak of "knowledge-in-action".' Helen says, 'I said be quiet!' I smile and start writing.

Helen talks first but then Jane cuts across, looking uneasy: 'Should we capture these so that others can get the benefit of our insights?' Gwen quite abruptly replies, 'I never learn very much from seeing others' learning like that.' Jane shrugs: 'maybe it's just me then.'

I start jotting down the difference of opinion. I know, and I think they know, that this is an 'arresting moment' when the taken-for-granted is exposed and we go on together in different ways. Jane's response is very typical of White Spirit. She interprets the difference as one of personal style, probably highlighting her qualities of practicality, concern for the whole, thereby inviting attention to seeking common ground and tolerance of difference. An alternative reading, in my view, is that this is a debate about how we learn and change practice and whether it is possible to change another's practice with 'distilled wisdom'. But they back off *as if the issue has no place in the discussion.*

This is the moment where I realized that *identity* is at issue as we discuss practice. Jane and Gwen are very good friends and I am very close to both of them. So I am very aware of the potential for conflict there is in that moment and how the White Spirit instinct, derived from its practice assumptions, is to pull back from the conflict and seek common ground. The maintenance of relationship is put over and above the exploration of the difference of opinion. Holding our relationships and identities intact prevents us from facing a difference generated by inquiry into taken-for-granted practice. However, the legacy of the past hangs over this moment, the current impact of a time when identity was more blatantly at issue as differences of opinion over practice were settled by calling intra-personal competence into question.

The conversation turns quickly to the reviews we hold at the end of each work day. The previous week, Helen had reported feeling flat. Several people mention that this new and complex work does not have a yardstick by which to judge ourselves. The conversation about yardsticks and feelings continues. It seems that we often judge a day by how we feel rather than by the quality of interaction with and among participants. This interests Alison and myself. We seem to be getting close to something that is core to our practice.

Jane says, 'It is unusual to review the day with Peter, the client, present.' Barbara says, 'It is a radical program and working closely with Peter is part of the newness, I wouldn't want to exclude him from the reviews.' I say, 'It is different in that with twenty to twenty-five people and four to five facilitators we are not working at the emotional or personal depth that we normally work, do we miss this in some way? Our practice is very much about working at depth. I wonder, do we get our satisfaction from this and not the type of reflective thinking we are facilitating in these Pharma programs?'

White Spirit hold that emotional blocks are 'behind' people's inability to act in ways they wish. There is usually some emotionally charged work involved in the release of these blocks and potentially more dramatic evidence of facilitation than the broad-ranging reflection we are encouraging at these events. I am beginning to realize that this 'depth' is related to the notion of a deeper self that is 'behind' behavior, an idea I am moving away from.

Gwen says, 'I check in with people regularly to see if they are alright.' Jane replies, 'I view it differently, I do not get close to people on this program, over three modules I found myself to be less intimate with these groups than with others.'

At some point during this conversation I had become very aware of the dual nature of our reviews: here and there at the events. The review discussions are a mixture of the need for assurance from one another that we are doing the 'right thing' and, at the same time, reviewing practice. The tone of these statements, it seems to me, is anxious and unsure. The mood is one of self-protection rather than examination of each other's practice. Responses do not seem to me to develop from a reflection on the previous comments. It is as if we are trying to figure out the right way to work with the Pharma people and checking anxiously if we have done the 'right thing'. This sense of a 'right thing' to have done is getting in the way of exploring differences in how we work. It is this pattern that gives us the feeling of stuckness and inability to really examine our practice. This is somehow fuelling my growing belief that power (constraint) and identities are at issue as we talk practice in a way that prevents reflection.

I think we are sounding a bit battle-weary and wonder whether we believe we are successful or unsuccessful in Pharma. I hold the question for a while, thinking it is important, and then ask the group. I am not sure if it is understood, or avoided, but the conversation continues uninfluenced by my question until Helen says, 'Yes! I am beginning to think this is a review indicating that things had gone wrong in the program. It is beginning to sound negative!' She had looked tense and flushed earlier. She is the client manager and leader of this whole project. I react silently, thinking that this is a surprise response but to say so now might be seen as a defensive maneuver by Helen. We each say that, of course, we had done good enough work and delivered the objectives. It has suddenly become a very White Spirit-type review, focusing on the achievements and strengths, but the energy and engagement have gone. While it was difficult, a genuine attempt to examine practice has been derailed. I conclude this because of the edgy nature of the conversation and the potential threat contained within it, but I am also aware that I have unintentionally contributed to the derailment! This is leading to my conclusion that we are all actively creating a sense of 'stuckness' including the possibility that my efforts to change may help create forms of stuckness.

Barbara tries to raise this with 'I was wondering what was behind the questions Helen asked?'

I am aware that she is indirectly surfacing an issue of leaders hijacking a good discussion. I am also aware that she is doing this in a very White Spirit way, pointing to the possible underlying issue with a well-crafted question. I admit that my earlier question was probably of the same type; however, I want to stay with the conversation, not step outside it or facilitate, so I avoid the question.

Someone says they need lunch to increase energy.

My reading of the Pharma narrative

How do I read this narrative? I am struck by the novelty of our getting together to reflect on the work we are doing with a client. I have rarely done this in White Spirit. However, we found it difficult to engage in a way that would illuminate something in our work. It seems to me that the purpose was not clear, or that there were many slightly different purposes. We seem to think that reviewing is about how we can do it better for the client, rather than my growing conviction that it is about understanding the nature of our practice.

I am emphasizing how our practice gets in the way of us examining our practice. Notice how Helen wanted to hear what everyone wants from the meeting, how a moment of reflection is suggested, how we value capturing the content to be brought to another meeting, how we attribute the cause of issues to personal styles and not shared practice.

The discussion of practice among members of a long-term community of practice raises questions of identity. As difference is expressed, we become aware of our identities and the potential threat to our fragile stability. If we accept that our identities are created between us, not residing within us, then as power relations change our identities are always at risk. In my view, we withdrew from the discussion because people were finding it difficult. That was when our style, one of attending to individual distress, clicked in, and we abandoned the discussion rather than wondering why discussing our work in this way was generating discomfort. I experienced this as an emergent pattern of preserving stability and not exposing the very ways of working we had adopted weeks earlier.

Contrasting views of practice, stuckness and joint inquiry

The concept of *practice* gives us a way to make sense of White Spirit, bringing to our attention what people do, day in and day out, and the meaning they attach to that activity. Recently, the concept of *community of practice* emphasizes how groupings emerge around a practice and generate common meanings or accounts of joint activity. Wenger defines practice by saying:

> the concept of practice connotes doing, but not just doing in and of itself. It is doing in a historical and social context that gives structure and meaning to what we do.
>
> (Wenger, 1998: 47)

Schön rightly points to the way professionals rely on their academic knowledge base and conduct a practice that, once established, irresponsibly closes itself from change through failure to reflect (Schön 1983). In my view he equates stuck with unreflective practice. He believes that unreflective practice arising as knowledge becomes ever more tacit or difficult to articulate. However, Shaw accounts for stuck practice differently. In her view,

> our professional practice is socially constructed meanings which are always open to further specification. A core of repetitively sustained, habitual ways of recounting and accounting are kept alive between increasingly clearly identified members of the profession.
>
> (Shaw, 2002: 96)

A discourse is developed, she says:

> which comes to police the way the practice is contested. Within the rationale of an accepted systematic discourse aspects of our experience become rationally-invisible to us, the discourse itself does not afford us opportunities to draw attention in certain ways and a certain voice is unable to speak. This sense of being constrained in a prison one is helping to sustain can affect all of us.
>
> (Ibid.: 96)

It is clear that our communities of practice are conversational processes where we develop, negotiate and share theories and ways of understanding the world: 'Practice is not immune from theory he says nor is it a realization of theory or an approximation of it' (Wenger 1998: 48).

On the issue of stuckness, Wenger maintains that communities of practice are not inherently unreflective, even though a particular practice may be more or less reflective. He says that practice includes both the explicit, and the tacit, in a socially negotiated context. He relates accountability to the stability of practice by saying that while some aspects of accountability may be reified – rules, policies, standards, goals – those aspects that are not are no less significant. Stability arises as a process:

> Becoming good at something involves developing specialized sensitivities, an aesthetic sense, and refined perceptions that are brought to bear on making judgments about the qualities of a product or an action. That these become shared in a community of practice is what allows participants to negotiate the appropriateness of what they do.
>
> (Wenger 1998: 81)

This regime of accountability becomes integral to the practice and may not be readily articulated. This is not a static process. He sees that relations of accountability are not fixed constraints but negotiable and moving the enterprise forward. He describes practice as a common history of learning and says that practice is not stable, but is constantly reinventing itself to remain as the 'same practice'. Learning is a source of social structure, not an object; it is emergent, inseparable from the process which gives rise to it.

Wenger explains what I would call stuckness through the idea of investment:

> In a community of practice, mutual relationships, a carefully understood enterprise, and a well-honed repertoire are all investments that make sense with respect to each other. Participants have a stake in that investment because it becomes part of who they are, from that standpoint, practice is an investment in learning.
>
> (Ibid.: 97)

He then says that the community will tend to react to novelty in ways that protect its investment. He goes on to say that this is an investment in interlocking identities and is about negotiating enough continuity to sustain these identities. So, rather than being unreflective, as Schön would argue, Wenger believes that practices protect their learning and interlocking identities.

There is a difference between Shaw's and Wenger's way of making sense of the impasse or prison of our making. Wenger's investment in learning approach overlooks the power relations at play. I tend to agree with Shaw that a certain dominant way of accounting for practice emerges which is actively policed.

Stuckness

The theme of stuckness through the narratives prompted my thinking about what is called, in management change literature, 'the current state'. This seems such an inadequate description of 'now'. Inspired by the theory of complex responsive processes, I have been thinking differently about organizations, now understanding change and stability as constantly and actively created through local interaction. However, the emphasis in the literature is usually on change rather than on stability. We are biased, because of our work, towards *changing* organizations. We overlook stability. Just imagine a chief executive saying. '*We must stay the same or we won't survive!*' I realize that if the future state is not predictable, then the present is not the *intended* outcome of some past actions, but it is the idea that we are active participants in the very stuckness we dislike that intrigues me most.

I think that stuckness is usually dealt with in the literature as 'resistance to change' (Block 1981; Nevis 1987). In other words, stuckness is thought of as a phenomenon that arises as someone tries to change things. This in turn follows from mechanistic notions of the current state as the system at equilibrium (Lewin 1951; Beckhard and Harris 1987). Argyris (1970) would see stuckness as an organization's 'theory in use' that becomes tacit or undiscussable.

To reiterate my own position, which is in contradiction to this mainstream line of thinking, I believe we need to account for both stability and change as arising from within the process of local interaction. In the same living present, using Mead's (1934) notion of time, both continuity and transformation arise as we relate, expressing our difference and so our identities. Therefore the experience of 'stuckness' or, atrophied practice, illustrated in the narratives so far, arises actively, created continually by members of the community. Patterns arising from local interaction are not the result of the predesigned interventions of any one person, so the stability and at times 'stuckness' that results is an emergent but not intended structure.

Stuck reflection

What do I mean by *stuck?* I have used the term in several ways to refer to:

- A collective practice that is repetitive, rote and lacking in spontaneity, while seeming to be responsive to the immediate situation but where the responses are actually generic, formulaic, even 'practised authenticity'.
- The active web of constraint that holds our practice within a domain related to our identities and implies the consequences of departure from that domain.
- The experience of fatigue and despair that arises from doing the same thing over again and failing to change, despite our 'best change efforts'.
- How I feel actively 'stuck' in the situation with Karl, within our attempted practice discussion or within our unreflective practice which has been highlighted for me by the Future Search conference.

Fundamental to the discussion is how Schön, Argyris and, to a certain extent, Wenger speak of reflection in the midst of action and to what degree, despite the assertion that all action contains reflection, some action seems devoid of reflection. They believe that it is by reflection in action, especially when made explicit, that professional competence develops. Much of the tacit/explicit distinction is premised on the inability of the practitioner to articulate his or her tacit knowledge. The implication is that tacit knowledge, although crucial, is somewhat inferior. I would say that when we separate thinking, action and speaking in this way we end up with false distinctions, which atomize what is a process of relating. Using Shotter's ideas I will account for the explicit/tacit distinction as more the *taken-for-granted*, but ever present, in our ongoing relating, from within rather than outside the interaction. Schön's emphasis on the individual leads him to the tacit/explicit dimension. When you deal with the individual in the classic individualist way, any gap in accounting for practice must be explained within the individual. I am arguing that if you start from the assumption of a social practice, then gaps in accounting or 'knowing more than I can say' are not fully my responsibility but must be more a result of a web of constraining relationships. Thus a practice that is stuck may not necessarily be unreflective at an individual level, but rather an emergent pattern of practice within the community which makes reflection together difficult. It is the link with power relations that I draw attention to, not an individual's inability to be explicit.

I think that what gets to be reflected upon, in public and in private, is political. The non-negotiation of certain aspects of practice supports the dominant way of accounting for practice which can be driven by fears about revenue generation as well as the identity the stability brings. This political aspect extends as far as clients who have interest in maintaining White Spirit Consulting as it is, in order to, I suspect, preserve their organizational credibility.

An alternative view of stuckness

I have used the ideas of Elias, Shotter and Mead as well as the collective thinking of Stacey, Griffin and Shaw as the foundations of the position I am developing. Elias says that in many processes of change, the unity is not due to any substance which remains unchanged throughout the process, but to the continuity with which one change emerges from another in an unbroken sequence. His view is summarized by Mennel:

'yesterday's unintended social consequences are today's unintended social conditions of intentional human action' (Mennell 1992: 259).

I take Elias to mean that there is no 'state' but rather continuous interacting and the socially constructed meaning we make of the continuity of the world around us. Our tendency towards process reduction reifies the present.

Shotter, exploring interaction, shows how, in our forms of inquiry, we take certain things for granted and that, in our everyday conversations, such things are so ingrained that to speak or even imagine otherwise would be difficult:

> In fact we hold each other to these forms of talk, to talk otherwise is considered a bit strange, as if one did not know what was involved in being a normal person.
>
> (Shotter 1993: 4)

This is not the 'tacit' realm of Argyris and Schön but a way of talking to and with others. However, Shotter goes on to say: 'talk that undermines the boundaries between our categories of things in the world, undermines "us", the stability of the type of beings we take ourselves to be' (ibid: 4).

Shotter makes an important distinction between the *representational* aspect of language and the *rhetorical*. By attending to '*words in their speaking*' (rhetorical) we notice he argues the emergent, relational situations created by those in communicative contact with each other. This third sphere, which he calls joint action, has been 'invisible' to us because of a scientific and everyday preoccupation with the '*words spoken*' (representational) objects of our conversation. He says, however, that this: 'joint activity between them and their socially (and linguistically) constituted situation "structures" what they do or say, not wholly they themselves' (Shotter 1993: 8).

Shotter explains how in the contested nature of words in their speaking we shape, or construct, but not fully intentionally, between ourselves, a sense of our own identities and social world. Interaction produces a situation:

> an organized practical-moral setting existing between all participants. As its organization cannot be traced back to the intentions of any particular individuals, it is as if it has a 'given', a naturally or an 'externally caused' nature; though, to those within it, is 'their/our' situation.
>
> (Shotter 1993: 39)

Here, Shotter, in similar ways to Elias, but vastly different to Argyris and Schön, accounts for the 'situation' the 'way things are' dynamically, and in a way that highlights how the present seems given, but is actually co-created in the living present.

Shotter describes, as 'a tradition of argumentation' or the 'rationally invisible', the 'tools' we use in accounting for ourselves in the disorderly zones of uncertainty. Similarly to Shaw (2002), he would explain stuckness as the process whereby the very nature of our accounting for ourselves becomes hidden from us. But his reason for this is different from that given by Wenger or Schön. It is because of the predominant tendency to concentrate on the rational-representational, the object of our conversation, to treat what we are hearing as an object of thought (e.g. OD models), to be formed as theory in order to form further action. It is because of this that we neglect the open-ended, dialogical, participatory nature of our joint action. Thus the overemphasis on *words spoken* rather than *words in their speaking* leads to the impasse.

Joint inquiry

I see possibilities for the transformation of stuckness through joint inquiry. This arises from how Shotter sees the nature of being 'struck' by moments of conversation. Shotter holds that within interactive moments, when there is a gap in the stream of communication of two or more speaking subjects, the bridging of that gap is an opportunity for a unique unrepeatable response tailored to the situation:

> By making these disorderly moments rationally visible, by critically describing them from within the event itself, *we can bring into view the character of the social negotiations, conflicts and struggles involved in the production, reproduction and transformation of our current social orders.*
>
> (Shotter 1993: 60; emphasis in original)

Thus, rather than the pessimistic view of Argyris and Schön's defensive reasoning, and closer to Wenger's notions of evolving practice, Shotter sees transformation as a possibility. However, I think Shotter is overly drawn to the *possibility* of these moments, not the *constraint*.

Using the ideas of Shotter and Elias, we can see that because of our mutual interdependence and therefore mutual constraint, people within a situation may prevent each other from exploring the tradition of argumentation because of the anxiety inherent in the unraveling of the identities involved. While this has this quality of being 'given' or outside the control of anyone within the situation, it is none the less an emergent property of the interactions within the community, each micro-interaction with its potential for change and stability re-creating the patterns forming that community.

But Shotter is adding the crucial idea that the 'tradition of argumentation' exists in the momentary, embodied, conversational, open-ended words in their speaking and not in the *results* of these conversations, the representational world they enable. It is this sense of being in the process of spontaneous relating and not knowing where it will take us, yet bringing into view the conflicts and struggles involved in the reproduction of our practice that I am proposing as being beyond *reflection in action* and that I am trying to express as I write my narratives.

The view I am proposing comes close to what Shotter and Katz call '*articulating a practice from within a practice*' (Shotter and Katz 1996). In ways very similar to Elias (1970) and to Mead (1934), Shotter is pointing to the structuration of the dialogue, in which, from within the interaction, both parties 'go on together' in new ways. I add to this the dimension that, as this joint action is how the background *taken-for-granted* nature of our practice comes into being, this *joint inquiry* is a potential transformation of practice that does not require further implementation like the classical process of reflection I have described. The very being 'struck' by aspects of the *taken for granted*, the reflexive noticing of connections, the further elaboration of the practice that occurs between practitioners within the dialogue opens up practice and, I think, results in a freshness of subsequent action rather than continued stuckness.

The intertwining of power and reflection

Questioning the nature of atrophied practice, however, creates difference, potential altering of power balances, and anxiety about potential unraveling or disintegration of identity. In addition, the standards by which we judge each other begin to transform, look less reliable, in turn offering some practitioners more promising horizons but others diminished standing. It is my belief that standards arise *within* collective reflection and ongoing practice rather than as externally given. Power relations constrain reflection and new sense-making within a community of practitioners.

However, I am arguing here that reflection shifts power relations. As the background *taken-for-granted* nature of practice comes into being through its history of relating, *joint inquiry* is a potential transformation of practice. The very being 'struck' by aspects of the *taken for granted*, the further elaboration of the practice that then occurs between practitioners, shifts the configuration of power relations. As the collective account of the efficacy of what is being offered as an appropriate practice is voiced, through detailed stories, that account is both re-created and potentially transformed. This fluidity is a shifting of power relations and is inevitably experienced by some as dangerous or threatening.

While adopting the role of questioner can seem powerful, this notion of inquiry and engagement means that the inquirer is both strong and vulnerable at the same time. The gesture of inquiry, as it is made, is incomplete, unknown in its trajectory, but I believe more likely to be fresh, enlivening, not stuck. I suggest connections between the way reflection is restricted through the constraints of doing business together and the emergence of stuckness and atrophy in a collective practice. Mead points out that it is the quality of reflexivity that marks the habitual from the intelligent and spontaneous. I suggest that the depth and detail of narratives is a key quality and that we need to be able to tell, evoke and provoke narrative descriptions and accounts of practice among our communities of practice.

New practice emerges

This meeting was discussed at the January Future Search and yet as I left my apartment at 6 a.m. it was May 2 and the sun was shining. The group that would gather in London were the impromptu group that had formed around the topic '*Becoming a leading edge consultancy*' on the final morning of that event. I had not wanted to set up a classic project group, so I suggested we get together informally to discuss our own practice. I had suggested some writing, perhaps a one-page piece on a particular moment of practice. I had sent out the short narrative about Karl, from earlier in this chapter, as a catalyst rather than an example to be followed. I had also attended the half-day discussion on practice in Scotland two weeks previously, so you can see that I am certainly entering into an inquiring process within White Spirit. Whether this is useful, or whether it will make a difference, is still unclear to me but I am enjoying the profound sense of doing something new and noticing that the movement of my practice is provoking my thinking, and that my searching for a particular type of engagement is my inquiry.

As we assembled in the conference room I remembered that we were in the same room where the Pharma meeting had been held, but that apart from Barbara this was a different mix of consultants. In the midst of a conversation, I mentioned to Barbara how difficult the Pharma meeting had been and that I was beginning to see how difference and our reactions to difference, as exemplified by Jane and Gwen's interchange, were holding us from really engaging in practice discussions. This led us into a surprisingly rich discussion on 'capturing knowledge'. I said that I did not have any need to capture our session today because the conversation is the inquiry and will inevitably inform how we are in other situations.

Barbara, though, posed some difficult questions which it seemed to me came from a different direction. How are we as a group to connect with other Future Search groups? What is their expectation of us? What is our output to be? I notice that we have quickly moved into the realm of organizational concerns about coordinating efforts of groups and expectations of outputs. The question seemed to paralyze us, as if it was not legitimate to have the quality discussion we have had so far in the meeting, unless we are connected to some strategy! Thinking stuckness, I said that I was beginning to think that many groups in White Spirit Consulting may have reached this point only to stall. I was beginning to wonder if the very practice of setting up groups to 'deliver' is something that keeps us stuck. 'My idea,' I said, 'is that several groups can form and discuss practice. There would be no definite outcome but rather a deepening inquiry, out of which may come an awakening and a freshness rather than a body of knowledge.' Barbara looked impressed, but I could read her subsequent expression as saying, 'It is not me you will have to impress!'

'I'd support that,' Sophie said, 'This is the first time since joining that I have been able to talk about what I do, or what I did before joining. All that gets squeezed out in the joining process.' 'Yes,' I respond, 'all the meetings until recently have been about organizational issues. It has been so rare to talk about what we do. I think people fear exposure.' I added that Wenger draws this interesting distinction between communities of practice and institutions. In doing this I am noticing how odd it feels but my intention is to give a voice to ideas, to locate our discussions in other debates. 'I am still uneasy,' says Clive. 'Is this it? Just talking about our practice? Surely this must lead to something, a new model or product. I am very interested in trying to see how people around the company are innovating and combine these into new designs that then can be used by all of us.'

I say, 'I think that what's going to be critical is that each of us identifies our question. What question is informing our practice? What themes do we come back to over and over again, then to inquire further in that area? For instance, I have heard you several times over the years, try to gather innovation and design a new offering. I think that is core to your practice, Clive. Maybe it would help to articulate your question further. But I am not going the intra-personal route here, as in why is that your question? I am rather trying to further your inquiry and to see this as part of our collective practice.' But the questions remain for me: Am I just raising awareness of what we do? Of what value is that? Perhaps I *will* make people less effective. What if this unravels things?

I was aware that some writing had been done and, if my own experience is anything to go by, there would be great reticence in sharing it. So I nudged it forward by inviting someone to start: 'It would be a shame if we didn't hear what has been written.' So Simon offered 'I just have some handwritten stuff.' 'That's great, read it out loud and if you find yourself wanting to fill in gaps do so, they are often where you haven't written all you need to say,' I added. I felt a moment of excitement as Simon began to read from his notes. I am aware how significant I feel this moment is. This is my contribution, my form of leadership emerging, something that I am introducing about inquiry and articulating the taken for granted.

Of course the others were engrossed in Simon's narrative. Interest started forming around the piece of the jigsaw for a consulting project that we call *design*. We were interested in how we do this designing. How do you decide what to put in? How do you know, in advance, what will be right on the day? How come my design would look quite similar to yours given what you have said about this group? How come the manager wanted to make progress on *business* issues yet you are doing *climate* building? Simon is trying to articulate his designing process: 'I know them very well and I have a real sense of what they need to do to proceed. I just need a framework to hang it all together. They know that we will probably depart from this.' I was struck by the recognition that by lingering on the theme of *design* and holding this conversation, awareness mounts in each of us that this is what we are coming to mean by practice development. This is not exactly what I had envisaged in some grand design, but it is how White Spirit Consulting are coming to engage with practice and how, as I reflect, I am further noticing how this is both repetitive and, at the same time, novel/full of potential. 'This is so central to our practice yet we never discuss how we design. We seem to lack the words. This is what Schön calls our *knowledge-in-action* where we know more than we can say and yet in us beginning to tease out these taken-for-granted areas we are changing collectively and individually. My belief is that we become less rote or unthinking if we explore our practice like this.'

This meeting built up my sense that I was engaging in ways that really mattered to me and in which there was movement.

References

Argyris, C. (1970) *Intervention Theory and Method*, Reading, MA: Addison-Wesley.

Argyris, C. and Schön, D. (1974) *Theory in Practice: Increasing Professional Effectiveness*, San Francisco, CA: Jossey-Bass.

Argyris, C. and Schön, D. (1978) *Organizational Learning: A Theory of Action Perspective*, Reading, MA: Addison-Wesley.

Argyris, C. and Schön, D. (1996) *Organizational Learning II: Theory, Method and Practice*, Reading, MA: Addison-Wesley.

Beckhard, R. and Harris, R. T. (1987) *Organizational Transitions, Managing Complex Change*, Reading, MA: Addison-Wesley.

Block, P. (1981) *Flawless Consulting: A Guide to Getting your Experience Used*, San Francisco, CA: Pfeiffer.

Elias, N. (1939) *The Civilizing Process*, published in 1982 by Oxford: Blackwell.

Elias, N. (1970) *What is Sociology?*, published in 1978 by London: Hutchinson.

Elias, N. (1998) *On Civilization, Power and Knowledge, Selected Writings Edited and with an Introduction by Stephen Mennell and Johan Goudsblom*, Chicago, IL: University of Chicago Press.

Goldstein, J. (1994) *The Unshackled Organization: Facing the Challenge of Unpredictability Through Spontaneous Reorganization*, Portland, OR: Productivity Press.

Goudsblom, J. in Mennell, S. (1992) *Norbert Elias: An Introduction*, Dublin: University College Dublin Press.

Lewin, K. (1951) *Field Theory in Social Science*, New York: Harper and Brothers.

Mead, G. H. (1934) *Mind, Self and Society: From the Standpoint of a Social Behaviorist*, Chicago, IL: Chicago University Press.

Mennell, S. (1992) *Norbert Elias: An Introduction*, Dublin: University College Dublin Press.

Nevis, E. C. (1987) *Organizational Consulting: A Gestalt Approach*, Boston, MA: GIC Press.

Schön, D. (1983) *The Reflective Practitioner: How Professionals Think in Action*, London: Ashgate.

Shaw, P. (2002) *Changing Conversations in Organizations: A complexity approach to change*, London: Routledge.

Shotter, J. (1993) *Conversational Realities: Constructing Life through Language*, London: Sage.

Shotter, J. and Cunliffe, A. L. (1999) 'Managers as practical authors: everyday conversations for action', in D. Holman and R. Thorpe (eds) *The Manager as Practical Author*, London: Sage.

Shotter, J. and Katz, A. (1996) 'Articulating a practice from within the practice itself: establishing formative dialogues by the use of "social poetics"', *Concepts and Transformations*, 1(2/3), pp. 213–237.

Shotter, J. and Katz, A. (1999) 'Living moments in dialogical exchanges', *Human Systems*, 9, pp. 8–93.

Stacey, R. (2001) *Complex Responsive Processes in Organizations: Learning and knowledge creation*, London: Routledge.

Stacey, R., Griffin, D. and Shaw, P. (2000) *Complexity and Management: Fad or radical challenge to systems thinking?*, London: Routledge.

Weisbord, M. and Janov, S. (2000) *Future Search: An Action Guide to Finding Common Ground in Organizations and Communities*, San Francisco, CA: Berret-Koehler.

Wenger, E. (1998) *Communities of Practice, Learning, Meaning and Identity*, Cambridge: Cambridge University Press.

Editor's introduction
to Chapter 5

In this chapter, Richard Williams, Principal and CEO of Westminster Kingsway Further Education College in the UK, explores how the social object (see Chapter 2 in this volume) of government policy on education is taken up by him and his fellow college CEOs in their local interactions with each other and with the Executive Director of the government body charged with overseeing their performance. He argues that these local interactions form, and are at the same time formed by, their identities. He describes the split to be found in the dominant discourse on organizations between identity and task. Here the individual is understood as having an identity, a reflection of the notion of a true self, which is independent of the work role of that individual, and what is required for the effective functioning of an organization is some kind of alignment between individual identities and the goals of the organization. Williams moves from this position to argue that our work roles are formative of who we are, and that our identities emerge and continue to be iterated in the interactions between us in our work roles just as much as in any other role we may experience ourselves to be in. Threats to our work roles are thus experienced as threats to identity with the anxiety, emotion and even trauma that this brings. This is a point of great significance because government policies are crafted within the dominant discourse and so, not surprisingly, when policy-makers set targets for managers in educational institutions they implicitly connect them entirely with work roles and take no account of the impact on people's experience of their own identities and the threats that unrealistic or meaningless targets pose to those identities. Such threats lead to responses that shut down the possibility of creative action.

Williams explores this contention in a detailed account of a single meeting, one of a regular series of informal meetings, between CEOs of further education colleges and the Executive Director. At the start of the meeting, the Executive Director invites comments on a recent major speech by the government minister responsible for education, but she does so in a way Williams finds manipulative in that the implicit message is that any form of dissent is barred. First, they talk about the substantial amount of new money the minister has promised for further education colleges. In the discussion it soon emerges, however, that most of the supposed new money has already been allocated. The conversation then moves on to new targets and performance measures which are soon to be imposed on them. Williams describes how anxious they all individually and collectively become as they attempt to make sense of the new performance measures in the context of few additional resources. The minister's announcements,

> it was feared, would potentially threaten all of the institutions represented in this meeting with being judged negatively. The perceived threat was that of being categorized variously according to the language codes of the scrutinizing bodies as 'unsatisfactory' or as having serious 'weaknesses' or as 'inadequate'.
>
> (pp. 125–126 below)

What Richards is drawing to our attention is the consequence of mainstream thinking in which it is taken for granted that a social object can be designed. From another perspective, all that ministers and policy-makers are doing is making a generalized, idealized gesture, the meaning of which is to be found only in the experience of many, many particularized responses. When policy-makers proceed as if they could do more than this and rigidly apply their prescriptions in a complex world, their actions produce many unintended, distorting reactions. In his narrative, Richards points to how the meaning of a statement on targets and new money in a minister's speech changes completely in another context, namely the micro-operational world of the college CEOs. As they discuss the promise of new money for the college sector, they realize that the minister's macro-level promise of new money turns out to mean no new money at the micro-level of the colleges. The intention of departmental officials to impose 'stretch' targets on the colleges sounds perfectly reasonable at the macro-level – who could possibly object to efficiency and improvement? In the actual micro-level context of the work of the CEOs, however, this reasonable requirement becomes an appearance which covers over the substance. In substance the 'stretch' targets amount to a persecutory, punishing action which threatens the

identity of the CEOs. Richards argues that the array of targets is so complex that members of the public who do not participate in the micro-detail of what these targets mean cannot understand what they really are, and this allows the government's onslaught on the public sector to appear reasonable. Richards shows in
his narrative the micro-detail of just how this attack on the public sector is sustained in the form of the twin cults of performance management and continuous improvement. It becomes clearer just how the social object of centralized control, as a form of emotional blackmail, is taken up in the detailed interaction of the college CEOs.

> As I walked back to my office in Victoria, I reflected upon what I feel to be the grinding poverty of imagination that lies beneath the surface of the performance management regime in the public sector. I thought too about the implications of having to factor the additional demands of these new targets into our management processes and find ways of making sense of these for the people working in the organization.
>
> (p. 128 below)

5 Experiencing national education policies in local interaction

Richard Williams

In this chapter I aim to explore some of the ways in which identities emerge in the context of relationships at work. In using the term 'identity' I am referring both to an individual's sense of self (a social object to oneself) and at the same time to a social object arising in the perceptual field of others. While the assumption of identity is therefore what enables us to become known to ourselves it is also what enables us to recognize and be recognized by each other as more than physical objects in our perception. Identity is social and relational in character. It is identity and the specific characteristics that this assumes for each of us in relation to one another which gives rise to our sense of individuality. An argument of this chapter is therefore that identity is a social process which entails an ongoing dialectical relationship between the *I* and the *me* together constituting the reflexive, social self of human experience. Identity,

I argue, is formed by and forming, at the same time, the social relations in which we are all at all times engaged throughout our life process.

I am therefore interested in the possibility of using my own experiences of being in a network of social relations at work to explore the ways in which identities are formed in processes of social interaction in organizations. I am seeking also to explore more fully the implications of this process for how we can *be* in the presence of each other as we engage in our various work roles.

As I think about these ideas I also think about the ways in which power relations enter into, are essential to, the process of identity formation and its ongoing reproduction in a context of social relations. It is because our life experiences are situated in contexts of power relating that our identities emerge. Power relations are what enable and constrain the way in which identities develop and come to be reproduced in our interactions. It is, for example, in the social contextual character of processes of power relating that the differentiated roles that we take up throughout our lives emerge: husband, parent, office worker, chief executive and taxpayer. Such roles provide contexts in which we enact patterns of behaviors that are also recognizable to others within our socio-cultural milieu. Roles therefore confer upon us a license to act in ways that are both enabled and constrained by rules of conduct that we know by virtue of other, generalized, processes of socialization.

It is also in the movement of the power relations associated with such roles that contexts arise in which our identities come to be threatened, and in relation to which we can experience great waves of emotional anxiety and/or trauma. Threats to identity therefore emerge in contexts where our habituated patterns of social relations are subject to change such that our familiar ways of doing things cannot be sustained. In organizational life these situations are exemplified in events such as reorganizations, mergers, or the appointment of a new line manager. Threats to identity can also take on coercive qualities that act powerfully to constrain the actions of individuals and so invoke compliant behaviors. Yet to understand the ability of such behaviors to constitute a threat it is important also to understand what it is in the relational dynamics of participation that confers this quality upon some gestures and not on others. Here it is important to understand something of what it is that individuals will have invested in their sense of the character of their identity. For a gesture to find its meaning in the arousal of an anxiety state, some other material (income, status, autonomy) or emotional (fear, humiliation, shame) consequence has to be anticipated.

I am arguing here that identity has to be understood as the product of human interaction. It is therefore made known both in the silent conversations we conduct with ourselves and in our public interactions with others who form the network of social relations in which we are participants. Our organizational lives are but one particularly significant aspect of such interactions. As we participate organizationally we enact figurations of relationships in which our identities are formed by and formative of those other identities we recognize within our network or milieu of acquaintance. There is, therefore, no juxtaposition in this process between our job roles and our individual selves. We do not take on these roles as if we are putting on a coat. As I argue this point, I am aware that I am adopting a position that is different from that of many other writers whose thinking greatly influences views about organizational life and leadership and management in the UK public sector at the present time.

Mainstream perspectives

In Senge's work, for example, there is a transparent differentiation between work roles and identities: 'We are trained to be loyal to our jobs – so much so that we confuse them with our identities.' Senge goes so far as to argue that such confusion needs to be understood as an example of the learning disabilities of contemporary organizations. Senge goes on to argue that the tasks associated with a job role should in some way be separated from the 'purpose' of the greater enterprise of which they are a part. Senge is arguing that identity can or should be attached to individuals' sense of purpose about their work but not to the performance of the tasks that go to make up their job. Put another way, notions of identity are not to be found in what constitutes the real lived experience of being at work but in a somewhat reified context of a sense of higher purpose (Senge 1990: 18).

This same juxtaposition is to be found in other writers of influence, such as Argyris, whose focus on organizational learning also leads to a perspective in which the individual in some way holds an identity that stands against the meta-identity of the organization in which they work. Argyris' work draws heavily upon personality theories in which individual action is assumed to be motivated by an impulse to self-actualization. The ideal of the fully self-actualizing individual is here accommodated by the implementation of *fusion* strategies that are intended to align organizational and individual goals. Here, too, there is a juxtaposition that presumes a monadic model of the individual. Argyris' subsequent theories of single- and double-loop learning are also attached to thinking about model leadership and management styles that may be used to condition the circumstances in which individuals' behaviors will be adjusted towards specific behavior outcomes. This is a model of agents acting in systemic part/whole relationships, not of actors engaged in processes of reflexive interaction (Argyris 1957; Argyris and Schon 1974).

From another perspective Charles Handy, writing about power and influence in organizations, describes also a context in which managers can elect to adopt a range of different situation-specific behaviors that will gain them influence in the workplace. In response to such behaviors, it is envisaged that subordinates will adjust their behaviors by the use of psychological responses that include compliance, identification and internalization (Handy 1999: 143). In this writing Handy shares an approach with that of the emotional intelligence theories of writers such as Goleman (1996). Goleman has attempted to identify good and bad emotional states that lead to high or low organizational performance. More recently Hirschhorn, also writing from a perspective that focuses on 'emotion', has explored the need to rework authority in what he describes as postmodern organizations. Hirschhorn's argument is that managers should make greater use of displays of feelings and engage in emotional risk-taking to create climates of engagement and participation for their subordinates (Hirschhorn 1998). The issue here is one of the relationship between a felt sense of personal identity in contrast with processes of identification with the goals and objectives of the organization.

Although these perspectives are taken from a relatively small sample of writers, they are representative of a dominant discourse within management theory that draws upon the traditions of philosophic liberalism, humanism, psychoanalysis and systems theory. As such there are a number of organizing themes within the arguments of these writers that recur in 'good practice' thinking about leading and managing in organizations today.

First, there is a common assumption that managers act from a position of being in control or with the capability (if they get 'it' right) of being in control of the intellectual and emotional worlds of their subordinates. This is in parallel with the assumption that they are also in control of the work of their organization. Second, managers' behaviors are assumed to be constrained by system blockages that are generally manifest in the non-compliant behaviors of their subordinates. This may be attributable to factors as diverse as organizational barriers to learning, communication difficulties or the repression of emotions. The manager's role is therefore in some way to unblock such problems in order to secure an alignment of attitudes, behaviors, resources and organizational performance. Third, the managerial task is therefore often also associated with the goal of attaining a symmetrical organizational culture within which individuals' attitudes and behaviors are aligned with the vision, mission and goals of the organization as articulated by the CEO and senior managers. Fourth, managers are always assumed to be observers and instigators rather than participants and subjects of the relational processes that characterize organizational life. In this sense the managerial position is always one that is situated outside of an envisioned context of interaction. Managers intervene as regulators and designers. My argument is that this is not the case. Leaders and managers are always caught up in an intense struggle of ongoing power relating in which their participation is wholly reflexive. In this regard senior managers are paradoxically in control and yet not in control of their situational context to the same degree as is the case for any other participant. Their organizational locus is also as constrained by power and threats to identity as it is for any other participant. The key differentiator for senior staff in organizations is that their power chances in these ongoing processes of interaction are weighted more heavily than for their subordinates.

The perspective of complex responsive processes

Since becoming engaged with the thinking that I associate with the idea of complex responsive processes I have become alert to the ways in which sense-making processes (how we order our experience, how we frame our actions) emerge in the conversations of gestures that are constantly iterated between people. When very senior colleagues meet together I now notice that very paradoxical occurrences emerge. For example, meetings between such people are not random. They appear in diaries well in advance of the occasion. They have an etiquette and structure that is highly formalized. In my experience of these events people generally arrive with a sense of agenda and an awareness (conscious and unconscious) of the conduct that they should observe throughout the proceedings. Yet from the moment of being together the interactions of such people seem to me to assume an order and flow that is never predictable and seldom, if ever, what was anticipated. In saying this I am not suggesting that it would be right to think of work meetings as free-form occasions. Organizing themes seem quickly to emerge. These too create patterns in these interactions. The conversations that take place are steered and yet not steered by the agenda at the same time. In the end, someone will often try to summarize what took place in such a meeting, as if to assert the legitimacy of their witnessing or participation in the events that have taken place. Others will consent or demur. Even at this point there is a process of negotiation taking place about what it is that everyone present has experienced. In the actions that flow from such occasions, further iterations of human interaction emerge. And so it goes on. The character of what is happening appears both constrained and unconstrained at the same time. So the conversational process always seems to be pregnant with risk, to hold the prospect of transformation in the ways in which participants make sense of what is happening around them and yet, finally, to be constrained within the conventions of the social relations that constitute the etiquette of how we in some way believe that we can be together (Shaw 2002; Stacey 2001).

This chapter departs from the themes of what I have described as a dominant discourse. My interest is in the identity formation issues that emerge in processes of interaction among senior managers. I participate in such a process when I am together with my peers. I observe and experience processes of *being together* in which we are all exposed constantly to identity threats associated with our situation. I recognize and feel the influence in this context of those power-dominant individuals who constitute the senior echelons of the civil service and government. I am interested therefore in the vulnerability of myself and of these individuals as this is *the* experience that I live and share in every moment of my working life. I am interested too in how, from the theoretical perspective of complex responsive processes, our participation together may be understood and described in a way that reveals something of the nature of power as a mediator in the process of our being together.

I have structured the chapter around an exploration of a series of interlinked themes which formalize a consideration of work meetings as a context relevant to a theoretical discourse concerning groups and group relations. First, I attempt to relate my own experiences at work to Norbert Elias' concept of figuration. Second, by pursuing G.H. Mead's phenomenological explanations of gesture (his conceptualization of objects and time in perception) I offer a socio-biological explanation for what in the Foulkesian tradition of group analysis is referred to as resonance. Mead's account of the way in which inter-bodily awareness emerges in our individual perceptual fields of experience is, I think, also akin to Foulkes' concept of the foundation matrix which he described as the background of common experience that is instinctively shared between us by virtue also of a common inheritance that is species- and culture-specific. This I believe to be important since the same insight viewed from different perspectives of causality gives rise to radically different explanations of what is going on in human interaction. Third, by shifting my attention from the foundation to the dynamic character of group processes I want to draw attention to Mead's conceptualization of the role of what he described as significant symbols in the conversational process of gestures passing between people in interaction. Here I will argue that Mead's organic and evolutionary explanations of the emergence of patterning themes in social interaction needs also to be complemented by a formal consideration of power. This is particularly with reference to the way in which political power comes to constitute a social object of our experience that is bureaucratized and reproduced in authority structures that constrain social processes of conversation and restrict (as against constrain) our capacity for creative action . By exploring these themes in this way, I think that it is possible to reconstruct the composite elements of a narrative of experience that in turn exemplifies Elias' idea of figuration. My interest is therefore in describing the process of identity formation as it emerges in the figuration of relations in contemporary organizational life.

A meeting

In the following narrative I describe a meeting in which I was a participant.

This was a meeting also involving several heads of large post-16 educational institutions in central London, of which I was one, and the Director of the local area Learning and Skills Council. Two of the Director's officials were also in attendance. The Director is the local head of the regulatory body that now oversees the work of all post-16 education in England excluding higher education. The Director in question is responsible for an annual budget in excess of £200 million. The Director is not the accounting officer for this money. Her role is to administer the arrangements by which it is committed in order to best achieve the targets set by the central Council. My institution accounted for 10 per cent of this local spend. In combination those present in the room represented a spending commitment equal to 85 per cent of the Director's annual budget. This meeting was of people who are recognized in their respective organizational contexts as having very considerable power and among whom complex patterns of interdependent power relations exist.

The iconography of power

We sat down around a block of tables that had been arranged into a square. The meeting began. The meeting was chaired by the Director. Flanked by her two officers she reminded those present that this was one of a series of informal meetings that we had agreed to have in recent months. As she mentioned the word 'informal', one of the officers started to circulate a written agenda while the other one moved his pen in what seemed to be to be a clear gesture of minute-taking. I wondered at the use of the terms 'we' and 'informal' to describe our proceedings and how the feelings of others in the room may have become affected by the mixed messages of the opening remarks and gestures. From the background conversations taking place between the principals in between these meetings I know that everyone else has said that they feel that these meetings are not an option: we have to be at them; we do not like them; we have no choice; these are her meetings not ours and so on. Prior to the formation of the LSC the principals of the large general further education colleges (GFE) would meet with the predecessor regulatory bodies as a discrete group. Now we meet with the Director in the company of other institutional heads who we do not regard as being a part of our particular area of what is now termed the 'learning and skills sector'. The seven heads of the GFE colleges continue to meet privately. We have formalized an identity for ourselves. This has been agreed through each of the college's boards and we have now developed our own distinctive brand name. This is intended to signify our intention to work collaboratively together. We try hard to do this but often struggle to establish real common ground that can be the basis of substantial collaborative work. Our commitment to each other is tempered by the underlying competition that exists between our institutions. At the same time, however, our brand identity helps us to cohere as a group relative to those whose desire it is to remove our claims to unique, different or special status in gatherings such as the one currently occurring. Our sense of solidarity therefore fluctuates according to context. Our ongoing relationships are therefore continuously and paradoxically collaborative and competitive at the same time.

I understand the collective feeling among the GFE principals to be one of resentment at the downgrading of our status with respect to the new regulatory body. The heads of very small institutions have been accorded equal voices in these provider meetings. We worry about the extent to which others, not visible to this meeting, may also have gained access to the Director and her regional staff team.

Both in her tone and in her reference to informality, I sensed that the Director was seeking to create an ambience of relaxed intimacy in the room in which she intended that we would all speak openly and contribute freely. My attention is always drawn to this feature of the Director's way of conducting business. She makes frequent references in meetings of this type to the idea that 'we must all work together in partnership'. Whenever she says this I find myself wondering what precisely she means as we are plainly not a partnership in the sense of mutuality to which this term most usually refers. I am aware that I think of this both as a gesture which is seeking consciously to manage the relations in the room and a signifier of her own unconscious anxieties borne of her role. This is to be often, at least with us, in a minority in the presence of a potentially hostile and untrusting majority. The Director is believed to be close to retirement age. She is ten or fifteen years older than the average age of the rest of the people in the room. The Director is also a highly experienced operator in this milieu. Prior to the formation of the LSC she had a national role in a predecessor body. Because it is believed that the Director could retire within the next twelve months a recurrent theme in the conversations of my peers is about what she is like and what her successor will be like. The successor always emerges in these considerations as a source of great anxiety among us. There is something about the context and the style of the Director's opening remarks that have a powerful effect in terms of laying the foundations for an emergent sense of we-ness being together in this room.

As we were still in the opening stages of the meeting someone drew attention to the fact that we were meeting in this room and not in our usual location. Normally we meet on the ninth floor of a large office building in central London. On this occasion we were in a much older building in another part of the city. There seemed to be a strong affectual awareness among everyone in the room of this different location.

Everyone noticed that this new room was extraordinarily well appointed. I remembered having been in this room a few years before when it was just a working office for a group of fairly low-grade officials working in an offshoot of a different government department. The cultivated drabness of civil service offices had now been replaced by décor and furnishings that communicated a sense of exclusivity. We were in the London office of the national Chairman. The Chairman is one of a number of private sector executives brought in by the government, as part of its wider reform process, to run major public sector operations. It was clear to all present that the Chairman's expectations of his working environment were not those of the previous occupants of the room. As this information was shared with the group it was apparent that everyone started to assume a great interest in the room itself. In simultaneous gestures of interest we made exaggerated motions of looking and noticing what was in the room.

The Director seemed self-evidently proud of the fact that she was the gatekeeper for this experience. That she had been allocated this room for a meeting when her own building was not available seemed to signify a proximity and/or intimacy on her part with the Chairman and the national center of power. She seemed to grow in presence by this association. There was a ripple of polite banter around the room about the Chairman as we all shared in the Director's more intimate associations with him. In the movement of these gestures I felt that we were in some way being drawn together in an inner sanctum of privilege. This seemed to strengthen the momentary feeling of we-ness among the group. Here was an invitation for us, present in this moment, to feel and be at one with the iconography of power that was signified by the room itself. As this awareness unfolded and moved around the room a collective group identity was being invited in the iteration of the action of noticing our location on the part of each participant. For each person the sense of being privileged over others was made concrete. For the group, this was a moment of private and shared experience through which some other more transient experience of solidarity could be aroused.

The emergence of organizing themes in the flow of conversation

The Director suggested to us that before we started on the agenda proper we ought to take a few moments to reflect upon the previous week's national conference of colleges and, in particular, the speech given by the

Secretary of State. As she extended this invitation I noticed that her body posture changed. She sat back slightly in her chair. Her expression suggested a benign half-smile. An air of expectancy descended upon the room. It was clear that we were being invited to participate in a celebration of this speech and to welcome the good news of the extra billions that, it was implied, would shortly be made available in our negotiations about the following year's funding allocations. There is something about the imposition of a ritualized celebration of ministerial speeches in these settings that I find disconcerting. I always feel that these invitations are confrontational. What is being presented in such invitations is an opportunity to make a gesture of public association (or disassociation) with the objectives of government and, *inter alia*, its agencies. Often, these invitations are associated in a semi-personalized way with the individual character of the minister or Secretary of State in question. There is frequently a knowingness of the other (conveyed in the solicitous tone of the invitation) that will be introduced to these moments. These invitations are often proffered, as in this case, by someone with a vicarious but direct association with the individual political play-maker or his or her immediate team of civil servants. I liken this experience to that of participation in a ritualized declaration of fealty. On such occasions I have the sense of being enveloped by the contemporary etiquettes of political power. At such moments, no gesture is insignificant. Every gesture conveys an attitude about association and belonging. Such moments are always a test of the insider/outsider credentials of those present. I noticed also that at such moments no one voices dissent or fundamental disagreement.

The immediate response to this invitation was oblique as someone interjected with the suggestion that a rumor had already started to circulate which suggested that the benefits identified by the Secretary of State might not be quite those suggested by the headlines in the education media. The mood in the room started to change and the Director, adopting a more formal posture, sat forward in her chair to listen. Someone in the room then asked if anyone else had confirmation of the suggestion that the Secretary of State met the lecturers' union ahead of the conference and agreed with them that the extra money being made available by the government would fund their current demand for improved pay. This it was said would explain the union's sudden and unexpected withdrawal of the threat of strike action. A third person then confirmed that they too had heard this rumor while at the conference. Another person then confirmed that they knew this rumor to be a true reflection of what happened. The weight of rumor and the certainty of the last speaker combined to convince those present that this was indeed an accurate version of events. A more somber mood descended upon the room as it was realized that a substantial element of the money promised as additional by the Secretary of State was already in circulation in the sector in the form of a special grant already linked to lecturers' pay. This was a centrally controlled grant offered to institutions on the basis that it was intended to create incentives for the introduction of a variant of performance-related pay: anathema to the trades' unions. At this point it was *apparent* to everyone in the room that references to 'new' money in the speech might, in reality, turn out to refer in the main to the consolidation of special grant monies already circulating in the system.

It is difficult to describe the atmosphere of despondency that descended upon the room at this point. The majority of the principals present have been in their jobs for some time. Everyone has had experience of making staff redundant in response to the cost-reduction measures imposed on the sector by government since 1993. It is estimated that this pressure resulted in a 16 per cent real terms reduction in funding over that period. Sitting in the room it was clear that those other than the LSC officers, who have no such responsibilities, felt immediately back in the familiar territory of having to grapple with the effects of policy statements that appear deliberately to mislead. Everyone believed that the Secretary of State had promised pay rises to the lecturers' union behind the backs of the college employers. In the moment of this meeting the *reality* to which we were attending was that the government had focused on the presentation rather than the substance of what we all saw to be a major problem.

The conversation in the meeting moved on. Much of the Secretary of State's speech had been centered on the implementation of the government's latest reform proposals (DfES 2002). One feature of these proposals is to introduce yet further performance targets for the post-16 sector. These include the introduction of floor targets (levels of performance below which institutions must contract not to fall) and stretch targets (differentiated improvement rate targets reflecting an individual institution's ability to 'stretch' its performance beyond its current baseline outcomes). In addition, the proposals include a new performance indicator to be described as a success rate. The threat of success rate measures is a cause of great anxiety among college principals as these have the effect of resetting baseline levels of measured performance to what will appear in public as being a very low level. This will create the appearance of great opportunities for improvement and establish a margin within which ever more intense processes of target-setting and scrutiny and orchestrated public opprobrium for failure will be applied.

The language game of common sense rhetoric

The manner of the introduction of success rate targets highlights the significance of the nuances of meaning that exist in language use between rhetoric and reality-congruent experience. By this I am pointing both to the distinction between what is said and what what is said means, and that which exists between presentation and substance. A proposition stated in one context of meaning (i.e. what Wittgenstein described as one particular language game) has a completely different meaning when it reappears in another. The issue of success rates is a specific example of this. In the language game of the public presentation of a political agenda for change, the idea of increasing the numbers of people who it may be said are achieving their planned qualification outcomes speaks to an idea of the social 'good'. As a proposition it appears absolutely reasonable. When we are able to move into the language game of specialist knowledge where both practical and technical meanings are combined with insight into the deeper significance of this as a statement of power, the meaning of the proposition becomes quite different.

In the extreme, a political proposition that speaks to the social good may be felt as a deeply threatening personal attack to those able to decode the specific action implications of what has been said. It is only those who are able to comprehend the significance of the nuances, the understanding of what 'what is said' means, who can be included in the dialogue. Non-specialists (including of course the majority of the media and the public at large) who operate in a linguistic field that is outside of the scope of this nuance may in general terms (perhaps from their own local learned experiences) distrust such presentations but they can only make sense of the headlines. The obtuseness of the special circumstances and practices that inform each branch and sub-branch of the management of the public realm, the essential preoccupation with a morass of micro-detail associated with the technocracy of the management process, is therefore isolating and thus silencing. The degree of explanation required to include someone from outside of the dialogue in an established point of shared understanding and meaning is too great. The political and thus media onslaught on public sector performance operates exactly in this way. No one can defend the accusation that performance is poor on a basis that illuminates the technocratic procedures used to inform such a judgment.

This dominant discourse is what constitutes the common sense of experience. Common sense is reproduced in a conversational process whose patterns of discourse are themed by an articulation of what Mead described as the cult values of the social milieu. What are truly dominant common sense propositions now (as witnessed in pages and pages of the media) are the twin cults of performance management and continuous improvement. This mechanism (i.e. the exploitation of the nuance of difference existing between language games) is the means by which these cult values are taken up in the active experience of professional roles. These themes were explored and developed extensively from a different perspective by the Italian philosopher Antonio Gramsci in his study of the relationship between ideas, language and the dynamics of hegemonic political power. Gramsci described common sense as a 'conception of the world that is followed in normal times' (Gramsci 1971: 327) where the 'principle of causality' is applied in a way that:

> identifies the exact cause, simple and to hand, and does not let itself be distracted by fancy quibbles and pseudo-profound, pseudo-scientific metaphysical mumbo-jumbo.
>
> (Gramsci 1971: 348)

In the irony of this statement, Gramsci characterizes common sense as a mode of discourse in which complex argument is treated dismissively and then dismissed in favor of truths self-evident from the experience of everyday life. Gramsci identified common sense as a central tenet within his theory of political hegemony. Common sense, argued Gramsci, 'does not permit of any action, any decision, or any choice and produces a position of moral and political passivity' (Gramsci 1971: 333). Like Mead, Gramsci saw conflict (in the realm of ideas) as being fundamental to processes of personal and social transformation:

> Critical understanding of self takes place therefore through a struggle of political 'hegemonies' and of opposing directions, first in the ethical field and then in that of politics proper, in order to arrive at a working out at a higher level of one's own conception of reality.
>
> (Gramsci 1971: 333)

The Secretary of State's speech is itself a powerful statement of both common sense argumentation and the character of the modern political process. The speech is structured in the form of a series of exhortations, instructions and the repetition of assumed statements of truth and fact. It is variously ingratiating of the audience, searching for solidarity, presuming of common ground and attacking (Clarke 2002).

Narratives and legitimating

The truth of this speech and its significance in praxis is to be found in the narratives of experience that emerge in the responses that are made to it. An important aspect of this narrative-building process is that of the interpretation of the policy context to which the speech refers made by both the LSC and the Department. The LSC's interpretation is conveyed in 'Circular 03/01: Success for All – Implementation of the Framework for Quality and Success' (Learning and Skills Council 2003). This was issued as a 'consultation' document in January 2003. It is a dense document packed with detailed information about the technical basis of the new performance management regime, the monitoring, supervision and intervention arrangements that will be established. It contains a considerable amount of information about the new 'trust in FE' agenda that is part of the Secretary of State's pledge to work in partnership. It also contains a great deal of information about the steps that will be taken when this assumed basis of 'trust' is found to have been breached by evidence of underperformance. Here it is evident that the penalties for failure will be in proportion to the level of expectation that a relationship based on 'trust' would assume. In reading 'Circular 03/01' it is hard to discern the hand of ministerial friendship that is conveyed in much of the speech.

Another stage in the narrative-building process is to be found in the ways in which the people sitting in the room with me are making sense of these developments. This was manifest in their individual and collective feelings of anxiety and their struggle to make sense of these meta-propositions about change and performance from within their local circumstances. The performance of inner city institutions always benchmarks at a level that is below that of others in the shires and provinces. The Secretary of State's announcements, it was feared, would potentially threaten all the institutions represented in this meeting with being judged negatively. The perceived threat was that of being categorized variously according to the language codes of the scrutinizing bodies as 'unsatisfactory' or as having 'serious weaknesses' or as 'inadequate'. The senior staff members present in the room were and remain very conscious of the potential consequences for them as individuals of falling foul of such categorization.

Further themes in the conversation of the group: insider–outsider relations

We were now well into the meeting. Talk of the introduction of yet more performance indicators elicited an outburst from another of the principals present. She expressed 'real concern' about the implications of all of this for her college, and asked the Director when we were to be given the detail of how these new arrangements would work. Two of the newer principals expressed their concerns more mutedly. In so doing, they adopted a demeanor towards the Director that was deferential. In the tone of their speaking they communicated their recognition that the Director held the ability to judge them. That she can give to and take from them. They appealed to the Director to 'give us all the support and information that we will need in order to respond to these new challenges'. This exchange introduced unexpectedly a new dynamic into the room. Enveloped by the informality of the meeting the Director suggested that she too was very unhappy with the development in relation to performance indicators. This she explained was because although it is the college's ('providers' in the new argot of the Learning and Skills Council) who have to 'deliver' these she and her team will be judged by the center to have failed if 'things don't happen' in 'our area'. This observation provoked some in the room to ask the Director about the pressures she is under. In response to this the Director shared with us several anecdotes from her own experience (having to seek approval for quite low-level decisions that should be taken locally, being forced to use standard letters written at the center in her local correspondence, being summoned to the center and told how to operate a variety of review procedures) in which she emerged as the victim of a dictatorial and centerist management process. It is on the basis of sharing this experience that the Director then made a direct appeal to us as a group to make sure that 'we get it right' in our locality. Acknowledging that she cannot deliver her targets single-handedly, the Director, I realized, was working hard to join us all together in a we-identification against a bigger 'they'. In this instance the outsiders became her senior managers, the central team at the national Council. As these anecdotes are shared, a bridge is created momentarily between the Director and everyone else. The anecdotes are also in their way minor indiscretions. The stories are disloyalties that communicate a sense of isolation and a need for belonging elsewhere with us. We, hearing these stories, took them up into our own narratives as we shared the Director's sense-making of her own position in her organization.

This gesture by the Director represented for me a sudden but fascinating movement of the power relations in the room. As we sat in relation to her, she now sat in relation to her own line managers. The Director's stories evidenced a dynamic of organizational power relations in which center and local exist in contradictory tension with each other. The Director's gesture of disloyalty, made in the exceptionally local context of this room, also drew attention to the systems, structures and anxieties that motivate national Council officers to behave towards her in a way which arouses in her the same feelings as are being felt by us. While the ED appears to have a power dominance in relation to us, this is a much more paradoxical relationship than the formal structures would suggest. These dynamics are reflected in the text of the Secretary of State's speech and in the documentation the DfES is producing to support its new *Success for All* strategy. I have therefore come to understand the Director's indiscretions as a response to the pressures being applied to her by senior LSC officers who, themselves, are in the grip of anxiety borne of the mistrust made public that now exists between their organization and the Department. Their ever more aggressive demands for the delivery of targets placed upon the Director and through her, us, is a function of their own sense of vulnerability to the judgment of those in the Department who are one step closer to the center of power. Sitting in this room in Victoria, it seemed clear to me that we are all enacting processes of gesture and response that combine into a particular figuration of power relations in which threats to identity are central to the dynamic of relational processes.

Encouraged by the rising feeling of fellowship in the room the conversation moved on to consider the detail of other targets that we would also be required to meet. These particular targets relate to the numbers of people participating in post-16 education in central London.

At this point, I asked the Director if she could bring us all up to date with the progress her team were making with establishing the numerical basis upon which we were going to agree the increased participation targets for the 2003/2004 year. As I introduced the question I explained the history of my attendance at earlier meetings where this issue had been acknowledged as being a major problem for the new Learning and Skills Council. I said that I wondered if, in the light of the new target-setting processes that were to be implemented, the issue of knowing where we were starting from and where we needed to end up had been resolved. If so could we have a copy of the analysis to help us with our own planning?

It was clear from her response that the Director did not particularly welcome this question. My compulsion to ask this question was borne of a desire to disrupt the mood of 'solidarity' that was present among those in the room. My question was intended to dislodge the fantasies that inform the performance management regime to which we are all subjected. I wanted to challenge the integrity of the idea of 'progress' that is so central to the justification of current practice in the administration of public services across the UK. I know that I feel some exhilaration, a sense of freedom and of being in touch with a personal core of motivation in the moment that I problematize, or disrupt, in a public way the fug of conformity within which my professional life takes place. I have a sense that such gestures are cumulatively career-limiting in their effect. As I speak, I am in touch with the idea that this intervention is reckless. I find myself, none the less, invigorated by taking the position of dissident. Without such opportunities for the expression of an alternative truth I would experience being no more than a cipher of processes with which I feel great disquiet.

Shortly after this interchange, the meeting came to a close. As I walked back to my office in Victoria I reflected upon what I feel to be the grinding poverty of imagination that lies beneath the surface of the performance management regime in the public sector. I thought too about the implications of having to factor the additional demands of these new targets into our management processes and to find ways of making sense of these for the people working in the organization. Finally, heading back past Victoria Station to my office, I tried to make sense of how my experiences of working between the institution and the agencies of public sector reform, at the interface of this politics, inform my relationships with those who teach and study at the college.

Foulkes and Elias: psychoanalytic and social paradigms of explanation

It seems to me that it is important to be clear about the implications of the explanatory paradigm for the way in which we make sense of experience. I have asserted the importance of understanding identity and group processes as phenomena of social interaction. But it would be possible to explain what was taking place in this room using insights drawn from a psychoanalytic paradigm that draws upon Foulkesian theories regarding group processes and the individual/group relationship. In this sense, the meeting could be treated as an exemplar of the Foulkesian concept of the matrix. This approach is potentially attractive because, unlike the dominant discourse of contemporary management theory, it draws attention to interaction in the construction of human experience and therefore raises questions regarding power and ethics in the conduct of relationships at work. 'Matrix' is suggestive of interdependency in human relations. This is qualitatively and significantly different from the perspectives on power, and therefore the assumed authority of the individual to act, suggested by the writers who I cited at the beginning of this chapter. The work of S. H. Foulkes, the acknowledged founder of group analysis, therefore points us in the direction of an explanation that assumes substantially different implications for power and power relations than would be found in the dominant discourse regarding the work of groups and teams at work. The reflexive quality of human interaction is fundamental to Foulkes' insights.

Thus Foulkes argued that as people come together, 'transpersonal processes' occur which give rise to what he observed and described as the group matrix: 'When a group of people, by which for our purposes I mean a small number of persons, form intimate relationships they create a new phenomenon, namely, the total field of mental happenings between them all.' In arguing for the idea that 'mind' is a transpersonal phenomenon Foulkes was also anxious to avoid the problem of collapsing the idea of 'mind' as process into the idea of 'mind' as object. To capture this view of 'mind' as a transpersonal process, Foulkes used the term 'dynamic group matrix'. Thus:

> I do not talk of group mind because this is a substantivation of what is meant and is as unsatisfactory as speaking of an individual mind. The mind is not a thing which exists but a series of events, moving and proceeding all the time.

> (Foulkes 1990: 224)

Although Foulkes was not consistent in the way that he treated this assertion (for example, he did make reference to the idea of a 'group mind') he also introduced the concept of resonance to describe the largely unconscious processes that constitute the ways in which people in a group sense and relate with each other. Resonance was the subject of another essay by Foulkes in which he developed this idea further and in the following terms:

> resonance is a good example of communication taking place without any particular message being sent or received, being in fact purely instinctive. In the group-analytic group individuals not only resonate on a large scale to each other, simultaneously and reciprocally, but also to the group as whole and particularly to the group conductor, who in turn is influenced by his own resonance.
>
> (Foulkes 1990: 299)

I want to argue here that Foulkes' concepts of the dynamic group matrix and inter-bodily resonance are valuable both in deconstructing and understanding our experiences of relating to others in the context of organizational life and specifically that of work meetings such as the one that I describe in the foregoing narrative. While Foulkes' conceptual frame is helpful, because he wrote from within a psychoanalytic paradigm, it was difficult, in the end, for him to fully elaborate these concepts as social and bodily processes of interaction. To explain these phenomena Foulkes therefore made recourse to a series of metaphors that describe the transpersonal occurrence of the matrix as being like X-rays which pass through individuals and of individuals in groups as being like the component cells of a more complex biological structure (Foulkes 1990: 229). In his essay on resonance Foulkes explains the feeling state of sensing other bodies also in terms of the metaphysical language of psychoanalysis. Resonance, he argues, 'has affinities and relationships to transference, projection or introjection' (Foulkes 1990: 300).

Other writers (Dalal 1998; Stacey 2003) have explored the tensions in Foulkes' writing between social and psychoanalytic themes in his explanations of group phenomena. It is the presence of this tension in Foulkes' writing that led Dalal to contrast his radical social perspective with his conservative Freudian view. While I do not intend to re-engage with the detail of these critiques of Foulkes' work, I do think that the concepts of matrix and resonance are helpful reference points for understanding further what was occurring in the meeting I described in the foregoing narrative. But to avoid the danger of lapsing into metaphysics I will set out to maintain a consistency of approach which treats these phenomena as social, biological and cognitive processes rather than as intra-psychic. Such an approach I believe to be consistent also with the conceptual framework of complex responsive processes. In this, as against the psychoanalytic paradigm, it is the thematic patterning of social interaction occurring between us in the living present of our experience together that forms and is formed by our feeling states and emotional responses.

In contrast with Foulkes' psychoanalytic approach to the group matrix, Norbert Elias' conception of figuration always remains social. Elias therefore substitutes a theory of human action linked to the occurrence of conscious and unconscious interpersonal processes, to an action theory that is consistently social. Within Elias' theoretical frame, power and power relations are always central to an explanation of what may be observed to be occurring between people acting in groups at any scale of social aggregation.

Elias therefore used the concept of figuration to describe patterns of interaction between people from which particular affectual predispositions (habitus) emerge. In Elias' work, habitus and figuration are dialectically related in that they form and are formed by each other at the same time. It follows that the idea of figuration is closely associated with that of power relations. I would argue that in Elias' work it is the configuration of power relations extant within an identifiable historical conjuncture (e.g. mediaeval Europe, late twentieth-century capitalism) that acts as the dynamic shaping figuration (Elias 2000). My narrative regarding the meeting in November is an example of this process. It is therefore the emergent character of the relative positions of the individual participants to flows of power and power relating that create the appearance of 'structure' in their relations with each other in this meeting and through which their relating together is mediated. We are there together acting in a way that pays regard to the Director's entitlement to regulate our conduct. Our behaviors towards each other are enabled and constrained by our sense of individual authority relative to each other. In part this is a function of the size of our institutions, but other factors are also in play. We recognize each other in terms of our length of service, our assumptions about each other's experience and professional competence. To some extent our presence at or absence from the AoC conference also conferred a status that affected our power relations together. Those who attended the conference had an immediate point of reference with each other (shared experience) and claim to truth in discussing the event (as witnesses). The statements of these individuals were, to some extent, privileged in the group relative to those who were not present. Insider/outsider relations were being played out in subtle but perceptible ways within the group all of the time that it is constituted in this room in Victoria. Group and individual identities are being constructed continuously in the ebb and flow of this relational process.

Two questions have arisen for me in reflecting upon Elias' theories of figuration. First, is it possible to understand our own immediate individual life experience in terms of Elias' concepts of figuration and habitus? Secondly, can I situate myself and, for example, my work experience within a concept of figuration? Writing of network phenomena in human relationships, Elias commented:

> To get a closer view of this kind of interrelationship one might think of the object from which the concept of network is derived, a woven net. In such a net there are many interwoven threads linked together. Yet neither the totality of the net, nor the form taken by each thread in it, can be understood in terms of a single thread alone or even in all the threads considered singly; it is understood solely in terms of the way in which they are linked, their relationship to each other.
>
> (Elias 1991: 32)

When I start to think myself into Elias' metaphor, I start to locate myself in patterns of personal/impersonal, direct/indirect, close to/far from relationships. I also start to recognize all my relationships as having all of these characteristics at different times and in different contexts. There are people with whom I have close and regular contact. I would say that they are integral to my everyday experience of being at work. I include my immediate team of five other people in this category. The Chairman and Vice-chairman of my governing body are also in this group. Most of my other immediate relationships within the organization are mediated through these relationships. I am aware that for much of the time I am at work others know me via the interactions I have with the few people who I manage directly. With some people, particularly those who have worked in the college for a long time, I have a relationship that they and I experience more personally but in a way that is not wholly aligned with the line management structure. With other new staff members this is not true and not likely to be possible. When I speak to small or large groups of staff or when I attend college functions, I am aware that I am present in a capacity that is paradoxically personal and impersonal at the same time.

As I reflect upon my work experience in this way and conceive of my participation in the meeting that forms my foregoing narrative account, I understand myself to be an actor in a figuration. My participation is forming this figuration. At the same time, the actions that signify my participation to others are formed by them and their interactions with others also present. In this sense, figuration becomes an exemplar of the iterative concept of human relating.

Objects, time and perception

Earlier in this chapter I drew attention to the room in which this meeting took place and to the fact that we were sitting around tables arranged in a square.

Looking around the room it was possible for the most part to see only those parts of people that were above the sight-line of the table top. For those people directly opposite it was possible to see more of their lower bodies but these were partially obscured by the depth of the table top and the angle of their seating positions. The overall effect of this seating arrangement, as in so many meetings of its type, was to reduce the physicality of interaction to gestures that are evidenced from upper body movements (including facial expressions) and speech. In this meeting, as in many others, no one got up from their seat or in any other way disturbed this established pattern. In reflecting upon this meeting I have found myself becoming increasingly preoccupied with this image. That is, the image of a group of people sitting in a room, dispersed in a formalized arrangement of the spatial structures of their interrelationship, immobilized in their seats and evident to each other only in the physicality of their upper bodies. At the same time as I describe this scene in a way that is limited and restrictive of certain possibilities for interaction, in my narrative I feel that I have hardly scratched the surface of what could be observed and described in relation to what occurred between those who were present.

I am struck by the significance of our non-verbalized gestures for the quality of our ongoing interactions. In this meeting, as in so many others, it was the minutiae and the nuances of the detail of these interactions that provided a source of tension to our drama of being together in a way that made the silent, but sensed, presence of others fundamental to our experience of being in the room. In my narrative, the Director's half smile, her leaning forward or backward, my silence, the deferential demeanor of others, the changing tempo of bodily movement in the room, the restrictions upon bodily movement are essential to the emergence of patterns of power relating that are taken up in later phases of the social act (the cycle of gesture and response that constitutes a conversational phase of interaction) that entails spoken dialogical communication. The immanent pathos of our being together was in the tension created in our bodily separation (our physical anomie) contrasted with our struggle to find meaning in our conversational interactions together.

It is therefore in the thematic patterning of our observations, the images that arise in our mental frame, that we come to recognize the identity of others. As in this process of recognition we come to know others, so we are able to recognize ourselves. This theme was represented by Hegel in his account of the dialectic of recognition in the following terms:

> Each is for the other the middle term, through which each mediates itself with itself and unites with itself; and each is for itself, and for the other, an immediate being of its own account, which at the same time is such only through this mediation. They *recognize* themselves as *mutually recognizing* one another.
>
> (Hegel 1998: 93)

While the act of observing is a function of biology, recognition is a social process. My narrative makes sense only if my description of the identities of the participants is in some way credible to those reading this script. By credible I mean that these descriptions hold together in a reality-congruent way that can be recognized from the manner in which I have connected these identity labels with descriptions of actions and interpretations of motives. This is a function both of the biology of perception and it is socio-culturally specific. At the same time, it is clear that I am using 'identity' as a word that is synonymous with particular sets of attributes and that I am not attempting to describe all the attributes that might be associated with the people who form the cast for my narrative. As I open up this line of thinking I feel myself being drawn to questioning what it is that I really am describing when I talk about being in a meeting with a cast of characters whose identities I describe with such confidence. The characters I depict remain physically fixed in time and space. They do not move relative to one another. Movement occurs in the thematic patterning of their processes of relating: these are perceptual, emotional and conversational. Identities form and re-form in the dialectic of recognition that goes on in the living present of their being together. The transformational character of this process is to be found in the feeling and knowing states of the participants as these are enacted in their ongoing relations with each other.

Take, for example, the Director's revelations about her anxieties about her own job role. In the moment of this revelation the Director's identity is transformed within the group. Her power relation to the rest of us becomes ambiguously framed as she takes up the role of one who is both in authority and fearful of those whose authority she represents in her relations with us. The meaning of her presence in the room is adjusted in ways that could not have been anticipated when we entered the room. Even now, in my act of writing about this event, I am reproducing an experience of this readjustment and recasting the Director's identity as I reconstruct it, and as my reflections are taken up by the readers of this chapter.

It seems to me that when we are in the act of participating in large or small group processes, of which meetings in organizational contexts are an example, we enact circumstances in which our action as living bodies always appears discontinuous. As our participation, our presence in relation to one another, is an unbroken process of being, feeling, emotion, gesturing, our experience of this and the experience of others with whom we are in relation is colored by the turn-taking character of our silent and public conversations. In this sense we encounter a world of gestures and one in which we always experience a sense of present and past. Our action takes place in a context of an anticipation of the future: what will happen or might happen next. As this world of gestures becomes more complex, non-verbal and verbal gestures combine to form the significant symbols of human interaction.

Significant symbols

As I reflect upon my participation in the event described in my narrative I readily relate to the Meadian account of the ways in which my feeling state (and that of others present) in that moment emerges in a social context. It is not the product of a single mind or located within a single physical body. I am aware, then, that my experience of being present in this situation arises from my responses to a complex range of signifying physical and social objects: the building, its location, the décor of the room, the formality of the setting, the clothing of the participants, the social objects of the roles they have taken up in society, an awareness of the wider patterns of conduct upon which the meaning of these roles is contingent, the fear of not behaving in a way that is consistent with this socially ordered pattern of conduct. My point here is therefore that it is in our cognitive and emotional responses to this emergent world of gestures that our identities also emerge as a continuous process of creative enactment.

Mead drew attention in his work to the difference between the ideas of gesture and significant symbol. He identified this difference as being brought about when a gesture from one to another:

> not only brings the stimulus-object in the range of the reactions of other forms, but that the nature of the object is also indicated; especially do we apply in the term significance that the individual who points out indicates the nature to himself. But it is not enough that he should indicate this meaning – whatever meaning is – as it exists for him alone, but that he should indicate that meaning as it exists for the other to whom he is pointing.
>
> (Mead 1922: 160)

For such a process to occur it is necessary for the individual to exist as a social object to his or her self. In order to use gesture in the significant manner described by Mead a reflexive awareness of oneself is a prerequisite. Mead's explanation of how such awareness arises for humans is both biological and social. Biological in the sense that the human brain has evolved to a point where it has the capacity to offer reflexive images back to the individual, and social to the extent that this reflexivity is nurtured as part of a wider process of socialization that occurs through childhood:

> The self arises in conduct, when the individual becomes a social object in experience to himself. This takes place when the individual assumes the attitude or uses the gesture which another individual would use and responds to it himself, or tends so to respond. It is a development that arises gradually in the life of the infant . . . and finds its expression in the normal play life of young children. In the process the child gradually becomes a social being in his own experience and acts toward himself in a manner analogous to that in which he acts toward others. Especially he talks to himself as he talks to others and in keeping up this conversation in the inner forum constitutes the field which is called that of mind. Then those objects and experiences which belong to his own body, those images which belong to his own past, become part of this self.
>
> (Mead 1922: 160)

Mead's comments regarding socialization and the reflexive nature of human consciousness as prerequisites of self he developed at length in *Mind, Self and Society*, and used also to elaborate his concept of the I–me dialectic (Mead 1934). This concept is fundamental to Mead's social psychological explication of the idea of identity and its emergence in patterns of social relations. For Mead 'me' was the reflexive representation of what he described as 'the organized attitudes of the others which we definitely assume and which determine consequently our own conduct so far as it is of self-conscious character'. In Mead's thinking, 'me' references the idea of the socialized individual whose patterns of conduct follow rules established within the social order. 'I' by contrast signifies the novelty arising from awareness of individual action: 'The novelty comes in the action of the "I", but the structure, the form of the self is one which is conventional' (Mead 1934: 209). Mead thought of 'I' and 'me' as phases of the self, and in so doing was proposing a dialectical process in which, at the same time, the individual and social character of self-identity is formed by and forming the social context of human action.

Earlier in this chapter I referred to Gramsci's conceptualization of common sense as a way of attempting to explain the social significance of the rhetoric of the Secretary of State's speech. I was interested in this from the point of view of the thematic patterning of what (after Wittgenstein) I described as the language game of performance management in the public sector. Situated in the theoretical context of Mead, these observations take on a specific meaning in that the rhetoric of this speech, which comes to constitute a common sense representation of the social object of the good in contemporary life, is a representation of what he described as a 'generalized social attitude'. These are the 'common responses' to situations that emerge in the interactions of collectives of individuals and which, once bureaucratized, come to constitute the social objects that we recognize as institutions (Mead 1934: 261).

Mead explained the existence of social institutions by reference to the same socio-biological thinking that informed his theories regarding the nature of individual selves. For Mead, the individual and the social are aspects of a single dialectical process of human action. For this reason he extended his observations regarding the constraining relationship that he observed between an organism and its physical environment to the social sphere. In his comments on America, for example, where he describes 'political control' in terms of the action of self-government as a 'generalized principle' of life for the whole community, it is clear that

Mead saw this as being analogous to the regulative relationships that exist in nature. To explain exactly how it is that individuals take on behaviors (taking the 'role of the other') which in their collective expression appear as socially ordered, Mead made reference to the significance of the moral authority that such 'generalized principles' or 'organized attitudes' come to assume in individual lives. Institutionalized responses become synonymous with the manners (or customs) of a community and come to be indistinguishable from morals. In the end, it is the moral authority of the generalized other, against which individuals critique and control their own conduct, allied to the charisma of leading individuals in society, that for Mead explains the phenomenon of society, social order and social stability (Mead 1934: 255–256, 263–267).

Truth, power, figuration and identity

Earlier in this chapter I drew attention to the emergence of themes in the interactions taking place within the group that created insider/outsider relationships. I suggested that this was what was happening in the way in which the Director moved towards us by challenging the legitimacy of the processes of her own organization. This gesture transformed the Director's identity within the group. She became, in a way that was never fully resolved, one of us instead of one of them, and yet not so at the same time. I also drew attention to the way in which the act of noticing the room in which the meeting took place had the effect of contributing to the emergence of something akin to a sense of collective identity. We, selected, privileged by virtue of our roles, to be present in this place at this time together. What I am describing here are processes that are both social and cognitive. There is a process of differentiation taking place that is social. This process explains why we are here: it is to do with our jobs and their contemporary relevance to the power relations that pertain to the administration of public education. At the same time, however, we noticed aspects of each other that in this specific context gave particular meaning to our being together. Our identities, limited in their character to our recognition of each other as senior officers, principals, CEOs, an executive director, meant that a particular kind of conversation could take place between us and one that we would not conduct with a different constituency.

As I return myself to the thought of sitting in the room in Victoria one November day, it seems clear to me that we are all engaged in an active process of figuration that is a local exemplification of Elias' bigger sociological argument. Everyone in the room has formal powers that are codified in statute. Our relationships are formalized by the frameworks of accountability that exist between the Secretary of State, the LSC and institutions. Our professional identities are contingent upon our ability to act in ways that remain consistent with this codification. Woven between us therefore are both the atavistic power relations of emergent human interaction (what will always be true) and the socio-specific relations that are a function of the political power structures of the present and the configuration of the organs of state. The Secretary of State's speech and our preoccupation with its meaning signifies the importance of state power and state truth to the ongoing viability of our present sense of ourselves. What is felt to be true is what emerges as the criteria determining what will or will not be selected or legitimated in the identity-formation process. Foucault offers an explicit rendition of this association in his narrative of the relationship between truth and power:

> truth isn't outside power or lacking in power; contrary to a myth whose history and functions would repay further study, truth isn't the reward of free spirits, the child of protracted solitude nor the privilege of those who have succeeded in liberating themselves. Truth is a thing of this world: it is produced only by virtue of multiple forms of constraint. And it induces regular effects of power. Each society has its regime of truth, its 'general politics' of truth – that is the types of discourse it accepts and makes function as true.
>
> (Foucault 2000: 131)

This speech requires us to make an accommodation to the truths that the Secretary of State articulates in our way of being together in the room and in our wider organizational relationships. His position in government gives him a command of the discourse of common sense to which none of us can aspire. The objects of our perception that form the institutions of power through which he operates and of which *we and the Director* are integral parts are therefore forced into our emotional world of experience. They give rise to our anxieties and the feelings of threat that we experience as we reflect upon our respective abilities to sustain the relational context upon which our identities are built. Our affectual conditioning arises from the interplay of these gestures (represented in the speech, the Circular, the Department's encoded messaging, the imposition of a more intense performance management regime) and our responses to them.

Elias made frequent references in his writing to the idea that civilizing processes flow from centrifugal and centripetal movements of power. The emergence of modern state structures is, for Elias, a function of the centrifugal movement of power. I think that this conceptualization is important also to understanding the interactions taking place in the meeting that I have described. My argument here is that we are currently living through a spurt in the dynamic of political power relations which in the UK context may best be described as centrifugal. The size of the political majorities of the Thatcher and now Blair governments has in turn led to the emergence of relations around the center of power that have all the characteristics of courtly life. The shift to the postmodern performative political focus of contemporary governments as described by Lyotard has been accompanied both by a focus on managerialism and access to power by merit rather than by election. The emergence of a new meritocracy has been accompanied by particular distortions in the political process. Progress by personal connection and recommendation has now become an endemic feature of public life in the UK where once it was the provenance of a social elite.

Everyone sitting in the room in Victoria can locate their position (professionally, personally) within this structure relative to the center of mainstream political power. These shifts to centralization have resulted also in the Center having a much greater interest in what is being said by and about people such as those sitting in this room. On a national scale, this grouping represents a power elite totaling no more than about 600 individuals. The Director is not very far removed from ministerial power. Between her and the relevant minister is the CEO of the LSC and a senior civil servant. Between the principals (especially those of the larger institutions) and ministerial power there is an equally short step. All these people intermingle in the social-political hubbub of public life that surrounds the conduct of mainstream educational practice in the UK. When the Secretary of State speaks to the national conference of college senior managers he is speaking to an audience that is more real in his mind than abstract. The politics of this meritocratic world therefore matter in a material way to the shaping of the realities of the life experiences of those present. It is in the sense that Foucault would apply the idea of *truth* that this power, reproduced in our social relations, comes in turn to animate the power relations at play between us in the room in Victoria.

References

Argyris, C. (1957) *Personality and Organization*, London: Harper & Row.
Argyris, C. and Schön, D. (1974) *Theory in Practice Increasing Professional Effectiveness*, London: Jossey Bass.
Clarke, C. (2002) Speech by the Secretary of State to the Association of Colleges Conference, 19 November, www.dfes.gov.uk.
Dalal, F. (1998) *Taking the Group Seriously*, London: Jessica Kingsley.
Department for Education and Skills (2002) *Success for All*, London: DfES.
Elias, N. (1991) *The Society of Individuals*, Oxford: Blackwell.
Elias, N. (2000) *The Civilizing Process*, Oxford: Blackwell.
Foucault, M. (2000) *Power, Essential Works of Foucault 1954–1984 Volume 3*, ed. J. Faubion, London: Penguin.
Foulkes, S. H. (1990) *Selected Papers*, ed. E. Foulkes, London: Karnac.
Goleman, D. (1996) *Emotional Intelligence*, London: Bloomsbury.
Gramsci, A. (1971) *Selections from the Prison Notebooks*, ed. Q. Hoare and G. Nowell Smith, New York: International Publishers.
Habermas, J. (1987) *The Theory of Communicative Action – Volume 2*, Cambridge: Polity Press.
Handy, C. (1999) *Inside Organizations*, London: Penguin.
Hegel, F. (1998) *The Hegel Reader*, ed. S. Houlgate, Oxford: Blackwell.
Hirschhorn, L. (1998) *Reworking Authority*, Boston, MA: MIT Press.
Learning and Skills Council (2003) Circular 03/01 Success for All – Implementation of the Framework for Quality and Success, www.lsc.gov.uk.
Mead, G. H. (1922) 'A Behaviorist Account of the Significant Symbol', *Journal of Philosophy* 19: 157–163.
Mead, G. H. (1934) *Mind, Self and Society*, Chicago: University of Chicago Press.
Mead, G. H. (2002) *The Philosophy of the Present*, New York: Prometheus.
Senge, P. (1990) *The Fifth Discipline: The Art and Practice of the Learning Organization*, New York: Doubleday.
Shaw, P. (2002) *Changing Conversations in Organizations: A complexity approach to change*, London: Routledge.
Stacey, R. (2001) *Complex Responsive Processes in Organizations: Learning and knowledge creation*, London: Routledge.
Stacey, R. (2003) *Complexity and Group Processes: A radically social understanding of individuals*, London: Brunner-Routledge.
Turquet, P. (1975) 'Threats to Identity in the Large Group', in L. Kreeger *The Large Group Dynamics and Therapy*, London: Karnac.

6 Technology as social object: a complex responsive processes perspective

Stig Johannessen and Ralph Stacey

The purpose of this chapter is to explore how technology features in our understanding of organizations. A number of different ways of understanding technology are first outlined, paying particular attention to how they encompass the social aspects of technology. It is argued that social interaction in relation to technology is not adequately dealt with. The chapter then suggests how one might understand technology from the perspective of complex responsive processes.

Complex responsive processes are processes of communicative interaction and power relating between human bodies in which thematic patterns of relating emerge as individual-collective identity. Such patterns, or identities, may also be described as social objects. These are generalized tendencies on the part of large numbers of people to act in similar ways in similar situations. They evolve in social interaction, forming that social interaction while being formed by it at the same time. We argue that technologies might usefully be thought of not simply as physical objects but also, at the same time, as social objects. While physical objects are to be found as things in nature, social objects may be found only in the experience of social interaction. This involves the particularizing of the general tendencies to act, which are social objects. That particularization takes place in the ordinary, everyday local interaction between people in the present. The consequence of taking this perspective is that attention is shifted from focusing on technology and competence as things or generalizations designed to achieve given futures, to focusing on the detailed interaction in which they acquire meaning as they are particularized and potentially transformed.

Before exploring the complex responsive processes perspective on technology, consider how it is viewed from some other perspectives.

The resource-based view of technology

One strand of thinking about technology and organizations derives from neo-classical economics in which technology was understood to be embodied in the physical objects constituting the resource called capital (buildings, plant and equipment). Technology was thought of in scientific terms and efficient ('if–then') causality, which it was believed made it possible for rational human beings to design and use technology in an instrumental way to control the environment in the pursuit of human economic interests. No attention was paid to the social aspects of technology use and development or the impact of technology on people. From this view, one technological solution follows naturally from the other. Technological development is linear. Technology must be at one level of sophistication before it can reach the next. It is not possible that history could have taken the course where computers were invented before the steam-engine. The laws of nature are revealed step by step, and technology as objects designed and constructed to control and display these very laws of nature reveal themselves through the scale, tempo and sophistication of a linear discovery process. This understanding has been taken up and developed in the resource-based view of organizational development (Penrose, 1959; Wernerfeldt, 1984), which focuses on how an organization's resources create competitive advantage. However, in an age in which human knowledge has become a more important resource than physical capital, the notion of technology has been developed to encompass the embodiment of knowledge in people. The creation, development and protection of core competences (Prahalad and Hamel, 1990) have come to be seen as key sources of competitive advantage, and it is the organization's managers who are responsible for sustaining and developing these core competences, as well as managing the creation of new knowledge upon which they depend (Nonaka and Takeuchi, 1995). Thus, from the resource-based view, technology is understood as a system amenable to intentional cultivation and management.

The instrumental approach of neo-classical economics to technology, mainly thought of as physical objects, has thus continued, but a social dimension has been added in the emphasis placed on the role of teams in knowledge creation and technology development, although human knowledge is still ultimately located in the individual. However, for reasons that are spelled out later in this chapter, we argue that the resource-based view greatly simplifies the connection between technology and the social, paying very little attention to how technology acquires meaning and so impacts on the manner in which people interact and experience themselves in organizations.

Furthermore, the move to competence and knowledge understood in terms of systems implies additional forms of causality, which are problematic. While the physical objects of technology continue to be thought of in terms of the 'if–then', efficient causality of the natural sciences, systems of knowledge creation imply formative and rationalist forms of causality (Stacey *et al.*, 2000). In rationalist causality, knowledge, competence and technology are all thought to develop as a result of rational choices made by inventors, scientists, investors or leaders. In other words, it is assumed that individuals choose, manipulate and control technological development. Much of the literature on innovation management and market-oriented product development, (e.g. Utterback, 1994) takes this view. This rational causality also frequently underlies debates about controversial technologies, such as biotechnology or nuclear technology. Many people call for the control of research and development in these fields and try, through laws or other constraints, to prevent the invention and use of new products. In doing this, they take the position that it is possible to choose and plan technological development.

In addition to this rationalist causality, however, formative causality is also implied. Resources, knowledge and technology are all thought of as designed systems, and this means that they must unfold the design already enfolded in them by their designers. In other words, the cause of technology development is the formative process of the system's operation. The resource-based view and linked developments of knowledge management are thus based on a dual causality, namely rationalist and formative. This dual causality is problematic because in the former, humans are doing the choosing, while in the latter, they are complying with the unfolding of the system and so, to that extent, they are not free to choose (Stacey *et al.*, 2000). Therefore, confusion arises as to the role of human agents in organizations and technology development.

Taking account of the social implications of technology: alienation and socio-technical systems

Other strands of thinking about technology and organizations originate in sociology and psychology. They pay much greater attention to the social implications of technology development. Some writers have pointed to the alienating effects of technology. For example, Blauner (1964) argued that technological development often destroys the dignity of people's work and the pride they take in it. The result is widespread feelings of alienation where people feel themselves to be powerless objects controlled and manipulated by technology. These feelings are exacerbated by hierarchical, bureaucratic organizational structures which create a mode of social domination (Weber, 1947).

The socio-technical tradition (Trist and Bamforth, 1951; Emery and Thorsrud, 1969; Trist, 1981) pays particular attention to the wider social dimensions of technology. In their study of the coal-mining industry, Trist and Bamforth (1951) compared the pattern of social relations of successful and unsuccessful teams and found that the cause of the success lay not in the technology, since both used the same technology, but in patterns of work relations. In successful teams, the members were very involved in detailed decision-making about how the technology was to be used in specific situations – they were self-managing teams. In the unsuccessful teams, on the other hand, members operated in a very hierarchical manner and displayed great dependency on the team leader. The self-managing teams were able to deal more flexibly with the complex details of specific situations and consequently felt safe in the dangerous conditions of underground mining. In the hierarchical teams, leaders were not able to provide all the control necessary to guarantee safety and failed to see that complex technology and role fragmentation made hierarchical control impossible.

These authors mentioned above concluded that technology, no matter how sophisticated, would fail if not mated with a social system designed to operate it. The requirement was for joint optimization of the interrelated technical and social systems, where the optimization of the whole might require less than optimization of the sub-systems taken separately. They argued that work relationship systems needed to be designed to bring the two sub-systems together. By reconciling human needs and technical efficiency many of the problems created by the introduction of new technology could be overcome. In this view, humans and technology are a whole (Emery and Trist, 1973). They function together and are dependent on each other, and must be seen as a whole system evolving together.

The result is a way of thinking about technology that incorporates the social in a much richer way than the resource-based view described above. However, the development of both the technical and the social systems is caused as much by human design as is the case in the resource-based view. It follows that the dual causality of the resource-based view continues to characterize socio-technical systems thinking. There are still rational designers, now designing both social and technical systems (rationalist causality), and there are still systems unfolding the enfolded design (formative causality).

Taking account of the social: actor-network theory

Actor-network theory is not one monolithic theory, since different authors use the main ideas in different ways and with different assumptions about causality. The main ideas were first developed by Latour and Woolgar (1979), and Callon and Latour (1981). They described how actors construct networks, where the network is composed not only of humans but also of non-humans such as technological artifacts. The theory claims that it is the actors, the network and the social relations between them that shape and constitute an organization. The interplay of technology, the objects it handles, and changes in knowledge and action are the outcome of a process of local struggle. Callon and Latour (1981) suggest that in network processes:

> The question of method is also resolved. How can we examine macro-actors and micro-actors, we were wondering, without

conforming differences in size? Reply: by directing our attention not to the social but towards the processes by which an actor creates lasting asymmetries. That among these processes some lead to associations, which are sometimes called 'social' (associations of bodies), and that some of the others are sometimes called 'technical' (associations of materials), need not concern us further.

(Callon and Latour, 1981, pp. 285–286)

Law (1992) explains that the object of actor-network theory is to explore the process of translation, which generates ordering effects such as devices, agents, institutions or organizations. The concern is with the description of the process in which translation of materials to actors takes place. This indicates a position of the researcher as an observer standing outside the process and describing it. Law also says that social structure is not free-standing, but is relational in that it recursively generates and reproduces itself. In this respect his view is similar to Giddens' notion of structuration (Giddens, 1984). However, both structuration and actor-network theory pay little attention to the detail of interaction between individuals as the process in which transformation emerges. They do not explain the transformation process. What is it that transforms social practices in their replication? What happens in the interaction? How does this patterning of interaction produce unpredictable transformation and the novelty of technology and organizations? The theories cannot answer these questions.

In more recent writings, Callon (2002) displays more clearly his view of organizations. He talks about management tools as important for managing and controlling complexity because they help to reduce and to simplify. He also talks about a dual process of 'complexification' and 'simplification', depicting an axis with the complex at one end and the simple at the opposite end. This loses the crucial aspect of paradox in the dynamics of complexity, as well as the phenomena of self-organization and emergence.

The different ways in which actor-network ideas are used imply at least three different views of causality. One is the implication of humans as rational designers (actors construct networks). Another is the formative causality where characteristics enfolded in the network are unfolded as actors are constructed. These two causalities are treated as dual when, for example, Law (1992) describes a network as a number of bits and pieces that are put together in different ways. Certain configurations are stabilized into actors, which are not only human beings but also human beings and their technological environment, so constituting a network. But since this actor-network is endlessly confronted with other actor-networks, there may be reconfigurations that will create new actor-networks. What is being described, then, is the enfolded characteristics of networks, which have the capacity of unfolding as actors. At the same time, it is possible for rational actors, by their operations, to influence the design and characteristics of the actor-networks. In addition, Fox (2000) talks about the way actor-network theory goes well with the notions of communities of practice (Brown and Duguid, 1991) and organizational learning. In this way, he places the theory in the tradition of systems thinking. The third causality is adaptionist; that is, chance operated on by competitive selection. A number of authors in *The Social Construction of Technological Systems* (Bijker *et al.*, 1987) base their description of the social construction of technology on actor-network thinking but also stress that the development of technological artifacts is an alternation of variation and selection, creating multiple possible directions in their development. This means that technological development occurs, to a significant extent, through chance.

This leaves us with confusing implications of people having choices as to overall technology design, on the one hand, and none, on the other. Actor-network theory loses the distinction between humans and things, and in the process turns the social into mere appearance. The theory does make the very important statement that people cannot be seen to operate in society separate from technology and materials. Technology and people are involved with each other all the time. Consequently, technological development is a social process. However, the way the theory incorporates this social process is through creating metaphors of physical objects, similar to the way Morgan (1997) does in describing ways of seeing organizations. In doing this, actor-network theory creates abstractions from the detailed social interaction of everyday life in which people's identities and technology interact, forming and being formed by each other at the same time.

Abstracting from the social: complexity theory and technology

The development of complexity theory in the natural sciences has also led to suggestions about how technology develops. The biologist, Kauffman (1995), demonstrates in his computer simulations of the evolution of life that a system, consisting of a large number of entities, or agents, interacting randomly with each other, is highly likely to evolve into a connected, orderly network in a relatively short period of time. This occurs without any design or blueprint for the network as a whole. Instead, the orderly patterning of the network as a whole emerges and is sustained in a self-referential or self-organizing manner through the local interaction of the entities prior to any competitive selection. The system becomes a complex adaptive system. Self-organization is held to be an inevitable dynamic, an intrinsic property of interaction, which causes the emergence of pattern. Instead of chance and adaptation, the first ordering principle of evolution, Kauffman argues that there is a more important second ordering principle, namely self-organization. He shows how the dynamics of a self-organizing network consisting of a number of entities is determined by the number and strength of the connections between these entities. For example, when the number of connections is low, the dynamics are characterized by stable patterns, and when the number is high, the patterns are unstable or random. In an intermediate state, between stability and instability, the dynamic known as 'the edge of chaos' occurs, which is paradoxically stable and unstable at the same time. At the edge of chaos, novelty emerges in a radically unpredictable way.

Kauffman suggests that technology could evolve in much the same way as organisms. This means that the evolution of technology is caused neither by chance, nor by the choices of managers, but by the nature of interaction, or relationship, between organizations. Organizations makes choices, trying to influence outcomes and the dynamics in which those outcomes emerge, but what transpires emerges from the conflicting constraints they place on each other and this is not the simple choice of any one of them. Kauffman's explanation, therefore, unlike the other theories mentioned earlier in the chapter, exhibits the main features of transformative causality (Stacey *et al.*, 2000). In his explanation, networks of networks are in perpetual construction moving towards an unpredictable future. The process of construction is that of forming and being formed at the same time, and it produces repetitive patterns always with the potential for transformation.

Marion (1999) uses the Kauffman approach to explain the development of the microcomputer industry. Marion describes a development in which there were a few people dreaming of microcomputers in 1974, a great many people wanting one by 1976 and explosive growth in the ensuing two decades. It looked as if microcomputers had suddenly appeared out of nowhere. However, the pieces were coming together long before microcomputers were ever envisioned: microcircuits, microprocessors, ROM and RAM memory chips were being used in calculators, while computer language logic was being documented in mainframes. Just as Kauffman argues that emerging connections between molecules became the chemical basis of life, so Marion argues that bits and pieces of already existing technology came together as emergent microcomputers. Marion shows how an industrial network evolves through its own internal dynamic to the edge of chaos. He emphasizes the radical unpredictability of such evolution and the continuing unpredictability when a network operates at the edge of chaos.

However, like Kauffman, Marion focuses at the macro-level of a whole industry and talks about a population of impersonal organizations interacting with each other in a self-organizing manner, driven by an urge to survive. He is talking about this population and the organizations of which it consists as if they were no different from a population of organisms. However, organizations are not organisms but, rather, patterns of joint human action. Marion reifies organizations and treats them as if they were things, or organisms, apart from, or outside of, humans, interacting according to principles that apply to them at a macro-level, split off from the humans that constitute them. The principles governing these systems are taken to be the same as those governing non-human systems. This approach, therefore, abstracts from the ordinary experience of social interaction.

Key features of the above theories of technology

To summarize, the key distinctions between the different views of technology described above relate to whether they see the evolution of technology as:

- Predictably determined by rational choice as in the resource-based and socio-technical systems (rationalist causality), or whether they see technology evolution as driven by chance and competitive selection, and so moving to an unknown future (adaptionist causality), or whether they understand technology development as the unfolding of characteristics enfolded by design (formative causality) as in different views of actor-network theory, or whether they see technology evolution as a self-organizing system moving to an unknown future (transformative causality) as in the theory of complex adaptive systems with heterogeneous agents.

- Not essentially involving social/psychological factors as in complex adaptive systems approaches, or involving the social/psychological as elements having very little difference to artifacts as in actor-network theory, or as involving the social/psychological in rather limited forms of teamwork as in the resource-based view; or as essentially involving the social/psychological as a separate system interacting with a technical system to form a whole as in socio-technical systems.

We turn now to another perspective, one that understands technology development as an essentially social process in which the causality is transformative. This makes the social/psychological central, as in socio-technical systems theory, but avoids any separation between the two and avoids thinking in systems terms at all. It also avoids any equation of human beings with artifacts in the evolution of technology, and explores just how one might think about the implications of technology for social evolution.

An alternative way of taking account of the social: complex responsive processes and technology

The theory of complex responsive processes of relating draws on a number of disciplines for its explanation of human action. One of these, the complexity sciences, provides a source domain for analogues with human action. Traditionally, the natural sciences have modeled the dynamics of natural phenomena in terms of movement to a pre-given state of rest or equilibrium. These models tend to focus on the smallest component of any phenomenon and when they do take account of ensembles of components they average out any differences between them and the events which they encounter, thus removing any micro-diversity. It is this removal of micro-diversity that leads to movement to a state of rest. This way of thinking also came to dominate the social sciences and is very evident in most of the theories of technology referred to above. Organizations and technology were treated as if they were only physical objects.

However, one of the principal complexity scientists, Prigogine (1997), departs from this way of thinking in two important respects. First, he argues that most phenomena in nature are constrained to a state far from equilibrium, taking the form of dissipative structures. These are paradoxical in that they are continuously dissipating energy while nevertheless continually renewing and thus retaining their form. Second, he identifies the importance of micro-diversity as a generator of change. He introduces fluctuations into his models, where fluctuations are non-average, apparently random events, 'noise' or disorder. In his experiments, Prigogine shows how this micro-diversity, or disorder, is essential to the self-organizing emergence of different dissipative structures as the unpredictable, spontaneous collective response to fluctuations in a far from equilibrium state. This phenomenon challenges the usual predictions in physics, and points to how nature paradoxically and unpredictably creates ordered structures in disorder. This amounts to a very different idea of causality compared to the efficient 'if–then' view of traditional sciences or the formative causality of systems thinking. The theory of dissipative structures points to transformative causality in which both repetition and potential transformation are generated at the same time.

Allen (1998a, 1998b) has clarified the importance of micro-diversity. He has shown that when the assumption of average components is abandoned, in addition to the assumption of average events, then phenomena display the capacity to evolve completely novel structures. The amplification of micro-diversity, or non-average behavior, is the source of transformation. The result is a theory of causality in which diversity is understood as central to the emergence of the novel. Nature is thus seen as being under perpetual construction and transformation in a fundamentally unpredictable way.

By analogy, human action may be understood in terms of transformative causality if one adds the attributes of being human. Two writers in particular, namely Mead (1934) and Elias (1939), have been used to add the attributes of being human and so construct a theory of complex responsive processes (Stacey et al., 2000) in which human interaction is understood as the perpetual iteration of continuity and potential transformation at the same time. Elias (1939) emphasizes human interdependence and shows in some detail how the self-organizing patterns of human society emerge in this interdependence. He argues that all human relating is power relating because in their relating people, at the same time, enable and constrain each other. Mead (1934) explains how mind, self and society all emerge in conversations of gestures between human bodies.

Taking a transformative perspective on causality, with its implication of fundamental unpredictability, leads to a substantial shift in thinking about organizations. In a world where patterns are emerging unpredictably, it becomes highly problematic to think of technology development as simply human choice or design. Instead, one thinks of technology and knowledge as being perpetually created in the power relating and communicative interaction between people in the living present. The focus is then on self-organizing processes, emergent results and different qualities such as participation, diversity, conversational life, and living with anxiety, unpredictability and paradox. The quality of relations creates the internal capacity for change and new patterns. This different understanding of organizing processes brings the insight that conversations are the basis of strategies and emergent new directions as the future is constructed in transformative conversational processes. It is in these conversational processes that the form of the organization continuously re-emerges and potentially changes. It is in these conversational processes that assumptions and ideas on how and why things are done are explored and challenged.

Examples of the way resources and technology have been incorporated into the theory of complex responsive processes are:

> Communicative interaction between people in organizations involves the use of highly sophisticated tools.
>
> (Stacey, 2001, p. 183)

> Meaning does not lie in the tools but in the gestures-responses made with the tools.
>
> (Ibid., p. 184)

> national and international financial systems can be thought of as tools in, as enabling constraints on, communicative interaction, so entering into the patterning of themes of communicative interaction. In fact, these tools shape the themes of communicative interaction, both enabling and exercising powerful constraints on that communication.
>
> (Ibid., p. 185)

Although this brief account does move away from a purely instrumental view of the use of tools in human action, it is inadequate in two ways. First, it collapses highly complex technological processes and real resources into the category of 'mere' tools (Johannessen, 2003). Second, although it points to the shaping effect of the use of tools on the thematic patterning of human action, it does not explain how this occurs. The rest of this chapter explores how these points might be addressed.

Social objects

In the theory of complex responsive processes, the account of the structure of human interaction is derived from Mead (1934). He understood individual mind and society as aspects of the same processes of communicative interaction between human bodies. The basic unit of analysis is the social act consisting of the gesture of one that evokes a response from another, which in turn is a gesture back to the first that evokes a further response in a continuing conversation of gestures. Meaning is not located in the gesture alone but is constituted by the whole social act. Furthermore, humans have the capacity, when gesturing to others, to call forth in themselves similar responses to those evoked in others to whom the gesture is directed. In other words, each can take the attitude of the other, where attitude means the tendency to act. The parties are then communicating in significant symbols and it is this that constitutes mind because now they can know the likely consequences of their actions. Furthermore, such gestures indicate to the other how the social act is likely to unfold further. Mind then is the activity of a body experiencing a similar attitude, a similar tendency to act, as others do in response to gestures that body makes. Mind here is clearly a social phenomenon. Mind is a private role play/silent conversation of a body with itself. The social is the public, vocal interaction or conversation of gestures between bodies.

However, Mead's main concern is not primarily with a dyadic form of communication but with much wider, much more complex patterns of interaction between many people. He is concerned with complex social acts where many people are engaged in conversations of gestures in which they accomplish the tasks of fitting in with each other to realize their objectives and purposes. People do not come to an interaction with each other afresh each time because they are born into an already existing socially evolved pattern and they continue to play their part in its further evolution. This leads Mead to his concept of the generalized other. In order to accomplish complex social acts, it is not enough for those involved to be able to take the attitude of the small numbers of people with whom they may be directly engaged at a particular time. They need to be able to take the attitude of all of those directly or indirectly engaged in the complex social act. It would be impossible to do this in relation to each individual so engaged but humans have developed the capacity to generalize the attitudes of many. In acting in the present, each individual is then taking the attitude of a few specific others and at the same time the attitude of this generalized other, the attitude of the group, the organization or the society. These wider, generalized attitudes are evolving historically and are always implicated in every human action.

Mead is making an important point here. In the evolution of society many generalizations emerge which are taken up, or particularized, in people's interactions with each other in the present. Mead is drawing attention to paradoxical processes of generalization and particularization at the same time. Mental and social activities are processes of generalizing and particularizing at the same time. Individuals act in relation to that which is common to all of them (generalized) but responded to somewhat differently by each of them in each present time period (functionalizing/particularizing).

Mead provides a number of formulations of these generalizing-particularizing processes. One such formulation relates to self-consciousness. Human society is a society of selves, and selves exist only in relation to other selves. Selves are social selves. In understanding self-consciousness, Mead talks about a person taking the attitude of the group to herself, where that attitude is the 'me'. Self-consciousness involves taking oneself as an object, a 'me', to one's subject, 'I'. One cannot, therefore, be a self independently of social interaction.

Mead's discussion of what he calls the social object is another formulation of this generalizing and particularizing process. Mead distinguishes between a physical object and a social object. A physical object exists in nature and is the proper object of study in the natural sciences. The social object is the proper object of study in the social sciences and social objects exist only in the experience of social relations. While the physical object may be understood in terms of itself, the social object has to be understood in terms of the experience of social acts. Mead refers to market exchange as an example of a social object. When one person offers to buy food this act obviously involves a complex range of responses from other people to provide the food. However, it involves more than this because the one making the offer can only know how to make the offer if he is able to take the attitude of the other parties to the bargain. All essential phases of the complex social act of exchange must appear in the actions of all involved and appear as essential features of each individual's actions. Social objects have evolved in the history of the society of selves and each individual is born into such a world of social objects as each individual learns to take up social objects in his or her conduct in ways that are largely unconscious. However, social objects are not simply forming action because they are at the same time formed by human action. In other words, individuals are forming social objects while being formed by them in an evolutionary process.

It is important to note how Mead used the term 'object' in a social sense as a 'tendency to act' rather than as a concept or a thing, which are meanings appropriate to physical objects. In a social setting, then, Mead used the term 'object' in tension with the usual understanding of object as a thing in nature. The pattern or tendency Mead calls an object is in a sense an object in that it is what we perceive in taking it up in our acting but this is perception of our own acting, not a thing. We seem to have a strong tendency to reify patterns of acting and this makes it important to emphasize that Mead's social object is not a thing.

Tools, techniques and technology

Mead's notion of social objects provides a way of understanding technology from the perspective of complex responsive processes. First, the social object of technology must be distinguished from technology as physical object. The tools involved in a technology may be understood as physical objects designed and constructed by people to purposefully accomplish their activities. As such, technology is to be found in nature as are other physical objects. However, techniques for using tools, that is, people's knowledge, skills, practices and methods of tool use, always involve complex social acts. As such, technology is a social object to be found only in experience. Technology in the form of physical objects is also, in use, immediately a social object; that is, generalized tendencies for large numbers of people to act in fairly similar ways in using the physical objects of technology. In their particularization these generalized tendencies evolve further as small differences are amplified – the causality is transformative. Technology is then understood, not simply as physical objects to be found in nature, but at the same time as social objects to be found in our experience of complex social acts. This provides us with an understanding of technology as being perpetually iterated in the particularizing of the generalized tendencies to act in the present.

An example is provided by Internet and email technologies. The tools are computers, servers and software programs. Their mere existence creates tendencies for large numbers of people to communicate with each other through email and accessing databases. This is the generalized tendency to act in similar ways. These generalized tendencies are iterated in each present as rather repetitive, habitual techniques. In their continual iteration, technologies are particularized in specific situations in the present. We send emails to each other and conduct transactions over the Internet, for example, with banks. Such particularization is inevitably a conflictual process in that techniques are adapted to the demands of particular situations with their specific understanding of the past and expectations of the future. For example, as the use of email spreads in organizations, conflicts arise as to the purposes it may be used for. People start using emails for personal use and this conflicts with business requirements, leading to policies specifying what uses are to be allowed or prohibited. The possibility of technological transformation arises in this particularizing as techniques are spontaneously adapted to variations in specific situations and then potentially amplified. For example, the Internet has become a means of transacting payments. Then there is the development of fraud and viruses and ways of dealing with them. Technology as social object exists only insofar as it is taken up, or particularized, in the ordinary everyday social interactions between people.

The relationship between people and technology: social objects and meaning

In the complex responsive processes perspective on technology outlined above, it is argued that humans do not have a relationship with things in anything like the same way as they have with each other, even though they may feel as if they do and metaphorically talk as if they do. People and things do not engage each other in the social act of gesture and response.

The gesture–response is an understanding of the detailed way in which humans interact with each other. It is not just one person doing something and the other reacting to it. In gesturing, one is taking a similar attitude to one's action as the other is taking to it. Furthermore, in human relating, one person is not simply taking the attitude of the specific other but always, at the same time, the attitude of the generalized other/me (which is the same as the social object). Both the gesturer and the responder are self-conscious and selves are social objects. Clearly nothing like this goes on when using a tool. The key point is that we are not interacting with or relating to a tool in anything like the sense we use these words with respect to human relating or interaction. What we are doing is using, even playing with, the tool.

However, tools and other physical objects in our environment are not just objects we operate with and upon because they have meaning for us, including highly emotional significance. The key point here has to do with *meaning*. We respond emotionally and intellectually to the *meaning* physical objects such as cars, mobile phones, clothes, jewelry, our own bodies, mountains, lakes and so on, have for us. However, Mead makes the profoundly important point that meaning cannot be located in a physical object. Physical objects have no meaning because meaning cannot be 'had'. For Mead, meaning is the social act and the social act is meaning. In this way of thinking, meaning is interacting and it does not exist anywhere, even as the vocal act of the word, let alone in a physical object. So it follows that a physical object can be meaningful only insofar as it is somehow taken up in our interactions with each other. Meaning arises as the particularizing of the social object in specific situations. Take a car as an example. The car in itself, as a physical object, has no meaning and can therefore arouse no emotion in those using it. However, a car is not simply a physical object but also, at the same time, a social object, that is, a generalized tendency to act which is common to a number of people. This generalized tendency could take the form of respecting those who own big cars, for example. What is evoking the response of respect here is not the physical object of the big car but the social object of 'big car'.

Thinking about technology in this way links to the fantasizing, imaginative activities of human minds. For example, it is well known that infants become very attached to particular objects such as a teddy bear or blanket. The psychoanalyst Winnicott (1965) referred to these as transitional objects because they were neither simply reality nor simply fantasy but both at the same time. However, the physical object of the blanket or teddy bear has no meaning in itself. The meaning is the infant's gesture together with the imagined response from the object – the meaning is constituted by the fantasizing or imagining activities of the body. In other words, meaning is not in the object but rather it is the activity of mind and there can be no mind without social interaction. Thus what is important is not the physical object of blanket or teddy bear, but the corresponding social object. Meaning lies not in the physical object but in the fantasy purpose for which the object is used. A similar argument could be made for adults with respect to the emotional attachments they create towards artifacts such as cars, mobile phones, musical instruments, clothes, jewelry and inanimate objects in nature, for example, a river or a mountain, or resources like money or oil. Thinking about technology in this way focuses attention not only on the physical objects of tools but also on the complex responsive processes of relating in which the generalized social object called technology is particularized. This brings to the fore questions of power, control and identity.

Consider some other examples. Reading and writing is a technology that is essential to scientific progress and the development of tools and techniques. However, reading/writing are also social objects. Abram (1996) points out how reading and writing have led to the replacement of the sensuous, embodied style of consciousness found in oral cultures with a more detached, abstract mode of thinking. When concepts such as 'virtue' and 'justice' are recorded in writing, they acquire an autonomy and permanence independent of ordinary experience. Abstraction becomes a way of thinking and speaking as well as writing. Donaldson (2003; and see Chapter 7, this volume) argues that reading and writing not only eclipse nature but also tend to eclipse local, bodily human interaction in the present. Drawing on Elias (2000), she suggests that a new technology (including writing and printing) may be understood as an unplanned process which transforms the society which has produced it. Drawing on Ong (2002), Donaldson points to how literacy and printing have influenced human patterns of relating. The technology of writing fosters logic and abstraction. Writing also sets up the conditions for objectivity. It fosters precision and what Ong calls 'sparse linearity' and distanced forms of communication between people. Writing led to a shift from 'hearing dominance' to 'sight dominance' and print continued the trend.

Modern technologies of information and communication are other examples of social objects that profoundly affect the pattern of our interactions and even the conceptions we have of ourselves. The development of computers has been accompanied by the development of cognitivist psychology in which mind has come to be thought of as an information-processing device similar to a computer. The mind has come to be thought of as models and maps, again reflecting technology. The development of the camera obscura some 250 years ago was accompanied by a view of mind as an internal world that made representations of objects in an outside reality. As social object, technology shapes our thinking in many areas apparently unconnected with that technology itself. Technology provides metaphors for our thinking about everything around us. Thus we think of organizations as machines or as ships to be steered by their leaders. The social objects of technology, therefore, affect how we experience ourselves, our identities, and they of course impact on patterns of social relations. One only has to think of the technology of fast foods and that of contraception to see what enormous shifts in social relations accompany the evolution of technology.

Consider finally a case described by Johannessen (2003) where the evolving strategies of a logistics company were studied. The logistics department was struggling to connect suppliers to the EDI (Electronic Data Interchange) system. They saw the technological system as crucial in the relationships with the suppliers. If the technology could help them control while at the same time aid them in becoming more efficient in supplying, then they would invest in such a technology. In this case, their understanding of the technology was crucial in the development of logistics actions towards the supplier. The meaning of the EDI system for efficient information exchange and flow in the supply chain, leading to a reduced need for large inventories, was created in their relations with each other. As a result of their communication with each other, and with other people in the organization, the meaning of the EDI system emerged as a way of controlling the supplier. The EDI system had no meaning in itself, it was the experience of the patterns of action in which the EDI system was included that the meaning of the system emerged and evolved. As time went by, and the relations between the partners who were going to use the technology evolved, there was also the possibility that the meaning of the technology would change. However, it was the meaning of the EDI system constructed in the relations within the company that was decisive for the patterns of action emerging as logistics activities between the company and the suppliers. This then became the actual strategy of the logistics department. When the implementation of the EDI system did not go according to plan, it was claimed to be due to the varying commitment among the suppliers. The particularization of the EDI system as social object differed. The people in the company did not work very closely with their suppliers. Consequently, the similar tendency to act with the EDI system had not emerged either. By working with the relations between people in the different companies there could be a possibility of creating such similar tendencies to act, although even then there would be no guarantee how the patterns of action would turn out.

The study suggested that it is inadequate to define and explain logistics activities in terms of operational models. They should rather be understood in terms of the way people in organizations establish meaningful and coordinated patterns of action and how these actions are formed in relating to each other. Logistics is thus understood in terms of participative action and complex self-organizing patterns involving people, technology, nature and resources, and not as a particular concept or object of manipulation and implementation. As people engage in using technological solutions, patterns of action are created in complex responsive processes of relating between people. These patterns self-organize and emerge in unpredictable ways. This means that the patterns of action are not organized by anyone or anything.

Concluding remarks

In this chapter we have argued that technology and the wider resources and competences of which technology is a part can all be thought of as social objects. These are generalized tendencies to act that are common to large numbers of people. Those generalized tendencies are only ever manifested in the experience of the social actors involved. This is the experience of particularizing the generalizations in specific local situations. The literature on technology in organizations tends to focus on the generalization and how such generalizations might be designed with a particular future in mind. The theory of complex responsive processes focuses attention on how social objects as generalizations are evolving, as they are made particular in the ordinary everyday local situations of the living present. This perspective suggests that we might obtain a deeper understanding of technologies if we direct attention to just how they are particularized. Such understanding is important and relevant for economic and organizational development, and as such is also an important issue for further research.

References

Abram, D. (1996) *The Spell of the Sensuous*, New York: Vintage Books.
Allen, P. M. (1998a) 'Evolving complexity in social science', in G. Altman and W. A. Koch (eds), *Systems: New Paradigms for the Human Sciences*, New York: Walter de Gruyter.
Allen, P. M. (1998b) 'Modeling complex economic evolution', in F. Schweitzer and G. Silverberg (eds), *Selbstorganisation*, Berlin: Dunker and Humblot.

Bijker, W. E. *et al.* (1987) *The Social Construction of Technological Systems*, Cambridge, MA: The MIT Press.

Blauner, R. (1964) *Alienation and Freedom*, Chicago, IL: University of Chicago Press.

Brown, J. S. and Duguid, P. (1991) 'Organizational learning and communities-of-practice. Toward a unified view of working, learning and innovation', *Organization Science*, 2(1), pp. 40–56.

Callon, M. and Latour, B. (1981) 'Unscrewing the big Leviathan: how actors macro-structure reality and how sociologists help them to do so', in K. Knorr-Cetina and V. Cicourel (eds), *Advances in Social Theory and Methodology: Toward an Integration of Micro- and Macro-sociologies*, Boston, MA: Routledge & Kegan Paul Ltd.

Callon, M. (2002) 'Writing and (re)writing devices as tools for managing complexity', in J. Law and A. Mol (eds), *Complexities: Social Studies of Knowledge Practices*, Durham, NC: Duke University Press.

Donaldson, A. (2003) 'The part played by writing in the organizational conversation', unpublished thesis, University of Hertfordshire.

Elias, N. (1939/2000) *The Civilizing Process*, Oxford: Blackwell.

Emery, F. E. and Trist, E. L. (1973) *Toward a Social Ecology*, London: Tavistock.

Emery, F. E. and Thorsrud, E. (1969) *Form and Content in Industrial Democracy*, London: Tavistock.

Fox, S. (2000) 'Communities of practice, Foucault and actor-network theory', *Journal of Management Studies*, 37(6), pp. 853–867.

Giddens, A. (1984) *The Constitution of Society: Outline of the Theory of Structuration*, Cambridge: Polity Press.

Johannessen, S. (2003) 'An Explorative Study of Complexity, Strategy and Change in Logistics Organizations', Ph.D. thesis 2003: 91, Norwegian University of Science and Technology, Trondheim, Norway.

Kauffman, S. (1995) *At Home in the Universe*, New York: Oxford University Press.

Latour, B. and Woolgar, S. (1979) *Laboratory Life: The Social Construction of Scientific Facts*, Beverly Hills, CA: Sage.

Law, J. (1992) 'Notes on the theory of the actor-network: ordering, strategy, and heterogeneity', *Systems Practice*, 5(4), n.p.

Marion, R. (1999) *The Edge of Organization: Chaos and Complexity Theories of Formal Social Systems*, Thousand Oaks, CA: Sage.

Mead, G. H. (1934) *Mind, Self and Society*, Chicago, IL: Chicago University Press.

Morgan, G. (1997) *Images of Organization*, Thousand Oaks, CA: Sage.

Nonaka, I. and Takeuchi, H. (1995) *The Knowledge Creating Company: How Japanese Companies Create the Dynamics of Innovation*, New York: Oxford University Press.

Ong, W. J. (2002) *Orality and Literacy*, London and New York: Routledge.

Penrose, E. T. (1959) *The Theory of the Growth of the Firm*, New York: Wiley.

Prahalad, C. K. and Hamel, G. (1990) 'The core competence of the corporation', *Harvard Business Review*, 68, pp. 78–91.

Prigogine, I. (1997) *The End of Certainty: Time, Chaos and the New Laws of Nature*, New York: The Free Press.

Stacey, R. (2001) *Complex Responsive Processes in Organizations: Learning and knowledge creation*, London: Routledge.

Stacey, R., Griffin, D. and Shaw, P. (2000) *Complexity and Management: Fad or radical challenge to systems thinking?*, London: Routledge.

Trist, E. (1981) 'The evolution of socio-technical systems', *Occasional Papers* No.2, Ontario.

Trist, E. and Bamforth, K. (1951) 'Some consequences of the Longwall Method of Coal Getting', *Human Relations*, 4(1), pp. 3–33.

Utterback, J. (1994) *Mastering the Dynamics of Innovation*, Boston, MA: Harvard Business School Press.

Weber, M. (1947) *The Theory of Social and Economical Organization*, London: Oxford University Press.

Wernerfeldt, B. (1984) 'A resource-based view of the firm', *Strategic Management Journal*, 5, pp. 171–180.

Winnicott, D. W. (1965) *The Maturational Process and the Facilitating Environment*, London: Hogarth Press.

Editor's introduction to Chapter 7

Alison Donaldson, an independent consultant working in England, considers the role of writing in organizational life. She argues that writing and printing are technologies (see Chapter 6, this volume) which have major effects on social interaction and our ways of thinking. For me, it then follows that these technologies impact on the very structure of the self. For example, we have come to think of ourselves as autonomous selves having minds inside which function like computers, processing and storing information received from outside us. Writing/printing, as technology, takes the form of physical objects, such as the written page, the pen, the printing press and the computer. But this technology is not only a physical object but also, at the same time, a social object (see Chapter 2, this volume). In other words, this technology is itself a tendency on the part of many people to act in similar ways in many similar situations. As social object, therefore, technology is constitutive of meaning in social interaction. Writing and printing foster precise, abstract thinking which enables people to distance themselves from their own momentary situations, so changing the meaning of what they experience. They encourage introspection and focus attention on the visible and quantifiable, which is recorded, fixed and repeatable. Writing also creates new meaning and stimulates learning. Writing and printing have thus brought enormous benefits and the scientific revolution is unthinkable without them. However, they have, at the same time, brought with them problems. Donaldson brings together a number of writers who describe how the move from an oral to a literate culture has distanced people from nature and to some extent their own emotional engagement with each other.

Donaldson then explores how the social object of writing is particularized in organizations today. In other words, people take up the technology of writing, as social object, in their local interactions with each other. What strikes me as I read what she writes is how in taking up technology as social object, people tend to focus on the technology as physical objects, for example, as tools of writing, as structures of written reports and as PowerPoint presentations of abstract frameworks. This focus of attention leads to our keeping rationally invisible to ourselves the technology as social object so that we pay little attention to the oral, social interactions in which the tools are being used. In organizations today, writing privileges certain kinds of participation. It privileges highly planned and structured meetings over improvisation and engagement in conversation. Generalized propositions and 'recipes' are privileged over narrative forms of communication, so that people tend to believe that they need frameworks models and 'tools' to do anything in an organization. The result is frequently a deadening experience, distancing people from participating, from talking to each other. Few organizations use writing intelligently for reflection and learning.

It is important to be aware of just how much we are conditioned by the technology of writing/printing for a number of reasons. First, it seems to me that this technology has something to do with the persistent tendency we have to reify what are actually temporal social processes. For example, it is extremely common to talk about an organization as a 'thing' that actually exists instead of perceiving it for what it is in our direct experience, namely patterns of relating between people. As soon as we do this, we naturally slip into a way of thinking of leading and managing as a rational activity of moving the organization, 'its' culture and 'its' values, about in directions we choose. The spatial nature of writing and printing encourages thinking about organizations and society using spatial metaphors which make it easy to slip into reification. This tendency to reify organizations, then, makes it easy to think in the magico-mythical terms Elias talked about (see Chapter 1, this volume) without even noticing that this is what we are doing because it is so covered over with rational-sounding jargon. In addition, the use of written records which are sent by one person and received by another makes the sender–receiver model of communication seem unquestionable. So we think that in a conversation one person translates his thoughts into words and 'sends' them to another. She then translates the words back into her thoughts and if the communication is effective the meaning passes intact from one to the other. This covers over the bodily nature of human communication and the way in which gestures evoke responses in which meaning emerges. We then come to focus all our attention on the 'tool' of reports and so on, becoming rationally blind to the much more complex processes in which we are engaged.

7 Writing in organizational life: how a technology simultaneously forms and is formed by human interaction

Alison Donaldson

- In what sense are we conditioned by the technology of writing?
- Ripple effects of writing and print
- The value of literacy
- How is writing used in organizational life today?
- How a report turned out not to be the whole story – a narrative
- What is writing exactly?
- New writing technologies

One day, I received a phone call from someone I knew (X) who occupies a senior position at a large UK health charity. She described to me a range of ways in which the charity was creating and funding a number of groups or 'communities' – of doctors, nurses and patients – with the ultimate objective of improving patient care. Each of these communities would meet regularly to share experiences and spread new ideas. These community-cultivating initiatives, X went on to explain, were a central part of the organization's 'medical strategy', and what she was now looking for was help in evaluating this strategy. Over the next few months we continued the conversation, involving a number of other people, exploring how this could be done. It soon became clear that what X had in mind was 'evaluation for learning' rather than 'evaluation for judgment', so we decided to drop the term 'evaluation' and adopt instead the phrase 'framework for learning'. I recall at some point probing to find out what 'learning framework' meant in concrete terms right now for the people in the room. X elaborated by saying that what they needed was 'a common language' so they could both understand what had been achieved and explain it clearly to other people. As we worked together over the subsequent months, the abstract concept 'learning framework' continued to evolve and take on specific meanings in each particular conversation.

My doctoral research had made me aware that abstract terms such as 'strategy' and 'framework' are characteristic of the 'text-formed speech' common in societies that have absorbed writing, writing technologies and literate ways of thinking. I am not criticizing X or her colleagues for using such terms (most educated people talk in text-formed speech at times). Rather, for me this story illustrates, first, the prevalence of writing-conditioned ways of thinking and talking in organizational life today; and second, the way in which we find ourselves needing to 'particularize' generalized concepts and reifications fostered by writing, in order to go on together.

There was an interesting further twist to this story: in a later conversation, X pointed out that she had used the term 'strategy' in order to gain acceptance of her plans from her Executive Board. It seems this was the kind of language they could relate to and take seriously. Yet many of the normal doctors, nurses and managers involved with the charity did not understand what 'the medical strategy' meant in practice. So, over and over again, X had to explain and illustrate the abstract term to these people.

In Chapters 2 and 6 of this volume, Ralph Stacey, drawing on Mead's thinking, refers to 'social objects', which are 'generalized tendencies, common to large numbers of people, to act in similar ways in similar situations'. The examples he gives for organizational life include organizations themselves (as collective identities).

As Stacey points out, social objects often emerge from the way we use technologies. Writing and printing, for example, paved the way for the emergence of social phenomena such as bureaucracy, regulation, management by targets, armies of people sitting in front of computer screens all day, as well as widespread tendencies to use email for exchange of information and opinions, and PowerPoint for presentations.

Further, we often employ the tools of writing to codify generalized tendencies or collective habits. The Ten Commandments was one of the earliest attempts. Written constitutions and statute books are further examples. More contemporary organizational examples include vision and mission statements and strategic plans. Thus, writing technologies (writing, print and computers) have allowed us to fix words on paper, *as if* we were fixing the very patterns of behavior themselves.

But writing and print have gone even further, as I will argue in this chapter. There is considerable evidence that these technologies have fostered generalized, abstract forms of thinking. Terms such as 'strategy' and 'culture' may seem very real in our imagination, despite Stacey's reminder (see Chapter 2) that 'The general is only to be found in the experience of the particular – it has no existence outside of it'. Indeed, people brought up in a literate society can conduct conversations about abstract, generalized concepts such as strategies and frameworks without necessarily referring to the particular interactions in which these generalizations become meaningful.

In what sense are we conditioned by the technology of writing?

As Norbert Elias (referring to transport) stated, a new technology can be understood as 'an unplanned process', which may set in train a transformation that 'reacts in turn upon the society which has produced it' (Goudsblom and Mennell, 1998: 223, citing Elias, *Technization and Civilization*). Most people would recognize printing and computing as technologies, but it may also be argued that writing itself is a technology.

In his last extended work *The Symbol Theory*, in which Elias explores the evolution and development of human communication, he devotes little attention specifically to writing (or reading), except to describe it as sound symbols in voiceless form, or as a way of replacing sound patterns with vision patterns (Elias, 1991: 104). For him, the development of 'learned language' (as opposed to the inborn language of animals) was the big breakthrough: 'The human form of communication by means of a learned language represents a unique evolutionary innovation' (Elias, 1991: 50).

While this makes sense, many have argued that the development of writing and printing has been as transformative as the development of human languages. There was a flurry of publications in the early 1960s illuminating the role of writing in society by studying societies that did not have this particular technology. Eric Havelock, in his book *The Muse Learns to Write*, dates the 'modern discovery of orality' to around 1963:

> Within the span of twelve months or less, from some time in 1962 to the spring of 1963, in three different countries – France, Britain, and the United States – there issued from the printing presses five publications by five authors who at the time when they wrote could not have been aware of any mutual relationship. The works in question

were 'La Pensee Sauvage' (Levi-Strauss), 'The consequences of literacy' (Goody and Watt, an extended article), 'The Gutenberg Galaxy' (McLuhan), 'Animal Species and Evolution' (Mayr), and 'Preface to Plato'.

(Havelock, 1986: 25)

What these scholars were asking was: 'What has it meant for societies and their cultures in the past to discard oral means of communication in favor of literate ones of various sorts?' and 'What precisely is the relationship between the spoken word of today (or yesterday) and the written text?' (Havelock, 1986: 24).

Nearly twenty years later, in 1982, Walter J. Ong published *Orality and Literacy*, a brilliant survey of the history of scholarship in this field. His work indicates that the technologies of writing and print have been essential ingredients in the development of modern society and science, and they have also introduced certain biases into the ways in which humans relate to one another. He argued that, growing up in a literate society, we are blind to the subtle influences of writing and printing on our way of life. I draw especially on the revised version of this classic, which appeared in 2002.

Before discussing Ong's work, it is worth noting that technological developments such as writing, print and computing do not represent static or complete phenomena, but rather 'unfinished processes' (Goudsblom and Mennell, 1998: 226–227, citing Elias, *Technization and Civilization*). The twentieth century saw the introduction of a whole range of new communication media – radio, telephony, film, television, computers – and we can only begin to make sense of the ripples that all this is sending through the patterns of human interaction (I touch on this again at the end of this chapter). First, however, let us start at the beginning – the invention of writing.

Ripple effects of writing and print

Writing . . . initiated what print and computers only continue, the reduction of dynamic sound to quiescent space, the separation of the word from the living present, where alone spoken words can exist.

(Ong, 2002: 81)

Walter J. Ong traces the way in which literacy emerged out of orality (Ong 2002: 76): 'Writing . . ., the technology which has shaped and powered the intellectual activity of modern man, was a very late development in human history. . . . The first script, or true writing, that we know, was developed among the Sumerians in Mesopotamia only around the year 3500 BC' (ibid.: 82–83). Ong warns that 'Fully literate persons can only with great difficulty imagine what a primary oral culture is like, that is, a culture with no knowledge whatsoever of writing or even of the possibility of writing', where no one has ever 'looked up' anything (ibid.: 31). He goes on to demonstrate that 'more than any other single invention, writing has transformed human consciousness' (ibid.: 77).

In the *Phaedrus*, Plato (427?–347 BC) has his teacher, Socrates (469?–399 BC), who was mostly non-literate (Abram, 1996: 109), say that writing is 'inhuman, pretending to establish outside the mind what in reality can only be in the mind' (Ong, 2002: 78). Over the last 2000 years, similarly strong objections have been voiced about the later technologies of printing (generally dated back to the invention of alphabetic letterpress print in fifteenth-century Europe) and computers.

So, what effects have writing and print had on the patterns of human relating? Drawing on Ong, Elias and other authors, below I pull together some influences of literacy and printing under six themes.

Theme 1: abstract and logical

> Writing fosters abstractions that disengage knowledge from the arena where human beings struggle with one another.
>
> (Ong, 2002: 43)

Abstract thinking is of course possible in spoken language. For example, the term 'tree' refers to a concept which is not any particular tree. George Herbert Mead calls such concepts 'universals' and even states that 'thinking takes place in universals' (Mead, 1934: 88). Elias too notes that language has made abstraction, or 'synthesis' as he calls it, possible. However, there are levels of synthesis (Elias, 1991: 45) or degrees of abstraction (Ong, 2002: 49), and writing has enabled humans to perform elaborate abstract thinking. While Elias does not attribute the capacity for high levels of abstraction to literacy, Ong does identify such a link. There is considerable literature, he points out, indicating that oral cultures tend to use concepts in situational contexts, anchored in the human lifeworld. For example, in A. J. Luria's work *Cognitive Development: Its Cultural and Social Foundations*, Luria's Russian illiterate (oral) subjects never dealt with abstract circles, but instead called them plate, sieve, bucket, watch or moon (Ong, 2002: 50).

Persons who have interiorized writing, in contrast, 'organize, to varying degrees, even their oral expression in thought patterns and verbal patterns that they would not know of unless they could write' (Ong, 2002: 56). Luria's work suggested that 'an oral culture simply does not deal in such items as geometrical figures, abstract categorization, formally logical reasoning processes, definitions, or . . . articulated self-analysis, all of which derive not simply from thought itself but from text-formed thought' (Ong, 2002: 54–55).

Formal logic, in particular, was the invention of Greek culture 'after it had interiorized the technology of alphabetic writing' (Ong, 2002: 52). Luria's oral subjects appeared not to operate with formal deductive procedures at all and seemed to find such procedures uninteresting. For example, when presented with the syllogism: *In the far north, where there is snow, all bears are white. Novaya Zembla is in the far north and there is always snow there. What color are the bears?*, a typical response was 'I don't know. I've seen a black bear. I've never seen any others. . . . Each locality has its own animals' (ibid.: 52).

The language of the twentieth (and twenty-first) century is 'rich in confused and confusing symbols of synthesis at a very high level' (Elias, 1991: 45). In organizational life today, not only do we refer to invisible, intangible concepts such as 'culture', but once they are written down they can be read by somebody who has never met us and who may have no direct experience of the culture in question.

David Abram, in his book *The Spell of the Sensuous*, argues specifically that writing has been a major factor in distancing humans from the 'more than human world'. Around Plato's lifetime (*c*. 400 BC), Greece was at the threshold between oral and written culture. It was in this period, Abram suggests, that the 'sensuous, mimetic, profoundly embodied style of consciousness proper to orality gave way to the more detached abstract mode of thinking engendered by alphabetic literacy' (Abram, 1996: 109). For example, prior to the spread of writing, 'ethical qualities like "virtue", "justice", and "temperance" were thoroughly entwined with the specific situations in which those qualities were exhibited' (ibid.: 110). As soon as such concepts were recorded in writing, they acquired an autonomy and permanence hitherto unknown. They were 'promoted to a new realm independent of the flux of ordinary experience' (ibid.: 111). Abstraction became a way of thinking and speaking as well as writing, maintains Abram. This ability to deal with abstract concepts has contributed enormously to scientific and technological progress. Large and complex organizations would be impossible to run without written communication. Indeed, the *Collins Concise Dictionary* reveals that the origin of the French word 'bureau' was a type of cloth used for covering desks. A desk is a writing surface, reflecting strong links between the written word and the evolution of large bureaucracies.

More than 2000 years after Plato, our ability to interact with our own signs in abstraction from our earthly surroundings has 'blossomed into a vast cognitive realm, a horizonless expanse of virtual interactions' (Abram, 1996: 265). We inhabit a 'global field of information'. But, as we sit at our computers, 'we do not notice that the chorus of frogs by the nearby stream has dwindled, this year, to a solitary voice, and that the song sparrows no longer return to the trees' (ibid.: 266).

Leonard Shlain is another author who addresses the shadow sides of writing (Shlain, 1998). He traces the history of writing from the cuneiform signs used in ancient Mesopotamia and hieroglyphs in ancient Egypt, through the invention of the phonetic alphabet (probably by ancient Semites in the Sinai peninsula), and its subsequent spread (via Phoenician traders) to the ancient Greeks and Western civilization as a whole. The phonetic alphabet (used today by so many languages, including English and other European ones) was a revolutionary invention, using a mere twenty-six symbols (give or take a few) to represent visually the whole range of sounds emitted in human speech, and enabling societies to 'elevate the written word at the expense of the image' (Shlain, 1998: 7). The phonetic alphabet, Shlain goes on to argue, has fostered abstract, left-brained ways of thinking (he is a brain surgeon as well as an author), and it was used to help establish all three patriarchal, monotheistic religions: Judaism, Christianity and Islam. Indeed, writing with abstract symbols (letters) spread from the Middle East outwards at a time when the many goddess images of the ancient world were vanishing. Tellingly, the first two of the Ten Commandments that God gave to Moses, according to the Bible, addressed monotheism and image respectively: (1) 'I am the Lord thy God. Thou shalt have no other gods before me'; and (2) 'Thou shalt not make unto thee any graven images, or any likeness of any thing that is in heaven above, or that is in the earth beneath, or that is in the water under the earth' (Shlain, 1998: 82, citing Exodus from the Old Testament).

> Each monotheistic religion features an imageless Father deity whose authority shines through His revealed Word, sanctified in its written form. Conceiving of a deity who has no concrete image prepares the

way for the kind of abstract thinking that inevitably leads to law codes, dualistic philosophy, and objective science, the signature triad of Western culture.

(Shlain, 1998: 7)

Theme 2: precise and sparse

Writing also fosters precision. There is more than one reason for this. First, the reader is usually absent when we write, so we have to work harder to make ourselves understood:

> To make yourself clear without gesture, without facial expression, without intonation, without a real hearer, you have to foresee circumspectly all possible meanings a statement may have for any possible reader in any possible situation, and you have to make your language work so as to come clear all by itself, with no existential context.

(Ong, 2002: 103)

Second, writing, unlike speaking, allows us to change or erase what we have just written before the reader sees it. Today, with word processing, this is more true than ever.

Elias too points to precision, again attributing this capacity to human language in general, not writing. One of the most pronounced advantages of human language over animal communication, he writes, is the 'relatively high precision of the information communicated from person to person' (Elias, 1991: 93). I would add that this is even more true of writing, which gives the author time to work out exactly what he or she wants to write, with added precision through grammar, punctuation, order, layout and so on. This remains true even if the precision is lost on the reader, who always interprets or makes sense in his or her own way.

Similarly, writing and editing are conducive to what Ong calls 'sparse linearity' (using 'linear' in the sense of non-discursive). Text can afford to be sparse because the reader can always go back to retrieve context and retrace the train of thought. In a primary oral culture – where an oral utterance 'has vanished as soon as it is uttered' (Ong, 2002: 39) – redundancy is common, offering the listener an opportunity to catch something next time round.

Theme 3: distanced and introspective

Human language, writes Elias, creates a 'comparatively high capacity for distancing oneself from one's own momentary situation. One can speak of the moon even if it is not visible, or a small herd of buffaloes not yet in sight' (Elias, 1991: 54). Similarly, 'Language has its origins in the face-to-face situation, but can be readily detached from it' (Berger and Luckmann, 1966: 52). Literacy, I would add, facilitates distance even more. 'Writing separates the knower from the known and thus sets up conditions for "objectivity", in the sense of personal disengagement or distancing' (Ong, 2002: 45). When we write we are taking time, at a temporal distance, to reflect on past (or future) events. Literature as an art depends on 'the human ability to imagine things which do not exist, events which do not occur and to communicate about them by means of appropriate symbols' (Elias, 1991: 72).

On a simple level, writing and reading are usually solitary activities. It is easy to see this in organizations today: for example, in meetings, when people are required to read a hand-out or a text slide on a screen, 'the unity of the group vanishes as each person enters into his or her private lifeworld' (Ong, 2002: 68). Ong was describing a school class, but his words fit the organizational context perfectly. In my own experience, the solitary nature of writing has been both a pleasure and a frustration.

Theme 4: visible and quantifiable

Writing initiated a shift from 'hearing dominance' to 'sight dominance'. This was a profound change: 'sound has a special relationship to time unlike that of the other fields that register in human sensation. Sound exists only when it is going out of existence. It is not simply perishable but essentially evanescent, and it is sensed as evanescent. When I pronounce the word "permanence", by the time I get to the "-nence", the "perma-" is gone' (Ong, 2002: 31–32). In contrast, while vision can register motion, it can also register immobility. Indeed, it even favors immobility (ibid.).

Print continued the trend from sound to vision. 'Deeply typographic folk forget to think of words as primarily oral, as events . . . words tend rather to be assimilated to things, "out there" on a flat surface' (ibid.: 32–33). Print technology, agrees Lanham, encourages the Platonic view that there is 'a "reality" which is somehow or another really out there' (Lanham,

1993: 214). This may in turn have contributed to the sense of meaning having an existence outside of any specific interaction.

Maps are a particularly interesting example of the shift to visual associated with printing. 'Only after print and the extensive experience with maps that print implemented would human beings, when they thought about the cosmos or universe or "world", think primarily of something laid out before their eyes, as in a modern printed atlas' (Ong, 2002: 72). Many habits of today's organizational life – such as organization charts, analytical frameworks and systems thinking – may be thought of as extensions of this map perspective.

Some of the earliest forms of writing preserved were lists, tables and accounts – all visual items, whereas orality 'knows no lists or charts or figures' (Ong, 2002: 97). Today, with word processing and PowerPoint presentations, we see a burgeoning of lists, bullet points, tables, charts and statistics. Again, these may be thought of as continuing a trend first made possible by writing and reinforced by printing. Calendars (and thus precise knowledge of date) are a further example.

Arguably all these visual forms born of writing and print, and intensified by computing, foster the emphasis in today's organizations on performance measurement and management.

Ong's argument that alphabetic writing marked a shift from the auditory to the visual may appear to contradict Shlain's view that writing elevated the written word over image. But on closer inspection there is no real contradiction: the images Ong was talking about were precisely the twenty-six abstract symbols of the alphabet, not images of gods or goddesses or anything else.

Theme 5: recorded, fixed and repeatable

> Writing moves words from the sound world to a world of visual space, but print locks words into position in this space.
>
> (Ong, 2002: 119)

This shift from sound to visual has many consequences. Take words: oral cultures have no dictionaries, so the meaning of each word is controlled by 'the real-life situations in which the word is used here and now' (Ong, 2002: 46). 'Word meanings come continually out of the present, though past meanings of course have shaped the present meaning in many and varied ways, no longer recognized' (Ong, 2002: 47). Print, on the other hand, 'encourages a sense of closure, a sense that what is found in a text has been finalized' (Ong, 2002: 129). A printed text can also be reproduced: 'The message of . . . typography is primarily that of repeatability' (McLuhan, 1964: 173).

The shift from oral to visual, and especially the impact of printing, is captured well by Dean Walker, paraphrasing Marshall McLuhan (Walker, 1968: 70):

> Western man's emphasis on the visual, especially after the invention of printing, changed him completely. . . . Before print, communicating involved him in living relationships with other people. Even in manuscript culture, writings were normally read slowly and laboriously aloud. But the invention of the printed, reproducible book let man into a new private world. Quietly and alone he could absorb the book's contents. His earlier communal consciousness and participation was replaced by a feeling of privacy, withdrawal, self-containment. Concepts such as freedom began to build. He put his faith into detached analytical knowledge.

Moreover, the 'fixity' of documents (Brown and Duguid, 2000) and repeatability of print seem to have influenced how we remember. Oral cultures had their own ways of remembering. For example, Homer's poetry (now thought by most scholars to have been created hundreds of years before it was written down) was full of verbal formulae arranged in a metrical way:

> In an oral culture, knowledge, once acquired, had to be constantly repeated or it would be lost: fixed, formulaic thought patterns were essential for wisdom and effective administration.
>
> (Ong, 2002: 23)

Thus, poems and history were retold over and over and remained enduring yet flexible. Sometimes melody helped the poet, and many traditional stories featured memorable larger-than-life characters.

Plato pointed to a link between writing and memory in the *Phaedrus*. The Egyptian king Thamus refuses the gift of writing offered to him by the god Thoth, commenting:

> If men learn [writing], it will implant forgetfulness in their souls; they will cease to exercise memory because they rely on that which is written, calling things to remembrance no longer from within themselves, but by means of external marks.
>
> (Abram, 1996: 113)

Even at the end of the twentieth century, the Aboriginal Australians evidently used their 'Dreaming' songs as an *auditory* memory tool to enable them to recall viable routes through harsh terrain, while the landscape itself provided a *visual* mnemonic for remembering the stories (Abram, 1996: 175).

In organizations nowadays people rely on note-taking and written records to spare themselves the effort of remembering. This reliance on the written word – something fixed and repeatable – may be partly responsible for the taken-for-granted way of describing memory as a store from which we retrieve things called memories. It is then only a small step to asserting that our minds have a limited capacity for receiving and storing information, as some writers have claimed (Shannon and Weaver, 1949; Miller, 1956; Minto, 1987).

Theme 6: prone to abstract categorization

Luria's research suggested that categorical thinking is characteristic of literate peoples, whereas his non-literates thought in situational patterns. They were convinced that categorical thinking was 'not important, uninteresting, trivializing' (Ong, 2002: 52):

> Subjects were presented with drawings of four objects . . . and were asked to group together those that were similar or could be placed in one group or designated by one word. One series consisted of drawings of the objects hammer, saw, log, hatchet. Illiterate subjects consistently thought of the group not in categorical terms (three tools, the log not a tool) but in terms of practical situations – 'situational thinking'. . . . If you are a workman with tools and see a log, you think of applying the tool to it, not of keeping the tool away from what it was made for – in some weird intellectual game. A 25-year-old illiterate peasant: 'They're all alike. The saw will saw the log and the hatchet will chop it into small pieces. If one of these has to go, I'd throw out the hatchet. It doesn't do as good a job as a saw'.
>
> (Ong, 2002: 51)

Thus writing in particular seems to favor abstract, analytical classification. While spoken language itself encourages us to classify or distinguish simply by naming, the ability to write down our categories and then return to them again and again has fostered abstract classification and given our categories an appearance of permanence.

The value of literacy

Ong describes writing as 'artificial' (i.e. created by humans), but is careful to add that this is not to condemn it but to praise it. 'Like other artificial creations and indeed more than any other, it is utterly invaluable' (Ong, 2002: 81).

It is worth distinguishing between two broad uses of writing: over the ages it has been used as a tool for organizing, on the one hand, but also as a method for reflection, learning – and of course literature.

A tool for organizing

'Writing was born of the urge to get organized. There's evidence to suggest that it evolved first as a memory aid, primarily for record-keeping and accounting purposes' (Poor, 1992: 87), states one of the many books on how to write effectively in the corporate world. The reason why writing is such an effective tool for these purposes really boils down to one word: 'list'.

> Comparative studies of literate and nonliterate societies . . . show that although narratives exist in both oral and literate cultures, three forms of text became possible only due to the existence of script: tables, lists, and recipes.
>
> (Czarniawska, 1998: 8)

It is safe to predict that writing will always continue to have many functions: some will be concerned with auditing, recording, planning, contracting, measuring and other transactions. But writing, if used intelligently, can act as a tool for learning in organizational life.

Facilitating reflection and learning

The value of literacy for learning rests on a range of characteristics. As we have seen, writing enables the author to develop precise and elaborate abstract thinking, essential to much of modern knowledge. In addition, writing enables us to make our thinking visible and thus available for further reflection and interaction. It also allows us to 'capture' stories and accounts that might otherwise be transient, overcoming some of the limitations of time and space. All these features increase our ability to share our thinking even with those whom we will never meet. Without any doubt, literacy has been indispensable in helping humans to share knowledge and pass on learning from one generation to another.

Ong pointed out that the advantages of written over spoken communication have paradoxical consequences:

> The deadness of the text, its removal from the living human lifeworld, its rigid visual fixity, assures its endurance and its potential for being resurrected into limitless living contexts by a potentially infinite number of living readers.
>
> (Ong, 2002: 80)

While Elias claims this knowledge-transmitting benefit for human language per se (Elias, 1991: 36), I would argue that not only language, but also writing and print (and now computers and the Internet) have made and will continue to make a huge contribution to learning, including intergenerational learning. Although knowledge defined as a relational process cannot be stored (Stacey, 2001), human beings can use stored symbols in the form of books, websites, audiotapes, videotapes and other artifacts, both to learn – which may be defined as developing new patterns of thinking – and to stimulate learning (to educate).

When we write we not only offer our thinking to the reader; we also develop our own thinking. Writing not only forces us to articulate and organize our thoughts, it also facilitates further reflection. Abram points out that, when we started writing down symbols (using the phonetic alphabet in the case of ancient Greek, English and other European languages), we were able to 'capture' our words in visible and fixed form, and this allowed us to see – and thus reflect on – our words in a way that was not possible before. 'The scribe, or author, could now begin to dialogue with his own visible inscriptions, viewing and responding to his own words even as he wrote them down' (Abram, 1996: 107).

There is a striking parallel with Mead's thinking. Mead argued that the vocal symbol (i.e. spoken language) enabled us to develop self-conscious thinking. When we speak, we can hear what we say. This enables us to respond to our own gestures as we speak, which in turn enables us to think or reflect (i.e. to conduct a continuous silent conversation or role play). Abram's observation similarly makes clear that, when humans started to write, we became able to enter a dialogue with our own written words. This makes writing and reading exceptionally complex and rich processes. We can even enter into dialogue with the words of Plato and Aristotle, who lived more than 2000 years ago. In short, writing is not only a way of recording, listing, accounting and measuring; it may also be used to stimulate learning and sense-making.

How is writing used in organizational life today?

As I have reflected on the way in which we use writing in organizational life today, I have become convinced that most people use it to control, plan and organize. Others view it primarily as a difficult chore. Few seem to use it fully for learning.

In my experience of organizations today, written communication often distances people from one another. Just as Abram argues that the world of letters, numbers and texts has contributed to the eclipsing of *nature* (1996: 123), I would argue that, in today's large organizations, the written word with its spin-offs (e.g. presentations, databases, analytical categories, measurement systems) distracts people from local, bodily human interaction in the living present.

An incident that occurred during my doctoral research laid bare the distancing potential of writing technology: a woman in an organization where I was working was struggling with a database that was supposed to record and systematize the staff appraisal process. Yet about two yards from her desk sat another woman at her own computer, who had told me earlier how demotivating she had found the appraisal meeting with her manager. This seemed a sad example of the focus on documents or tools taking people's time and attention away from talking directly about their experience.

Also striking was an article that appeared in *The Financial Times* on 16 April 2003 headed 'Whitehall "fails to use" research costing £1.4bn a year'. A report by the National Audit Office (an independent body that scrutinizes public spending in the UK) had revealed problems in ensuring that, once government-funded research was done, policy-makers were made aware of it and then used it. 'There are few knowledge transfer mechanisms in place to ensure effective communication and dissemination', said the NAO report. To me, this problem seemed likely to be a symptom of the over-reliance on written reports as a tool for changing behavior. The quotation also raises questions about how abstract generalized terms such as 'knowledge-transfer mechanisms' or 'dissemination' might be particularized or put into practice.

I would like to offer a number of further examples of how our use of writing privileges certain forms of participation.

Writing privileges planning over improvisation and engagement

I was helping a major UK insurance company plan how to communicate some IT changes within the organization, which included several thousand employees. I was struck by the sheer amount of time (about four weeks) it took to draw up a 'communication strategy', which involved going through every 'stakeholder group' we could think of and asking ourselves how they would be affected by the changes, what their perspective might be, how we could involve them, and so on. I recall walking towards the office one day thinking what a military-like procedure this seemed, and yet I had to admit to myself that it was probably indispensable in such a large organization. We had to write the information down in order to be more sure of including every group that mattered. And the process of articulating and discussing the needs of the stakeholder groups forced the team to give them some thought. Yet I could not help noticing at the same time that the climate was very inhospitable, full of secrecy, distrust and personal criticism, with everyone apparently glued to a computer screen, and nowhere to go for a proper conversation (except the local café outside the building).

In the same organization, there was a project team member who seemed to spend all his time updating a project plan. Every time he saw me he would ask me if I had any new 'milestones' he could enter into his computer. Again, I found myself wondering if this was a good use of his time. On one occasion, out of this person's earshot, I heard a colleague humorously cursing all the documentation of procedures he was required to do for the same project.

If writing encourages planning, this can be at the expense of improvisation (by which I do not mean 'muddling through' but being present and ready to act into each human encounter). As musical improviser Derek Bailey writes:

> improvisation embraces, even celebrates, music's essentially
> ephemeral nature. For many of the people involved in it, one of the
> enduring attractions of improvisation is its momentary existence: the
> absence of a residual document.
>
> (Bailey, 1992: 15)

Writing privileges structured meetings over free-flowing conversations

Some time ago, I co-hosted a day of collaborative inquiry with a group of colleagues at my house. The invitation was to explore structure and improvisation in conversation. Instead of sending around an agenda, we simply emailed a selection of potentially interested people, posing a question that we hoped might spark their interest. Ironically and not surprisingly, a discussion immediately arose about whether and how we should 'organize' a day devoted to improvisation and structure. I realized that one option would be to write an agenda for the day, indicating what we would talk about when, which 'exercises' we might do, and so on. Instead we continued the pre-conversation, by phone and email, which helped to develop themes that later influenced what we talked about on the day. In the end, the only written 'agenda' that was necessary was to coordinate, and perhaps allay anxiety, in the form of an email confirming the date, starting time and directions to my house.

With this experience in mind, I was struck by some of Ong's words (distinguishing between the 'primary orality' of societies that have never used writing and the 'secondary orality' that we are experiencing today thanks to telephone, television and multimedia computers). The new, electronic media, he wrote, foster 'a new, self-consciously informal style' (Ong, 2002: 133) where:

> primary orality promotes spontaneity because the analytic reflectiveness implemented by writing is unavailable, secondary orality promotes spontaneity because through analytic reflection we have decided that spontaneity is a good thing. We plan our happenings carefully to be sure that they are thoroughly spontaneous.
>
> (Ong, 2002: 134)

Thus, for me, the preparation for this day of inquiry was an exercise in thinking carefully about how best to use the written word as a form of preparation. Given that a written agenda seemed inappropriate, but we did want a pre-conversation, we had a choice between email and telephone. An inclusive exchange was most feasible by email (which could be sent to everyone in the group, and did not require scheduling as did, say, a teleconference), though I also continued one-to-one phone calls with some members of the group. Email even made it easy to keep involving two people who were interested in the topic but could not make it on the day. I copied them into the continuing email conversation, and they continued to contribute for some time. The email exchanges also generated suggestions about further people, not known to me or to my co-host, who were interested in participating. One person who did not participate actively in the email conversation decided – after I had asked her on the phone what she thought of it – to circulate a note saying that she preferred to meet people first face-to-face.

My doctoral study with the University of Hertfordshire provided another example of how a relatively unstructured, free-flowing meeting could produce 'results'. When my 'learning set' (i.e. supervision group) met, we usually spent two whole days together without any written agenda, though of course the need to make progress with our thesis-writing gave us some focus. On the first morning we often just continued the conversation from breakfast for a good hour before anybody attempted to steer us towards the 'business'. Our supervisor also expressed a wish to avoid mechanical turn-taking (e.g. by going through each person's draft paper strictly in turn and for a set length of time). Accordingly, we followed the interest and energy of the participants, while staying conscious that everybody needed sufficient time to talk in depth about their work. The comparison between learning set and normal organizational meetings made me more aware of the anxiety about structure and results that so many of my clients express. As my own anxiety about structure or productivity in meetings subsided, I sensed that I was freeing myself from the need for plans that my own writing and print bias had fostered in me.

Writing privileges abstract categorization over direct experience

The habit of abstract categorization may be seen in the many tools and 'frameworks' circulating in the organizational world. Examples include two-by-two matrices, the McKinsey '7 S' framework (for analyzing organizations), as well as psychological tools such as learning styles and personality types. While I would argue that this categorizing habit has been fostered by writing, this is not the only reason why people persist with it. For example, I have heard consultants from the big consulting firms say that they need analytical frameworks so that inexperienced consultants 'know what to do' when dealing with senior executives.

At a recent conference on story-telling in organizations I was a little disappointed to discover that the two days were devoted mainly to platform speeches in which the expert on story-telling would tell us that there are X main forms of organizational story, or that a narrative must contain Y key elements. *Harvard Business Review* articles typically tell the reader there are three (or five or seven) key steps needed to solve any particular problem. For example, in the May 2004 issue, Steve Denning, writing about story-telling in organizations, distinguished seven types of organizational stories, recommending that leaders and managers use the appropriate narrative to achieve the results they are after.

These tools, classifications and golden rules focus our attention on certain aspects of our experience. In the case of Myers Briggs, we focus on whether somebody is an ENTJ or an ISFP, rather than noticing how their difference is manifest now in our current interaction. The tools may create a scientific impression (the Myers Briggs indicator was developed from some of Jung's thinking) and give people a license to talk about personal differences in an apparently objective way. However, they can distract us from noticing what is occurring between people in the moment, observing, for example, non-verbal communication, and also the way in which we mutually constrain ourselves in what we say.

In addition, I believe there is a more insidious effect of all these tools, frameworks and step-by-step techniques. They encourage us to believe that we can only understand or manage a situation if we have the right model or framework. We do not trust ourselves simply to talk, listen and pay attention to our experience. Just engaging with people in ordinary conversation, noticing what a complex process this actually is, is not considered sufficient. (I write with feeling on this because it has taken me years to recognize how I have felt disempowered by all the techniques I was not familiar with.)

Writing privileges propositional over narrative forms of communication

Once, after my colleague and I had started working for the health charity mentioned at the beginning of this chapter, we were waiting to interview someone in the organization as part of our 'learning framework' project. I recall that I was eager to invite this person to give us her account of working with the medical strategy, whereas my colleague was more keen to use the interview to identify 'recipes' for the future. My thinking was that general principles and recipes represent a writing-conditioned approach – nothing wrong with that in itself. However, the potential drawback is that, first, the past is not necessarily a guide to the future and, second, some people resist recipes about how they should behave. Narrative, on the other hand, leaves listeners or readers more room to make sense in diverse ways. And by asking an interviewee for specific stories and examples, one creates an opportunity to explore with them the particular interactions out of which generalized lessons emerge. After some discussion, my colleague and I agreed that we would look to develop a combination of story and recipe, in the expectation that this would allow us to cater for a range of needs.

When looking at human language, it is helpful to distinguish between abstract form (e.g. generalizations, principles, theories, propositions) and narrative form (in the sense of stories connecting specific past, present or even future events in order to make sense of them). In organizational writing and business books today, the propositional (often prescriptive) form is dominant. Undoubtedly abstract/propositional writing has its place – for example, in order to reach a 'point of view' (however temporary and subject to further evolution) we have to abstract and thus decontextualize.

On the other hand, narrative has many qualities that are absent in abstract forms of communication. It can retain context, history and non-linearity, and can arguably therefore better reflect 'the unavoidable complexities of concrete human experience' (Toulmin, 1990: 201). This makes it particularly suited to 'teaching' situations, since human learning is contextual. A narrative can also 'resonate' for the reader, meaning that readers tend to recognize patterns and connections from their own past experience, and often to learn from the comparison. This quality of narrative rests strongly on the way humans think in patterns of association and can compare one pattern with another – hence our quick grasp of analogy and metaphor. In addition, narrative allows people to select, fill in meaning and draw their own lessons, and to make sense of what they read or hear. It does not impose a single moral or answer on the listener/reader, but leaves them freedom to associate and connect and conclude.

There is overwhelming evidence that narrative is a natural and very old form in human thinking and communication. Very young children can understand complex matters presented as stories when their powers of comprehending general concepts are almost non-existent. We experience the events in our life as connected and occurring over time, we dream in stories, we spend huge amounts of time devouring stories in the form of films, novels, television and so on, and we tell each other stories (i.e. give accounts) every day at work and at home and in the local shops. Research has also shown that oral societies use narrative to remember, as in the case of the Aboriginal Australians, mentioned above.

Writing privileges written record over memory and conversation

I have come to think that the practice of recording and 'capturing' the 'outputs' of a conversation on a flipchart or in a meeting note has less value than commonly supposed.

Flipcharts are a useful informal medium, which we can use, for example, to explain something that is otherwise highly conceptual and difficult to grasp. The conventional wisdom seems to be that taking notes in a meeting in this way helps focus participants' attention, reassures them that their points are being heard and registered, and appeals to those with visual learning styles. All of these arguments have some merit. However, I have recently become acutely aware of just how distracting the flipchart habit, so common in organizational meetings, can be, and how it diverts energy away from the direct face-to-face interaction. Besides, bullet points recorded on flipcharts and dutifully typed up invariably seem lifeless after the heat has gone out of them. The context has changed and the transient meaning that emerged in the meeting has become elusive.

I recall how one manager, responsible for buildings and facilities in a large organization, was running a meeting in which he was supposed to be collecting suggestions from staff. Every time somebody made a suggestion, he made a note on a pad on the table in front of him, saying, 'I'll take that away'. In effect, he gave himself a lengthy to-do list which he would never act upon.

In a contrasting example, once I worked with a group of six 60-something about-to-retire executive coaches, who had been asked by their younger colleagues to share some of their knowledge or wisdom before leaving the firm for good. As a writer and consultant, it would have been easy for me to suggest interviewing each of the six 'wise men' and writing case studies to be put on a database for colleagues to consult. That is not what we did. I was aware of the risk that few people would read written accounts, and I was eager to explore face-to-face story-telling as a form of 'knowledge sharing'. So what we agreed was that initially I would conduct conversations with each of the six coaches to draw out stories from their lives and work. In two cases I invited in another of their colleagues, to give him an opportunity to participate and listen – otherwise there was a danger that only two people (the coach and myself) would learn anything.

One of the most striking aspects of this process was how easy it was to get some of the men to tell colorful coaching stories, but how hard it was with the others, who seemed to feel compelled to abstract key principles from their experience. I encouraged the stories, with all the context, humor and personality that can get lost when you abstract. We ended up with twenty-four written stories, based on the conversations. Two members of the group later added these stories to a database of coaching tools and techniques, with a handy index allowing someone with a particular coaching issue to find both a technique and a relevant story.

However, we also got together face-to-face as a group, at which point we agreed that the most important lesson we had learned was the value of taking time to have these kinds of learning/story-telling conversations. They resolved next to 'do an Alison' and conduct similar conversations with their younger colleagues, but this time with a twist: they invited their colleagues to tell the stories themselves. They also took a half-day slot at a conference of the whole firm to share their experience of story-telling with their colleagues, and to urge them to make it an organizational habit.

Temptation to focus on the tools of communication rather than on human relationships

When we focus our attention on reports, plans, presentations, databases and other 'tools of communication' (Stacey, 2001), we risk losing sight of the quality (or poverty) of our working relationships. In the following narrative I explore a situation where a report was the immediate focus of attention, but turned out to be just part of a far more complex relational picture or process.

How a report turned out not to be the whole story – a narrative

I was asked by a client, director of communications for a major international company, if I could help her new deputy write a report for the Chief Executive (CEO). I went along for an initial conversation with the deputy, whom I will call Jo. She felt that, despite many years of experience in PR and press relations, she was ill-equipped with the skills needed to create what she referred to as a 'business report'.

I remember at one point asking Jo what 'business report' meant to her and she said she associated it with something worthy, loaded with detail, based on financial certainty, probably with graphs and an appendix of some kind.

It transpired that this particular report was to be about the organization's internal marketing services (e.g. events, market research) – a topic that was not part of her normal area of work. When I asked her why the CEO had none the less asked her to write it, she quoted him as saying, 'it doesn't matter if everyone ends up hating Jo'.

By now she was clearly feeling guilty about the fact that, although she had done a great deal of research, she had not yet produced a draft. The CEO had asked for it some months before and had recently enquired about its progress. Jo talked about the CEO being, in Myers Briggs terms, an 'ISTP', whereas she was an 'ENTP'. This way of classifying a human being, so popular in organizations, did not seem to help her much in deciding what to do next. I already had some acquaintance with the CEO and had the impression he was not the easiest person to please. I also discovered later that Jo's boss was concerned about Jo's relationship with the CEO.

So already I could see that the task of coaching Jo in how to present information in a report was only a part of the whole story. It seemed to me that the relationships between Jo, the CEO and the rest of the organization were far more significant.

Right now, however, it made sense for us to focus on what Jo could do next. She told me she wanted to spend part of the approaching weekend gathering her initial thoughts, so that she could present them to the CEO the following week and get his reactions. She wanted to send me the report once she had written it, but I suggested that she and I meet at the beginning of the week, so she could bounce her thoughts off me before approaching the CEO. In other words, I was suggesting we view the process of writing as just that – a process, in which she formulates something, gauges reactions, then takes the next step – rather than planning the entire report on her own in advance.

So Jo and I met again the following week, as I had suggested, to talk through her initial thoughts. As we sat together in the canteen, she showed me her preliminary draft, which followed the common, rather dull headings of purpose, methodology, findings and recommendations. I suggested what I thought would be a better structure, which she adopted readily. Essentially, her next draft retained the introductory text about the purpose of the review and the number of people involved, and then launched into five main themes – which were all suggestions to the CEO about what the organization might do next in this area. My sense was that the CEO would appreciate seeing straight away some ideas about where he might focus his attention. The methodology would sit best at the end of the report where he could refer to it if he wished.

During my conversations with Jo, I found myself interested not only in the task of writing a report but also in the relationship difficulties she was having. The report we had been asked to work on became just one strand in a complex weave of relationships, motives and meanings – the 'whole story'. Sadly – despite Jo's feeling that her meeting with the CEO went well – I heard from her boss shortly afterwards that the CEO's opinion had not changed for the better. Jo had been hired because she was thought to have the skills for the job, but had then found herself in a relationship context in which she could not succeed. This illustrates for me how both the skill of writing and the meaning of a report are highly dependent on the relationships and interactions around the text.

What is writing exactly?

In this chapter we have seen much evidence that those of us who live in literate societies are conditioned by writing technologies. Above all, writing has fostered elaborate abstract, generalized ways of thinking and even speaking, and it has privileged certain habits in organizational life. In order to understand more fully the way we use writing technologies in organizations today, it helps to reflect on what actually happens when we write. What goes on in the writer's mind? How does the reader respond? What, if anything, passes between them? What and where is meaning?

Sending and receiving messages

When people talk about communication in organizational life, they almost always use sender–receiver terminology. A 'sender' sends a 'message' to a 'receiver'. (The root of the word 'message' is the Latin *mittere*, to send.) And, depending on the quality of the communication channel and the amount of 'noise', the message either arrives intact or with something missing. Thus we say things like 'they didn't get the message', or 'the statement contained bad news', or we talk about 'information flows'.

Metaphors tend to stimulate a range of associations in people's minds, sometimes referred to as 'entailments' (Lakoff and Johnson, 1980). If we examine the entailments of the sender–receiver metaphor, we discover that it focuses our attention on some aspects of communication while overlooking others. It leads us to think (consciously or unconsciously) of ideas (or meaning) as objects, communication as sending, and words and documents (and even human beings) as containers, conduits or channels. Thus, we talk about capturing, transferring and stealing ideas; and we view documents as having 'content'. The metaphor locates meaning in the word or the document.

The implicit comparison is with a postal service, telegraphy, telecommunication, radio transmission, or possibly computer code. It is worth looking at what is really being compared. For example: a postal service delivers something physical – a letter or a parcel – which is supposed to remain intact during its transport and delivery; a radio transmission is a technical process, whose quality can be improved in various ways, such as making the signal stronger or louder. This does not do justice to the complexity of human communication.

If these are some of the entailments of the sender–receiver metaphor, what does it play down or distract our attention away from? *Ambiguity*, for one, has no place in sender–receiver language. Either the message arrives or it doesn't. If it becomes scrambled it is the fault of the sender, or noise, or a poor communication channel, or misinterpretation by the receiver.

Long before today's computers were invented, humans were physically sending written messages to one another. Ong argues convincingly, as we have seen, that we are conditioned by literacy or writing (he calls it 'chirographic conditioning'). He also gives this as the reason for our willingness to live with what he calls the 'media model of communication' (Ong, 2002: 173). He points out that literate cultures regard speech as informational rather than performance-oriented (unlike oral societies). Furthermore, 'the written text appears *prima facie* to be a one-way informational street, for no real recipient (reader, hearer) is present when the texts come into being' (ibid.: 174).

Legacy of information theory

It is instructive to review a seminal work associated with this way of thinking, namely Shannon and Weaver's *Mathematical Theory of Communication* (Shannon and Weaver, 1949). Of the two essays in the book, Shannon's solely addressed the 'engineering problem' encountered in fields such as telegraphy, telephony, radio and television, stating that: 'The fundamental problem of communication is that of reproducing at one point either exactly or approximately a message selected at another point' (ibid.: 31). He noted that 'frequently the messages have *meaning*', but concluded that the 'semantic aspects of communication are irrelevant to the engineering problem' (ibid.: 31).

Weaver, in his essay, however, went so far as to argue that the mathematical theory of communication is helpful in considering *both* the technical and the semantic problem. He suggested making 'minor additions' to the model, which consisted mainly of adding new boxes labeled 'semantic receiver' and 'semantic noise' (ibid.: 26), and made only fleeting mention of the 'influence of context' on meaning (ibid.: 28). Weaver also used the technical observations as a direct analogy for human communication. For example, technically, when one tries to crowd too much over a channel, error increases and fidelity decreases. He then extrapolates, saying, 'if you overcrowd the capacity of the audience you force a general and inescapable error and confusion' (ibid.: 27).

Information theory is of course essentially about information. But what is information? The word comes from the Latin *informare*: to give form to. Typically, information consists of visual forms (e.g. words) that we create and point to, and which *evoke* meaning. In reality, the only 'thing' normally transferred by a text is some black marks on a white page.

Shannon and Weaver's work was much influenced by the relatively recent invention of the telephone, television and the birth of computing. Having read the theory after my acquaintance with the writings of Stacey, Mead and others, I realized just how important it is to think about human communication as involving interdependent beings with unique histories, feelings and self-consciousness. A critical reading of Shannon and

Weaver's work made it clear that, while there is a legitimate field of communication theory concerned with the technical transmission of symbols, human communication is *not* a matter of engineering.

A complex responsive processes perspective

If meaning is not a 'thing' and is not located in the word or text, what is it? I will explore this question with the help of a number of writers (Mead 1934; Shotter, 1997; Stacey *et al.*, 2000; Stacey, 2001), who offer alternative but complementary ways of thinking about this subject.

Stacey and colleagues suggest we focus on *conversation* as 'the central activity of organizing' (Stacey *et al.*, 2000: 132). Stacey applies the term 'communication tools' to the documents or written artifacts so often used in conversations in organizations, including reports, plans, agendas, slide presentations, databases and intranets. He suggests that we focus less on the tools themselves and instead pay attention to how they are used (Stacey, 2001). Put another way, it makes sense to view written communication as part of the 'complex responsive processes of human relating' or as part of the 'organizational conversation'. The intention to write a document always emerges out of a web of previous conversations; and once a piece of writing has been created it may be used to stimulate further dialogue and change.

Such a 'process view' of writing takes into account that any utterance *is a link in an ongoing chain* or web of responsive relating. As Shotter puts it, 'just as the effect produced by poking a stick into a stream of water depends upon the whole character of the flow of water at the time – with different effects depending upon the power (or lack of it) already in the stream's flow – so for us, the effect of our words depends upon where in the stream or communication they occur' (Shotter, 1993: 54–55). One major implication is that it is important to distinguish *writing as a process* from the *artifacts* it produces; Yet many people apparently continue to think of meaning as contained within documents and other tools of communication.

Writing – a silent conversational process

The way in which Stacey and colleagues understand communication is strongly influenced by the thinking of George Herbert Mead. Mead sees meaning as arising from within the social act of gesture and response, and he describes mind as an internalized conversation with the generalized other. (See Chapter 2 above.)

If we apply Mead's theory to writing, what do we learn? When I first came across Mead's thinking, I thought of a document as a form of gesture which would stimulate some kind of response. However, the more closely I studied *Mind, Self and Society* (Mead, 1934), the more I came to think of writing itself as a conversational process: the writer while writing conducts a silent conversation – with some combination of the generalized other and the specific reader(s). As this conversation moves along, the imagined responses act back on the writer, who may change what he or she was intending to write. Eventually, the writer finishes writing and may send the text to someone, at which point the reader's response becomes real. This actual response then continues to change the meaning of the writer's gestures. In other words, the meaning of a text is not fixed.

Nearly everything that Mead writes about communication is as true for written communication as it is for spoken. The act of writing is part of a social act, usually preceded and followed by spoken communication. Writing employs 'significant symbols', that is, the writer is aware of the meaning of what he or she is writing. This meaning does not lie in the text but moves constantly in the light of both the reader's response (imagined and real) and the writer's own response while writing. None the less, the meaning also has a certain degree of stability, if we accept that a significant symbol arouses a similar response in all members of a community.

Ong's account of communication echoes Mead's:

> Human communication is never one-way. Always, it not only calls for response but is shaped in its very form and content by anticipated response. . . . Some recipient must be present, or there can be no text produced: so, isolated from real persons, the writer conjures up a fictional person or persons. The writer's audience is always a fiction. . . . The fictionalizing of readers is what makes writing so difficult.
> (Ong, 2002: 173–174)

One factor that particularly sets writing apart from talking is the delayed response of the reader. If the reader is absent physically while we are writing, we can only adjust to their *assumed* or *imagined* attitudes. This is the fictionalizing of the reader that Ong refers to. A related advantage of writing is that it offers us an opportunity to 'take our time' – organizing, testing and finally selecting our gestures. As Mead points out, without delayed reaction, no conscious or intelligent control over behavior could be exercised (Mead, 1934: 99). Writing could be described as one form of delayed reaction.

When we are writing, the thoughts that appear on the page are probably just a fraction of our thinking, which Norbert Elias describes as the 'rush of telescoped reasoning' (Elias, 1991: 69). It is not surprising that 'people have difficulties in translating the rush of telescoped reasoning into the step-by-step language required for communication' (ibid.).

Looked at from the reader's point of view, when a person starts reading, the words enter and disturb his or her own silent conversation. A conversation with an email, report or book can alter our patterns of thinking. This is learning.

The written text has traditionally been constrained by an absence of visual, auditory and other cues, yet even a black-and-white text can stimulate the imagination to such an extent that the images and connections created by the reader seem positively colorful and vibrant.

Other authors offer explanations that are consistent with Mead and Ong. Elias, for example, writes: 'The meaning of an action for the actor is codetermined by the meaning it may have for others' (Elias, 1991: 49). John Shotter portrays meaning as a fluid feature of human communication, rather than a thing. He writes that humans involved in joint action are 'not so much acting "out of" any of their own inner plans, or scripts, or suchlike, as "into" a situation or circumstance already partially shaped by previous talk-intertwined activities of others' (Shotter, 1997: 5). What is so special about joint action is 'that its overall outcome is not up to any of the individuals concerned in it; it is entirely novel; its outcomes are as if they have "come out of the blue"' (ibid.). Bakhtin also emphasizes the 'out-of-the-blue' nature of meaning: 'An utterance . . . always creates something that never existed before, something absolutely new and unrepeatable' (Bakhtin, 1986: 119–120).

It follows that meaning is fleeting and ephemeral. It cannot be sent and received, nor can it be 'delivered intact'. At best, it makes sense to *act as if* we could formulate and 'convey messages' to another person.

In summary, it is useful to view writing as theoretically similar to talking, even though it has some important qualities and biases of its own, as we saw earlier in this chapter. Moreover, once we grasp the complex, conversational nature of both writing and reading, and the way in which they can alter patterns of thinking, we can better appreciate the power of writing as a tool for learning and 'knowledge sharing'.

New writing technologies

In this chapter we have seen that writing and print have been strong forces in the evolution of society. What then can we begin to discern about the newer, electronic writing technologies associated with computers? This is not the place to discuss whether writing standards are loosening, internet fraud is growing, or personal security is threatened by electronic records. Instead, I would like to make some final observations relevant to the arguments of this chapter.

Co-existence of print and newer media

Ong suggests that the new medium reinforces the old, in that computers are actually producing more documents, not fewer. The 'electronic transformation of verbal expression has . . . deepened the commitment of the word to space initiated by writing and intensified by print'. At the same time, however, it has also, together with the telephone, radio, television, tape-recording, CDs, DVDs and so on, brought us into 'a new age of secondary orality' (Ong, 2002: 133). Whereas societies characterized by primary orality have never encountered or used writing, our current society is 'based permanently on the use of writing and print, which are essential for the manufacture and operation of the [electronic] equipment and for its use as well' (Ong, 2002: 134).

Similarly, Lanham argues:

> [The] shift from print to the computer does not mean the end of literacy. What will be lost is not literacy itself, but the literacy of print, for electronic technology offers us a new kind of book and new ways to write and read.
> (Lanham, 1993: 213, citing Jay David Bolter 1991: 'Writing space: the computer, hypertext, and the history of writing')

The pendulum may be swinging away from the static, monochrome structures of print towards more fluid, multi-sensory patterns. We are witnessing a revolution in terms of the use of image and sound, with millions of people now able to create, distribute and manipulate digital pictures and sounds. Whereas in the past many reports and books have consisted largely of black-and-white symbols, technology is now re-introducing other sensory experiences.

In short, we may indeed be moving out of the age of print or the 'Gutenberg era' (McLuhan, 1964: 95), but this does not mean abandoning literacy in favor of orality. In any case it makes little sense to view orality and literacy as polarities; they co-exist in today's organizations and society.

Further distance between people?

Finally, one of the arguments in this chapter has been that the way we use the technologies of writing and print frequently alienates us from one another. It is therefore worth asking what influence the newer forms of writing may be having.

I have pointed to one occasion where a performance management database seemed to divert attention away from the quality of work conversations, and over and over again I have seen people use PowerPoint presentations come between people. There are also frequent examples of people emailing a colleague who is sitting a few yards away. On the other hand, there are equally common examples of people using the internet successfully to find other people with similar interests, regardless of physical location – after all, an email can be anything from cold and impersonal to warm and intimate. It seems that, as one would expect, there are multiple and contrasting influences.

None the less, on balance I am inclined to support Ong in his view that computers are reinforcing many of the patterns and biases that began with literacy and print. I am thinking primarily of the tendency to use elaborate abstract language and thus distance ourselves from our momentary situation, but I am also mindful of the current widespread use in the public sector of written targets and measurement. The one thing that is clear is that, like all 'social objects', the global patterns of behavior fostered by writing, print and electronic media will continue to emerge out of – and act back on – millions of particular human interactions.

References

Abram, D. (1996) *The Spell of the Sensuous*, New York: Vintage Books.

Bailey, D. (1992) *Improvisation: Its Nature and Practice in Music*, London: The British Library National Sound Archive.

Bakhtin, M. M. (1986) *Speech Genres and Other Essays*, Austin: University of Texas Press.

Berger, P. and Luckmann, T. (1966) *The Social Construction of Reality: A Treatise on the Sociology of Knowledge*, London: Penguin Books.

Brown, J. S. and Duguid, P. (2000) *The Social Life of Information*, Boston, MA: Harvard Business School Press.

Czarniawska, B. (1998) *A Narrative Approach to Organization Studies*, Thousand Oaks, London, New Delhi: Sage.

Elias, N. (1991) *The Symbol Theory*, London: Sage (paperback edn 1995).

Goudsblom, J. and Mennell, S. (1998) *The Norbert Elias Reader*, Oxford: Blackwell.

Havelock, E. (1986) *The Muse Learns to Write*, New Haven and London: Yale University Press.

Lakoff, G. and Johnson, M. (1980) *Metaphors we Live By*, Chicago, IL: University of Chicago Press.

Lanham, R. (1993) *The Electronic Word: Democracy, Technology and the Arts*, Chicago, IL, and London: The University of Chicago Press.

Larkin, T. J. and Larkin, S. (1994) *Communicating Change: Winning Employee Support for New Business Goals*, New York: McGraw-Hill.

McLuhan, M. (1964) *Understanding Media*, London and New York: Routledge (published in Routledge Classics 2001).

Mead, G. H. (1934) *Mind, Self and Society: From the Standpoint of a Social Behaviorist*, ed. Charles W Morris. Chicago, IL, and London: The University of Chicago Press (paperback edn 1967).

Miller, G. A. (1956) *The Magical Number Seven, Plus or Minus Two: Some Limits on our Capacity for Processing Information*, Harvard: The Psychological Review, Vol. 63, No. 2, March 1956.

Minto, B. (1987) *The Pyramid Principle: Logic in Writing and Thinking*, London: 1991 edn. BCA by arrangement with Pitman Publishing.

Ong, W. J. (2002) *Orality and Literacy*, London and New York: Routledge (first published 1982 by Methuen & Co).

Poor, E. (1992) *The Executive Writer: A Guide to Managing Words, Ideas, and People*, New York: Grove Weidenfeld.

Shannon, C. E. and Weaver, W. (1949) *The Mathematical Theory of Communication*, Urbana, Chicago, IL, and London: University of Chicago Press.

Shlain, L. (1998) *The Alphabet Versus the Goddess: The Conflict Between Word and Image*, London: Allen Lane The Penguin Press.

Shotter, J. (1993) *Conversational Realities: Constructing Life Through Language*, London, Thousand Oaks, CA, and New Delhi: Sage.

Shotter, J. (1997) *The Social Construction of our Inner Lives*, (Journal of Constructivist Psychology).

Stacey, R. (2001) *Complex Responsive Processes in Organizations: Learning and knowledge creation*, London: Routledge.

Stacey, R., Griffin, D. and Shaw, P. (2000) *Complexity and Management: Fad or radical challenge to systems thinking?*, London: Routledge.

Toulmin, S. (1990) *Cosmopolis: The Hidden Agenda of Modernity*, Chicago, IL: The University of Chicago Press.

Walker, D. (1968) 'Executives who want this man's insights will get them only on his own terms', in G.E. Stearn (ed.) *McLuhan Hot and Cool*, Harmondsworth: Penguin Books.

Whyte, D. (1997) *The Heart Aroused: Poetry and the Preservation of the Soul at Work*, London: The Industrial Society.

Index

values 10, 30, 34

Waldrop, M. M. 10
Walker, D. 177
Weber, M. 145
Weisbord, M. and Janov, S. 87
Wenger, E. 80, 95, 96–7
Wernerfeldt, B. 143
whole 4, 22, 25–6, 36–7, 41
Winnicott, D. W. 158
work roles 108, 111, 112, 113
writing/printing 159; as abstract/logical 171–4; background 164, 167–9; and categorization/direct experience 184–5; and co-existence of print/newer media 196–7; and codification of generalized tendencies/collective habits 168; complex responsive process perspective 193; definition of writing 190; development of 171, 173; and distance between people 197; as distanced/introspective 175; and facilitating reflection/learning 179–81; and legacy of information theory 192–3; and meaning 176; new technologies 196–7; and orality 169–70; in organizational life 181; and planning/improvisation, engagement 182; as precise/sparse 174; as prone to abstraction 178; and propositional/narrative forms of communication 185–7; as recorded, fixed, repeatable 176–8; reliance on 178; report example 189–90; ripple effects of 170–1; sending/receiving messages 191–2; as silent conversational process 193–6; as social object 164–5; spatial nature of 165; and structured meetings/free-flowing conversations 183–4; as technology 164, 169; as tool for organizing 179; and tools of communication/human relationships 188; transformative nature of 169–70; and use of abstract terms 168; and value of literacy 179–88; as visible/quantifiable 175–6; and written record/memory, conversation 187–8